DEFIANT PEACEMAKER

Number Seventeen:

The Elma Dill Russell Spencer
Series in the West and Southwest

Defiant Peacemaker

NICHOLAS TRIST
IN THE MEXICAN WAR

Wallace Ohrt

Texas A&M University Press
COLLEGE STATION

Copyright © 1997 by Wallace Ohrt
Manufactured in the United States of America
All rights reserved
First edition
04 03 02 01 00 99 98 97   5 4 3 2 1

The paper used in this book meets the minimum requirements
of the American National Standard for Permanence
of Paper for Printed Library Materials, Z39.48-1984.
Binding materials have been chosen for durability.

∞

Library of Congress Cataloging-in-Publication Data

Ohrt, Wallace.
    Defiant peacemaker : Nicholas Trist in the Mexican War / by Wallace Ohrt. —
1st ed.
       p.   cm. — (Elma Dill Russell Spencer series in the West and
Southwest ; no. 17)
    Included bibliographical references and index.
    ISBN 0-89096-778-4
    1. Trist, Nicholas Philip, 1800–1874. 2. Diplomats—United States—Biography.
3. Mexican War, 1846–1848—Peace.   4. United States—Foreign relations—
Mexico.   5. Mexico—Foreign relations—United States.   I. Title.   II. Series.
E415.9.T84039   1997
973.6′22′092—dc21   97-35669
    [B]   CIP

FRONTISPIECE: Nicholas Philip Trist at age 35.
Painted in 1835 by John Neagle.
Courtesy Monticello/Thomas Jefferson Memorial Foundation, Inc.

Who steals my purse, steals trash;

'tis something, nothing;

'Twas mine, 'tis his,

and has been slave to thousands:

But he that filches from me my good name

Robs me of that which not enriches him

And makes me poor indeed.

—WILLIAM SHAKESPEARE, *Othello*

CONTENTS

INTRODUCTION

A century and a half ago, during the James K. Polk administration, the boundaries of the United States spread so dramatically that in less than three years the nation grew in size by two-thirds, literally extending "from sea to shining sea." Today the configuration of our country is so familiar, so *right,* that the notion of a truncated America, bounded to the west by the Rocky Mountains, is unthinkable. Yet, however much we may approve the acquisitions made by President Polk, the process called Manifest Destiny was not as noble as its early proponents declared. The vast region of the Southwest that encompasses Texas, extends west to the Pacific and spreads north to the latitude dividing California and Oregon was unwillingly sold to the United States in 1848 by a sullen, beaten Mexico. Only the work of one rather eccentric idealist, a Virginian named Nicholas Philip Trist, enables us to consider what happened during the Mexican War without what historian Robert Arthur Brent has called "a thorough revulsion."

This biography could, and perhaps should, be subtitled *The Man Who Would Be Jefferson,* for Trist idolized and did his best throughout his life to emulate the sage. He married Jefferson's granddaughter, studied under Jefferson himself, and when Jefferson died, administered his debt-ridden estate. In some respects he was more consistent than his model in adhering to Jeffersonian ideals, for Jefferson the statesman often found compromise necessary, whereas Trist, the radical idealist, never compromised.

Our third president was not the only great influence on Nicholas Trist, who could claim acquaintance—and in some cases intimate friendship—with at least half the presidents between Jefferson and Lincoln, most notably Andrew Jackson. He also knew a host of other distinguished Americans, many of whom admired and even loved him. Indeed, an apparent anomaly in a man as unbending as Nicholas Trist is the number of friends he acquired and the warmth of their affection for him. Still, there were many who despised him, and on two unrelated occasions eight years apart, he was the most controversial figure in America.

Trist was a man much beloved by good women, not as a romantic Don Juan but as a devoted son, grandson, son-in-law, husband, and father. The voluminous correspondence between Nicholas and Virginia Trist reveals a couple battered by every kind of adversity and frequently separated for long periods of time, yet deeply in love and selflessly committed to each other and their children.

For all his admirable qualities, Nicholas Trist was in some ways his own worst enemy. His lifelong fear of illness drove him to adopt ludicrous health practices and avoid unwholesome climates, even when opportunities beckoned. His judgment was often faulty, especially in business dealings. An astonishing arrogance in a man of relatively modest station enabled him to condescend to presidents, quarrel with military commanders and hurl insults at the House of Lords; yet his opposite numbers in Mexico admired and respected him for his unfailing patience and courtesy under the most trying conditions. At times, when confronted by aggressive opposition, he took refuge behind lengthy written counterattacks, displaying an insecurity that was usually concealed by iron self-control. His insecurity probably resulted from an unstable childhood, for he was made to call three men "Father" by the age of ten.

At the end of his life, Trist was considered by some an object of pity. His career was so thoroughly destroyed by its one great defining achievement that he was reduced to working long, exhausting hours at humble jobs even into his seventies. Others, however, saw him as one of the most distinguished men of his time. If his vision did not soar as high or his language inspire as movingly as his grandfather-in-law's had done, Trist was successful by his own standards and in the eyes of many of his fellow Americans. In 1870, Gen. Thomas Kane wrote to President Grant: "I am old enough to remember when Mr. Trist was even more intimately in the confidence of General Jackson than . . . any of your military family . . . in yours."[1]

The quintessential character of Nicholas Trist can best be distilled in a tribute he paid to General Winfield Scott—the highest compliment of which he was capable: "He is . . . a true lover of Justice." Much has been made of the famous feud between Trist and Scott that preceded their life-long friendship, but, significant as that historic quarrel was, it pales in comparison with Trist's incredible defiance of a direct order from his commander-in-chief, Pres. James K. Polk.

Mr. Polk is generally considered by historians to be the strongest president between Jackson and Lincoln. Some rate him "near great," and nearly all grant him high marks for his phenomenal success in achieving seemingly impossible goals. Yet, Polk labored under burdens that were often self-imposed. His actions were invariably shrouded in secrecy, and he tended to assign responsibilities unaccompanied by trust. He sometimes underestimated quite seriously the difficulties confronting his agents. Although surrounded by gifted aides, he insisted on doing too much of his administration's work himself. He held himself to the highest ethical and moral standard but found little virtue in those around him. Of all the troubles that plagued him, faulty communication, frequently of his own doing, was the most damaging.

Polk's exaggerated reliance on secrecy left later historians, as well as his contemporaries, uncertain about his intentions. His aggressive expansionist policy was formerly assumed to be political opportunism, reflecting the national appetite for land. Twentieth-century scholarship reveals, however, that Polk was intent on building international trade, the full potential of which, he understood, would depend on acquisition of the fine natural harbors of the Pacific Coast. (As part of his maritime plan, for example, he hoped to acquire transit rights across the narrow, low-lying Isthmus of Tehuantepec for the construction of a canal, but that development would have to wait for another administration—and another isthmus.) Well aware that he had both Great Britain and Mexico as adversaries, and having set himself a limit of one term, Polk drove himself to exhaustion and early death trying to achieve his goals.

Polk's greatest fault was a lack of those ordinary human qualities that Americans expect and demand in their leaders: trust, warmth, candor, kindliness, generosity, and patience. Had his personality permitted him the comfortable relationship with Trist that Trist had earlier enjoyed with Andrew Jackson, our history might have turned out quite differently.

DEFIANT PEACEMAKER

CHAPTER I

Louisiana

"The world still presents many other resources of happiness," wrote forty-year-old Thomas Jefferson to his younger friend James Madison, who, having been spurned by a lovely sixteen-year-old Philadelphia socialite named Kitty Floyd, was suffering the pangs of unrequited love. Jefferson wrote out of an even more painful loss: the recent death of his beloved wife of ten years. The two Virginians, both delegates to the Constitutional Convention, lodged while in Philadelphia at the excellent boardinghouse of Mrs. Mary House. His wife's death having left him responsible for two young daughters, Jefferson brought the elder, Martha (called Patsy), to Philadelphia during his extended stays in that new federal capital while leaving the younger, Maria, in the care of trusted household slaves at Monticello. Mrs. House's married daughter, Elizabeth Trist, took charge of the high-spirited Patsy and soon came to be like a surrogate mother to her. She also became a close friend of Thomas Jefferson, with whom she corresponded, although infrequently, for more than thirty years.[1]

Elizabeth Trist's husband was an English immigrant named Nicholas Trist, a restless, wandering man who spent much of his time on the western frontier, where he acquired several large tracts of land somewhere in the wilds of the Mississippi Territory. He died in 1784, leaving Elizabeth with their only child, a son named Hore Browse Trist.

In 1797, Hore Browse Trist, then a young man, traveled to England to search—as it turned out unsuccessfully—for some vaguely described properties to which he believed himself the heir. Returning to America, he married Mary Louisa Brown. Soon the couple settled in Charlottesville,

Virginia, where Trist first studied and then practiced law. Here were born two children: Nicholas Philip Trist in 1800 and, two years later, another Hore Browse Trist.

When it became apparent that Virginia was oversupplied with lawyers, Trist began casting about for a more promising means of earning a living. By 1802, Thomas Jefferson was in the second year of his presidency and, having maintained close ties with the Trist family, felt some obligation to offer assistance. Even so, appointive positions were not unlimited, and many clamored for the more remunerative posts. Trist had to settle for the position of revenue collector at Natchez, a raw new settlement overlooking the Mississippi River. His acceptance of the appointment was motivated in part by the opportunity it afforded to locate the land he had inherited from his father.

Trist was appalled by the barbarous conditions at Natchez and decided not to subject his wife and infant children to the rugged life of the frontier. Instead, he chose to bide his time alone in the hope that another post at a location more suitable for his family might soon arise. He consoled himself by writing long, reflective, sometimes doleful letters, filling pages with indignant comments on the villainy of mankind and upbraiding his poor wife for her few brief replies. Politically, Trist was an anti-Federalist; by temperament if not by training, he was something of a philosopher. Although a newcomer, he appears to have assumed some community responsibility, for in one letter he wrote: "The [infamous *New York Herald* is] designed to have a coveted effect upon these ignorant and credulous people. As credulity and ignorance always go hand in hand, a reformation can only be expected by the establishment of schools generally throughout the Territory. This desirable objective we are endeavoring to effect. . . ."[2]

After some months of privation, Trist's letters took on a plaintive note: "Two posts have arrived without a line from you. . . . My greatest pleasure . . . is in holding sweet converse with you in my dreams. Frequently have I [held] my boys on my knee; twenty times a day do I see them." He also wrote about his health, which was not robust: "I have recovered again in a great measure my strength, at least as far as a debilitating climate will permit—My eyes are also free from inflamation."[3]

A few more months of neglect intensified his loneliness. His letters became more florid and took on a note of reproval for Mary's reluctance to engage in long-distance romantic exchange: "You need not the pen of Sterne to give a reciprocal feeling of sentiment to your expressions—the tender glow of virtuous attachment, in whatever form expressed, will always convey to the sympathetic mind that portion of Ethereal spirit which such only are capable of receiving—such only capable of communicating. . . . The polish of the diamond adds to its lustre, but in lessening its bulk destroys in part its original value. The value of our expression is its sincerity. . . ." Abruptly descending to earth, he added apologetically, "When I mention this my love do not suppose I have not a proper appreciation of the little leisure that a mother has. . . ."[4]

Mr. Trist's letters were invariably filled with complaints about the irresponsible and chaotic way in which the federal postal service was often conducted in the territories. Flooded rivers, storms, piracy both ashore and at sea, and not infrequently the rascality of local officials made intercourse by mail haphazard at best. At the dawn of the nineteenth century, less than two decades into the infancy of the new nation, federal bureaucrats believed there were more pressing problems than the carrying of letters. A strong temptation toward mail tampering lay in the general shortage of hard money and the scarcity of consumer goods, as well as in the common practice of sending small luxuries and valuables with personal letters despite the well-known risks. Some of Trist's most overwrought prose dealt with this matter: "I have again to complain my beloved wife of some postmaster who has detained my letters for three mails. . . . I am almost induced to believe that man is dishonest of nature, & that corruption in all variety is implanted in his disposition, never to be eradicated. Else why should we so often find him acting thus, even when no possible benefit can result and receive pleasing satisfaction at the [consternation] he creates in his fellow man. . . . Have I not seen Duplicity, meanness, [lack] of principle at the rich table, enjoying without thought the comforts obtained by dishonesty, corruption, oppression, selfishness—where then was conscience?"[5]

In this same letter, dated August 5, 1803, Trist lauded his benefactor for negotiating the Louisiana Purchase from France, a stupendous bargain at $15 million for a vast, rich territory that approximately doubled the size of the United States. He wrote: "Mr. J has . . . clinched the nail of immortality for certainly his country is indebted to him. . . . Independence and the acquisition of [Louisiana Territory] will render his pyramid of fame as durable as to mean in after ages his name shall be called 'wonderful, Counselor.' . . . This also determines I suppose my station, as the position will be changed. . . . I will hold myself in readiness. . . . I understand that applications are showering upon the President for my Office already—but ineffectual I hope . . . for there is not one of them who has not an enmity for republicanism."[6]

Trist's speculations concerning the effect of the "Acquisition" upon himself were soon borne out. Shortly he would have little time for gloomy reflection on the folly and infamy of man. He had scarcely signed his name to the above letter when he received directions from Secretary of the Treasury Albert Gallatin to prepare for a larger assignment of the same nature at New Orleans.

The vast domain acquired by the United States in 1803 stretched from the Gulf of Mexico to the present boundary with Canada and from the Mississippi River to the Oregon country. Its acquisition was an incredible piece of luck, analogous in modern terms to finding a winning lottery ticket in the street. The vaguely defined empire belonged at the time to Spain—and Spanish officials still ruled in New Orleans—although an earlier agreement, soon to have been in effect, would have transferred the whole tract to France. However, Napoleon found that he had his hands full with European wars. In addition, his earlier attempts to send troops to Haiti had turned out badly, causing him to shy away from further adventures in the Western Hemisphere.[7] Not wishing to have such a stronghold fall into British possession through his own inability to defend it, he ordered his foreign minister Talleyrand—who was at the time negotiating with James Monroe for the relatively minor turnover of French interest in New Orleans—to offer the American envoy not merely New Orleans and its environs but the entire territory called Louisiana at a price not even a fool could refuse. Monroe was no fool, and Talleyrand, who valued the territory more highly than did Napoleon, was a reluctant seller, but eventually the deal was struck: for $15 million the United States acquired the prize package and even the privilege of defining its boundaries! Jefferson, of course, got the credit.[8]

When Trist received his new commission, he was both stunned with apprehension and transported with joy at the effusion of new titles that came with his appointment. He immediately informed Mary that her husband was to be "Collector, Administrator, Treasurer . . . with full authority . . . as to the revenues of Louisiana."[9] Another communication soon arrived from the president, accompanied by fuller instructions from the treasury secretary, directing him to proceed without delay to New Orleans (or send his deputy in his place) and to convert the Revenue Department from the Spanish system to the method required by the United States government.

Mary Trist lost no time gathering up her two small sons, her mother-in-law, and their belongings and booking passage on a sailing vessel to

New Orleans. Though concerned about pirates, the two women suffered only moderate seasickness before arriving without incident to a joyous reception by the lonely collector of revenues.

The time that followed was the happiest period in the life of Mr. Trist and, perhaps, of his wife and mother as well. The boys, now active, cheerful toddlers, filled the little house with merriment. The city was then emerging as a gateway to the new territory while still clinging to its colorful past. Pirates and gamblers strolled the muddy streets shoulder to shoulder with settlers, immigrants and planters, while gangs of slaves loaded and unloaded vessels along the riverfront. Host businesses were operated by French and Spanish owners, who continued to use the language and coin with which they were familiar, leaving newcomers to discover for themselves the ways of this exotic city.

At night the great homes of the rich blazed with parties, for the turnover of government was a natural occasion for social festivities. Trist was now important enough to receive a fair share of invitations, and at these levees he was usually accompanied by his wife and mother. Elizabeth Trist, whose letters made up in general interest and good sense what they lacked in punctuation, wrote to Thomas Jefferson: "God be thanked we have at present nothing to apprehend from the Spaniards. Governor Williams has been in Town about a fortnight if we may Judge of the festivity that has taken place he must be very popular he may be a very good man and possess a strong mind but I wish . . . that he had the advantage of education. . . . Governor Claiborne brought him to see us I could not but make a comparison which is in favor of our own Governor. . . . the summers are made [miserable] by the Muscketoes. . . . I hope that my constitution [will] become creolised as they term it. . . ."[10]

The little family's happiness was short-lived. During the steaming summer of 1804, Trist was stricken with yellow fever, and he died on August 29. Desolate with grief, Elizabeth wrote to her sister, ". . . my Son, my support, my all in all in life was wrested from me."[11] To Jefferson, her "Dear and Hon'd friend," she wrote: " . . . these operations of nature lean not equally hard, when the support of a family is taken how truly deplorable. My lot is among the hardest an only child on whom my dependence for comfort and support in my decline of life rested, his wife and Infant children what a change in their situation, a very short period since prosperity and happiness expanded to [them] but now all is gloom. Small I fear is the means left them for support, what there is left them is in England but whether we can command it I know not."[12]

Elizabeth Trist's influence with the administration secured the post vacated by the death of Trist for the widow's brother, William Brown, who brought his and Mary's mother to live with the family for a time. He of course contributed to their support. Trist's personal estate was barely sufficient to settle outstanding debts; however, the land he had inherited from his father passed to his infant sons in accordance with territorial law and would one day prove vital to their welfare. Meanwhile, the devastated family struggled on.

Then, with what Elizabeth regarded as scandalous haste, Mary Trist found a new husband. Scarcely more than a month after Trist had been laid to rest, she became the wife of Philip Livingston Jones, a prominent New York lawyer who had made his way to New Orleans and established a thriving practice. Jones was a good husband and father, though he suffered from an unhealed wound received in a duel in which his opponent had been killed. At times he brooded over having taken another man's life, but for the most part the atmosphere was cheerful, and the new family adjusted rapidly. The boys, now four and two, had no trouble learning to call Jones "Father," and a loving parent he proved to be.

Never an enthusiastic correspondent, Mary left to her mother-in-law the responsibility of maintaining contact with friends and relatives in the East. An interesting letter from Elizabeth Trist to President Jefferson bears the date October 27, 1807. The letter was motivated by a desire to warn Jefferson against the traitorous Gen. James Wilkinson, who for a time was suspected, along with Aaron Burr, of plotting to separate the western lands from the United States and place Burr as emperor of the new nation thus formed. Her letter reads in part:

My Dear Sir—I have been desirous of writing to you but the insecurity of the mail has made me afraid to attempt it as not half of my letters are received, friendship now induces me to obtrude on your time for I am sensible that you have too much at this moment to occupy and perplex you. I have heard with much surprise of Burr's acquital [sic]. . . . I fear that this country is not secure against [traitors], there are a horrible set of unprincipled men throughout the United States and I suppose they will be soon flocking here. . . . what angers me at this time is a report that Wilkinson is to return to take the command in this country [Louisiana Territory] if so I . . . definitely and devoutly believe him to be as traitorous a character as we have in America . . . he [is] a man of deep intrigue. . . . I was [formerly] rather prejudiced against him but in his discovering the plot that was to disunite our country I believed him honest and I felt grateful for his exersions [sic] . . . but many of his transactions have since transpired as to induce me to change my sentiments . . . most powerfully . . . was his consumate [sic] duplicity with regard to yourself. To your friends he always spoke of you with the greatest respect and veneration, to those inimical to the present administration his conversation was quite abusive of you. For instance, speaking of you to a gentleman . . . [who asked] what effect [Wilkinson's] arrival here had on you he replied that he had frightened the damn'd old rascal. . . ."[13]

History has confirmed Elizabeth's suspicions, but it has not wholly explained Jefferson's reasons for retaining the rogue general in supreme command of the nation's army despite convincing evidence of his treachery. Jefferson was aware of the plot from other sources; he remained watchful of Burr, who was tried for but never convicted of treason, but inexplicably disregarded the warnings of Elizabeth Trist and others concerning Wilkinson. Perhaps the president's hatred of Burr was stronger than his distrust of Wilkinson and he hoped to use the latter to trip up the former.[14]

Soon Nicholas and his younger brother (hereafter called Browse) were old enough for school. Mary was determined that her sons should receive the best education that Louisiana Territory could provide. With the family now comfortably situated in Philip Jones's New Orleans home, the boys were enrolled in a "classical school" operated by a Mr. Debecour. Even before commencing each day's lessons at this academy, they reported for an hour of dancing instruction at the home of a Mr. Digrain. Both boys proved apt scholars and were eager to learn. Nicholas was the more facile in the study of languages, which he mastered with ease and fluency. Browse, stolid and thorough, showed the greater aptitude for practical learning.

In 1808, while the family was enjoying a visit to New York, Nicholas wrote a letter to his grandmother Elizabeth, now returned to Charlottesville for a long stay with relatives. At eight he had already mastered the beautiful penmanship that would distinguish his letters throughout his life. He wrote: "It was my Mother's intention to place us under the care of Parson Chase, who promised to take us for eight hundred Dollars a year, Dancing and French and washing, was to have been a separate item but the parents of the young Ladies who reside with him objected to our sex."[15]

The New York trip was cut short when Philip Jones suffered a severe attack of gout. When the painful symptoms persisted, the family was forced to return to New Orleans. Although the boys welcomed the resumption of studies and youthful activities, their parents found their lives permanently blighted. Chronic gout and the insidious effect of his old wound reduced Jones to invalidism. In the spring of 1810, his pain-wracked body gave up the struggle. The end came in May.

In June, Elizabeth, who was then at Charlottesville, wrote a consoling letter to Nicholas, commending him for

> your application to your duties, which from your mother's lamentation for the loss you had sustained in the death of your father and in her inability to pay the attention you required, made me conclude that yourself and Brother were not as obedient and attentive as you ought to have been but I am very glad to find that was mistaken, as I was much mortified to be impress'd with such an Idea. . . . if you do not turn out clever fellows I should be humbled to the last. I am much pleased to hear that you are learning the Spanish language it will more than probable be of greatest advantage to you [prophetic words!]. . . . your dear Mother will strain every nerve to give you an education and when you know how to provide for yourself and conduct yourself with honor you will be respected by everybody. . . .[16]

Although his life would be influenced by many distinguished benefactors, Nicholas owed none more than he owed his loving grandmother.

Within a few months Nicholas, now ten, and Browse, eight, were once more required to call a stranger "Father." In the fall of 1810 their mother again remarried, this time to an amiable Frenchman, St. Julien Tournillon, whose son of the same name was several years younger than Browse. Tournillon was a well-to-do planter, occupied with the cultivation of sugar and cotton. For a time the new family lived on in New Orleans, where the boys continued to attend Mr. Debecour's school.

After two years Tournillon found it necessary to change his residence to Donaldsonville in order to be near his plantations. The Trist brothers, now enrolled at Orleans College, were placed in lodgings in the city. It was their first separation from their mother.

Mary House Trist Jones Tournillon was throughout her life a reluctant correspondent and, therefore, appears at times a somewhat shadowy figure. Her prompt replacement of each departed husband with an affluent successor tempts one to regard her as callous and materialistic, unless one remembers the comforting words of Elizabeth Trist to her grandson: "Your dear mother will strain every nerve to give you an education. . . ." The times were difficult for an indigent widow with small children, especially if she entertained lofty ambitions for their careers. Again quoting Elizabeth: "Small I fear is the means left them for future support. . . ." Mary had to consider not only the boys and herself but her mother and mother-in-law as well, for Elizabeth spoke the truth when she wrote after her son's death, ". . . my support, my protection, my all in all was wrested from me. . . ." There was then no safety net to catch those who fell into penury following the death of a breadwinner. Few employment opportunities existed for widows, even if they were fortunate enough to find someone to care for their children. For a woman in Mary's circumstances, marriage was usually the only solution; that she was able to make two suitable matches, each in a very short time, says as much for her charms as for her resourcefulness.[17]

At the college Nicholas pursued with characteristic diligence his interest in languages and also discovered an enthusiasm for history and government. Browse, two years his junior, was fully his equal as a student but had yet to demonstrate a special aptitude or interest. The boys, now dependent on each other, forged a bond of trust and affection that was to endure. Free of parental restrictions but exceptionally self-disciplined, they took to staying up until nine rather than retiring at eight, their former bedtime. They formed the curious habit of rising at four on Wednesday mornings for long walks in the country, where they sampled oranges from roadside trees as they strolled and talked.

Nicholas struck up a friendship with a youth of his own age named Lewis Livingston, whom he described in a letter to his grandmother as one of the finest boys he had ever known. Before long young Lewis invited his new friend home, where Nicholas met Lewis's father, Edward Livingston, a lawyer of national renown. Livingston was much taken by the slender, dark-haired youth, whose poise and formal demeanor were noteworthy even in that era of polished manners. Nicholas was invited again, and in continuing conversations the lawyer spoke at length about his profession. These talks made a lasting impression on Nicholas, who remembered that two of his three "fathers" had been lawyers. As time went on he gave increasing consideration to the law as a means of earning a living.

When their studies permitted, the brothers took a riverboat up the Mississippi to Donaldsonville for visits with the family. During one such stay Browse wrote to his grandmother: "I have the pleasure to [inform you] . . . that Mother presented us with a brother last thursday [sic] who is the image of his father." This announcement is remarkable in that the newcomer soon thereafter was named Mary! The discrepancy can perhaps be attributed to youthful inexperience, for Browse was twelve at the time. Elsewhere in the letter, Browse wrote, almost casually: "General Jackson has taken Pensacola. He sent word to the Spaniards that he came there as a friend, but that he would treat them as enemy's [sic] if they made any resistance. . . . He entered it peaceably and the english [sic] betook themselves to their ships and fired two or three guns when they were out of reach. The Spanish and American flags were flying amicably together. . . . though we have not experienced the horrors of the war [of 1812] we feel the inconvenience of it."[18] Although not yet expert in distinguishing gender, Browse already displayed a command of language and a skill in communication that would enliven his later correspondence.

Tournillon's fortunes were improving so steadily that in 1816 he moved the family to his newly acquired plantation at La Fourche. He had purchased the property for $30,000, a princely sum in that era. By all appearances, Mary's struggles were over. Appearances, however, can be deceiving—especially in times of wild speculation.

La Fourche is located twenty or so miles down the bayou of the same name. Once the main channel of the Mississippi—before the river carved a new bed and left its old waterway a pastoral stream—La Fourche Bayou deepened as it approached the Gulf of Mexico. With two or three exceptions, the families living along its banks were French Acadians, refugees of the lingering warfare between the French and English in eastern Canada. They were easygoing Catholics, generally small farmers, dependent on their own labor for the cultivation of cotton, the main cash crop and principal material for homemade clothing, rather than on that of slaves, whom they could not afford anyway. These were the true "Cajuns," a word corrupted from "Acadian"[19] but not to be heard for another half-century.

Tournillon, though French, was not of the same stock or temperament as his neighbors. His aspirations were much more ambitious, and he was already looking beyond cotton as a source of income, though large-scale sugar planting was still a few years away. He owned slaves and was prepared to buy more when his projects warranted their acquisition. He viewed as his own the undeveloped lands in Mississippi that Mary had inherited from her first husband.

By the spring of 1817, Nicholas had absorbed all that Orleans College could offer him and was looking for a suitable provider of further education. His friendship with the Livingstons had deepened his early interest in the law, and he was strongly inclined to pursue a legal career. He hesitated, however, to commence his studies in Louisiana, for he hoped to return to his birthplace, Virginia, both to study and later practice. He investigated the College of William and Mary, but an expense list provided by the institution discouraged that hope. In a restless mood he considered joining the navy, a notion that alarmed his mother. She wrote: ". . . it has always been my wish that you should study law, yet you must be sensible my dear child. I only desire to advise . . . you in the choice of a profession, . . . you are too young to decide. . . . I hope you will lose your predilection for the navy which has been created by your intimacy with Gaston [a school friend] . . . . and apply yourself to finish your studies. I have such hopes for you that I know not how I should [escape] being disappointed."[20]

Gaston's influence soon faded. The brothers returned briefly to the family circle, and while at La Fourche, Nicholas received a letter from another college chum, a youth named Dumoulin. From it we glimpse another side of the serious young scholar. "I go there [New Orleans] occasionally in the evening, as of course in various other places to see the pretty *Demoiselles* of the City. . . . A number of young ladies have been asking for you and have [said] what a *jolie garcon* you were at college—I could not but in justice add that was the least of your praises and that you would be soon in town. About six days since a fine young Frenchman shot himself with a double barrel gun. . . . He was about 20 years of age and one of the handsomest young men I have ever seen—What crimes the Frenchies have been guilty of. I hardly know which is the worst race [French or Spanish]. . . ."[21]

While waiting at La Fourche for a chance to settle his fate, Nicholas learned from Browse, still attending college, that a yellow fever epidemic "raged with great fury in New Orleans carrying off from 3 to 400 a month."[22]

Shortly before Christmas a door was opened that would change the brothers' lives. In March of 1809, upon completing his second term as president, Thomas Jefferson retired from public life and gratefully returned to his beloved Monticello. Here he occupied himself with his vast library, his voluminous correspondence, the management of two large farms and his other innumerable interests. Despite his assurances to her that having a baby was "no more than a knock of the elbow," Maria Eppes, his beautiful younger daughter, had died after giving birth to a child.[23] His elder daughter, Martha Randolph, was the wife of Congressman and future Governor of Virginia Thomas Mann Randolph and mother of eleven children—thirteen, counting two who died in infancy. Martha adored her father above all other beings and served as his household manager. Hers was a task of heroic dimensions. To be both mistress of Monticello and mother of her own brood, she arranged, with her father's enthusiastic concurrence, to have her children live with her at Monticello. Her husband joined her there when his official duties allowed.

Who was this famous ex-president, and what impression did he make on his neighbors now that he had returned to private life? In the words of Edmond Bacon, his farm manager, he was "six feet two and a half inches high, well proportioned and straight as a gun barrel, like a fine horse he had no spare flesh."[24] The reddish hair of his youth and middle years had gone white. Never athletic, he was nevertheless vigorous and strong, though his gait had slowed; now his exercise consisted of a daily ride around his estate. On these rides he inspected his crops, livestock, nail factory, and other enterprises.

His dress was casual, sometimes downright shabby, and his daily habits simple. He usually wore overalls during the day. A favorite evening costume consisted of a red vest and threadbare red knee breeches, even though by this time most gentlemen of his standing preferred the new long trousers. After seeing to the affairs of the farm, Jefferson regularly retired to his library to immerse himself in study and correspondence. He scrupulously answered all of his mail, which daily poured in from statesmen, philosophers, and scholars throughout America and Europe.

For relief from his intellectual pursuits, Jefferson liked to join the young people who swarmed over the house and grounds in the late afternoons and evenings. Two older grandchildren, Anne Carey Bankhead and Thomas Jefferson (Jeff) Randolph, were by this time married and living apart, but a host of teenaged grandchildren and their friends were invariably on hand to make the stately mansion echo with laughter and music. Picnics, singing, dancing, card games and conversation were their customary recreations. The dignified old gentleman loved them all and never tired of entertaining them with his violin and sharing their company for an hour before returning to his books and papers. Late in 1817, he decided to invite the grandsons of his old friend Elizabeth Trist to Monticello for an extended visit.[25]

The invitation from their grandmother's distinguished friend reached the brothers shortly before Christmas. The prospect could not have been more welcome or the timing more propitious. Nicholas and Browse had absorbed most of what the college could offer and, at ages seventeen and fifteen respectively, were eligible for university enrollment. They were aware that their prospective host was the leading spirit in a campaign to establish what everyone believed would be one of America's finest institutions of higher learning, and they hoped that somehow they might enroll there. Their parents, of course, warmly approved of the visit.

Elizabeth Trist was overjoyed at the sight of her two grandsons, now tall and startlingly mature since she had last seen them. Their hostess, Martha Jefferson Randolph, welcomed them warmly and introduced them to her own numerous brood and to their assembled friends and relatives. Most were young people, the Randolphs and their cousins and neighbors who constituted their social set. The young males eyed the brothers with open curiosity, the girls with equal interest though veiled with suitable modesty. The two visitors endured this inspection with commendable poise and did their best to remember names. They were impressed by the number of girls, most of whom seemed to be named Randolph. Ellen, eldest of the sisters present, was easily the prettiest, but it was sixteen-year-old Virginia who caught and held Nicholas's eye. Taller and more poised than the other girls, she radiated gentle friendliness without a hint of coquetry. As Nicholas held her slim hand—a trifle longer than convention required—a thrill went through him that was utterly new to his experience.

The introductions were interrupted when a servant opened a door and ushered in the master of Monticello. Thomas Jefferson acknowledged the respectful murmur of the assembly with a courtly nod and approached his guests. In his seventy-fifth year his carriage was still erect, his eye clear and his voice strong, though his mottled skin and stiff, deliberate movements betrayed his age.

Mr. Jefferson observed his young guests keenly. Elizabeth Trist and her daughter had done well, he decided. Both boys carried themselves like gentlemen, and the elder looked like a lad who might go far. Nicholas Trist had reached his full height, about six feet, and was slim and straight as a rapier. His hair was black and slightly curling, his features were chiseled and his dark eyes direct and flashing. Browse, equally slender and an inch or two shorter, gave an impression of sober stability unusual in so young a lad.

The period that followed was a time of carefree happiness that would excite the envy of high-spirited young people in any era. Christmas, already at hand when the Trists arrived, was a round of parties and festivities, with feasting and dancing and much innocent revelry. (Mr. Jefferson held strict convictions about drinking and would not even serve wine except to mature guests.) There was music, both amateur and professional. The host, resplendent in his red vest and knee breeches, brought out his famed violin and showed that age had not diminished his talent. Through the winter there were sleigh rides and skating parties with bonfires on the river bank; in the spring, fox hunts, bird watching, and nature walks. Summer brought picnics and rides through hills and fields.

The days rushed by and the months flowed together. In late summer Nicholas grew restless, realizing that the question of his education seemed to have been forgotten. One day Jefferson summoned him to his library for a serious conversation. What occupation did young Mr. Trist intend to pursue? Nicholas spoke of his interest in the law as theory but admitted to reservations concerning its practice. What were those reservations? The moral compromises that seemed inextricably associated with the law bothered the young idealist. What means did he possess to pay for an education? None, Nicholas confessed, for by now his stepfather was heavily in debt due to speculation in sugar planting and was not likely soon to recover. The old philosopher regarded him thoughtfully for an uncomfortable length of time and at last brought forth a startling suggestion: What would the young man say to a free education in preparation for a professional military career? At a momentary loss, Nicholas stammered that such a possibility would certainly deserve consideration.[26]

What Jefferson had in mind, of course, was an appointment to the fledgling military academy at West Point,[27] for he recognized in Nicholas a first-class mind and a singularly staunch character, qualities he did not wish to see wasted. After a few minutes' reflection, Nicholas discovered an enthusiasm for the military life he had not known he possessed. With a faint smile, Jefferson said he would see what could be done.

Shortly thereafter, Nicholas Trist, Esq., was informed by a letter from the secretary of war that he had been accepted for enrollment at West Point. He was directed to report to the superintendent for the fall term, and the date specified was only weeks away.

A matter of utmost importance to Nicholas remained to be settled before his departure, a matter that made his young heart quake. He could not muster the courage to approach Virginia directly, so he did what many another lovesick swain has done before and have done since. He wrote to her mother.

The probability of an absence of some length from Albemarle has induced me, Dear Mrs. Randolph, to take a step which I had, a short time since, resolved to defer until I should have attained my twenty-first year, a step which if it does not entirely meet your approbation, I pray you at least not be offended at. You may possibly have perceived that an attachment has existed for some time, in my bosom, to your daughter Virginia; that the attachment is strong, and *must* be lasting, I am fully convinced.

Hoping that my sentiments may be agreeable to yourself and Mr. Randolph, I address you these lines to request the permission of making them known to Miss Virginia.

Accept, dear Mrs. Randolph, for yourself, the Colonel and family; assurances of perpetual gratitude and devoted friendship of

NichoP. Trist[28]

18th September 1818——

Martha Randolph was extremely fond of young Nicholas and fully aware, as he had suggested, of his growing love for Virginia, who was now a month past her seventeenth birthday. Martha was also a clear-eyed realist. She wrote a gentle, motherly reply expressing her opinion that Nicholas and Virginia were "both too young to be entangled in an engagement . . . and that [since] a change of sentiment is pardonable," Nicholas would be wise to defer for the present an open declaration to Virginia.[29] He immediately wrote again to assure her that there was not the slightest possibility of a change in his sentiments, but that he would nevertheless honor her wishes and offer heart and hand to Virginia only when all parental reservations had been erased.

And so, with the matter of greatest concern still unresolved and officially secret, he set off for West Point at the end of September 1818.

CHAPTER 2

West Point

The departure of Nicholas Trist cast a pall of deep gloom upon the usually exuberant young spirits at Monticello. His absence also affected their elders and even the domestic servants. Browse and Francis Eppes hid their grief by going into Charlottesville to observe the workers building the new university. Wandering by the riverbank, one of the Randolph cousins found the initials VJR freshly carved in an ancient beech tree near the picnic ground. Elizabeth Trist wrote a tender letter to Nicholas warning him to protect his health "in that cold climate," then added ". . . Mrs. Randolph in speaking of you her eyes filled with tears she said she felt the regard of a mother for you and Browse and since you left the whole family lost their spirits."[1]

Had he known what awaited him, Trist might well have entertained second thoughts about the academy, for West Point was a smoldering bomb, soon to explode. The fuse had been lit a little more than a year earlier, on July 28, 1817.[2] On that date Maj. Sylvanus Thayer leaped from the deck of a Hudson River sloop onto the North Wharf, climbed the hill well remembered from his cadet days, entered the superintendent's office without knocking, and confronted the glowering officer he had come to replace.

Until that moment Capt. Alden Partridge had served as acting superintendent, although "acting" was an unwelcome part of his title and one he invariably ignored. Partridge had been at the academy almost from its modest inception in 1802, when the crumbling ruins of General Washington's Revolutionary War headquarters had been renovated for the purpose of training army engineers. After graduating from the school he stayed on as an instructor, and when that ill-starred and much abused facility teetered on the brink of oblivion—at one point only Partridge and one cadet remained—he assumed the role if not the official title of superintendent.

Early in his administration, Pres. James Madison gave his strong support to the academy, and West Point again began slowly to rebuild its enrollment, still without an officially sanctioned head. Meanwhile, "Superintendent" Partridge continued to run the place in his customarily chaotic, arbitrary, and capricious fashion, varying each day's program according to the weather or his own whim. At the time, the minimum age for enrollment was fourteen, although some cadets were younger and one was only ten. Partridge pandered shamelessly to these young boys, showing favoritism and playing up to their childish fancies much as an untrained governess might cater to an infant. As a consequence he was popular with some and hated by others. To make matters worse, his immediate superior, General Swift, commander of the Corps of Engineers, loyally protected Partridge from the increasingly disenchanted War Department. Matters came to a head when a group of unhappy professors sent a heated letter to Pres. James Monroe, who by this time had succeeded Madison, detailing the numerous causes of their discontent. When the letter was routed back through channels to Captain Partridge, he promptly arrested the disgruntled professors, who were the cream of the faculty. At this point Secretary of War John C. Calhoun ordered Sylvanus Thayer home from a two-year study tour in Europe and directed him to take charge at the military academy. Thayer's first challenge was to dispossess his defiant predecessor.

The two officers were nearly of an age—Thayer thirty-two and Partridge a year older—but in all other respects they were as dissimilar as two men could be. Where Partridge was disorganized, temperamental, and mentally untidy, Thayer was disciplined, visionary, and deeply committed to an ideal. He carried in his head a precise blueprint of the military academy he intended to build, and he would allow nothing to obstruct his plan. He was also a patient realist who understood that no good could come of wresting the superintendency from the recalcitrant Partridge, who clearly enjoyed a measure of popularity with many of the cadets; forcing the issue would only create a serious division of loyalties. Thayer reported the situation in a letter to General Swift and retired to New York to await orders.

General Swift, still loyal to his friend, persuaded President Monroe to accompany him to West Point, hoping that a personal inspection would cause the president to revoke his order and allow the beleaguered Partridge to remain. But nothing of the sort happened. Thayer's appointment remained in effect.

Incredibly, Partridge continued to resist the inevitable. When Thayer took possession of the superintendent's office, Partridge demanded that he be allowed to occupy it and even threatened to seize it by force. More than that, he actually did so by ordering a junior officer to read aloud an announcement that Captain Partridge was reassuming command. Conscious of the jubilant cheers of those cadets who had enjoyed Partridge's favor, Thayer again calmly retired from the field of battle after first reporting to the secretary of war. But arrogance alone would not carry the day, for by this time the administration had endured enough of Partridge. He was arrested, court-martialed and cashiered from the army, though his patron, General Swift, succeeded in reversing the latter action and allowing Partridge to resign, still bellowing defiance.

Superintendent Thayer quickly instituted a series of reforms designed to bring order from the chaos that was threatening the survival of the academy. The minimum age was raised to sixteen, although younger cadets who were currently enrolled and otherwise able to meet Thayer's standards were allowed to continue. The annual summer vacation, in Thayer's opinion a source of trouble and a temptation to waste time in vice, was canceled in favor of a more restrictive policy: after successfully completing three years training, cadets would be eligible for furlough. Parade ground drill, formerly suspended during colder months, became a year-round event except in the most inclement weather. Academic standards were stiffened, with dismissal facing chronically weak students. More new regulations were introduced with alarming frequency. These unfamiliar strictures seemed excessively draconian to young men thoroughly spoiled by the sloppy Partridge system.

Trist arrived at the end of the first vacationless summer. Cadets smarting over this denial of their "rights" were also getting acquainted with a new instructor of tactics. Capt. John Bliss was a hard-boiled martinet who demanded perfection on the drill field. He possessed the vocabulary of a mule skinner and employed it freely to instill fear and discourage inattention. Cadets long accustomed to straggling through simple maneuvers found themselves on the receiving end of a sulfurous tongue-lashing for anything less than machinelike precision. One day an unfortunate youth named Edward Nicholson committed some infraction in ranks, then compounded the offense by dragging his feet when ordered back to barracks.

Nicholson was summarily jerked out of formation by his collar and treated to a withering blast of profanity.

Two days later, November 24, 1818, five cadets came to the superintendent's office and introduced themselves as a committee elected by the cadet corps to protest the "attack" on Cadet Nicholson and to submit a long list of other outrages allegedly perpetrated by Captain Bliss. The group's speaker, Thomas Ragland, and another committee member, Wilson Fairfax, were brilliant students who had recently been appointed acting assistant professors. Nathaniel Loring was a cadet captain. All but one of the five were Partridge favorites. They handed the superintendent a round-robin petition signed by 179 cadets, many of them sons of influential families.

Thayer received the delegation with glacial formality. Recognizing some legitimacy in their complaint, though outraged by the form in which it was tendered, he informed them that complaints brought to his attention by individual cadets would be given fair consideration but round-robin petitions would not be tolerated. He dismissed them with a stern warning not to make the same mistake again.

With astounding bravado, the committee returned the next day with another round-robin petition, this time accompanied by a threat of mutiny by the entire corps if their charges were not taken seriously. Ragland, again acting as speaker, had apparently deceived himself into thinking that his honorary position as post adjutant afforded him all the privileges of a commissioned army officer. Superintendent Thayer ordered them to leave the post within six hours and to remain at their homes awaiting further notice.

At the time this crisis arose, Nicholas Trist had been at West Point less than two months. The rigorous academy program had taken its toll on his nonathletic body. He was shocked to discover that a full ten pounds had departed his already slender frame. Always apprehensive about his health, especially about a tendency toward respiratory ailments, he fretted over the constant exposure to cold and fatigue, and not without reason. Long hours of drill on the sometimes icy parade ground left the cadets shivering in their poorly heated two-man rooms, where they slept on a floor cushioned by a thin mattress or a blanket. They studied by candlelight, cold feet pressed against the bumper of a tiny fireplace, until the "Lights out!" order was given.

Although Trist rankled under the stiff discipline, there is no record of his active participation in the "insurrection." Still, he sympathized with its objectives and undoubtedly signed the two petitions. In the short few weeks before the confrontation, he had formed a lasting friendship with Wilson Fairfax. Fairfax was typical of the many young men who would be attracted to Trist: bright, bold, aristocratic, well educated and fiercely independent, like Nicholas himself. When the banished five withdrew, still defiant and full of fight, to try their influence on Congress and the administration, Fairfax maintained contact with Trist by mail,[3] seeking what inside information he could obtain and expressing a confidence that faded with the fading hopes of the insurrectionists as Washington frowned disapproval on the uprising.

Secretary of War Calhoun and President Monroe understood that they had a rare gem in Sylvanus Thayer, and they backed him to the hilt. As for Congress, the insurrection confirmed its persistent suspicion that West Point was a nest of rich, spoiled brats and a waste of taxpayers' money. Though there were never quite enough anti-academy votes to shut it down, that perception would remain until the Civil War finally erased lingering doubts about the value of the academy. Thayer emerged a clear winner. Captain Bliss was less fortunate; Secretary Calhoun concluded that he did "not appear to possess a sufficient command of his temper" and ordered Bliss transferred.[4]

A splendid academic institution was emerging at West Point, although the challenges of the classroom were, if anything, more frustrating than those of the drill field. Luckily for Trist, the crux of one institutional weakness lay at the point of his greatest strength. From its inception, the military academy has been primarily a training school for engineers.[5] In the Napoleonic era, the best military engineers were French officers, and the best textbooks on the subject were all written in French. President Jefferson, who authorized the academy, was an ardent Francophile as well as a champion of higher education. When the faculty was selected, the choice for professor of engineering fell to a veteran of the Napoleonic wars, one Claudius Crozet.[6] Textbooks in French were being translated into English, but no English translations existed in engineering or mathematics. Crozet spoke little English; his pupils, except for Trist, spoke even less French. One may readily imagine this tall, heavily built academician toiling at a blackboard, his face alight with enthusiasm for his subject while the faces before him were, alas! wreathed in perplexity; for not only did they comprehend scarcely a word being said, but most of them also lacked the bare rudiments of the science under discussion.[7] As Crozet labored to make himself understood, Trist, who was fluent in French, articulate in English and quick to learn as well, repeatedly came to his rescue. Crozet was understandably grateful.

Although history tells that Trist served as an instructor in French, he was, like Ragland and Fairfax, only a teacher's aide, or "acting assistant professor," to use the academy's term. Soon Major Thayer became aware of Nicholas Trist and, being dependent on all available resources, undoubtedly valued his ability as translator.

Trist enjoyed his special status, but his combative spirit soon got him in trouble with some of his instructors. The recurring cause of friction, which was not limited to him but affected many high-spirited cadets, was regional hubris. The cadets came from three fairly evenly represented sections of the United States: North, South, and West. Northerners were mostly from New England and most were sons of merchants, lawyers, doctors and politicians. They were, on the average, better educated than the other boys; however, some had already absorbed the strident new philosophy called Abolitionism, and even those who had not were considered boorish and ungenteel by the southerners. The westerners were for the most part hearty, good-natured fellows, generally as lacking in scholastic ability as their southern brothers but much admired by all the cadets for their frontier manliness. The tension lay, as it would for decades to come, between North and South. Trist entered the fray with reckless enthusiasm.

The reader may have detected that Nicholas Trist was something of a snob. Even though he had spent most of his eighteen years in Louisiana, he considered himself a Virginian, and in his view Virginia, birthplace of presidents, surely needed no defense as a place far superior to anything the North might offer.[8] His opinion found little favor with some members of the faculty. When complaints about Trists's unrestrained regionalism began pouring into the superintendent's office, Major Thayer regretfully began toying with thoughts of dismissal.

The superintendent customarily informed the family of an endangered cadet that the young man faced dismissal, for he knew that often early notification was all that was needed. Unfortunately, Trist's family mistakenly believed the complaint had something to do with the recent highly publicized insurrection. The reaction was swift and highly charged. Elizabeth Trist fired off a letter declaring "if . . . you put yourself in any measure that would have occasioned your expulsion I should have been mortified to the Soul."[9] His mother echoed these alarms, admonishing him to "be consistent." Levelheaded Browse, always his staunchest supporter and severest critic, wrote: "I read with great interest the pamphlet published in justification of the conduct of the Cadets. . . . Doubtless you all acted perfectly right in adopting some measures to redress your grievances, but I think those Cadets whom Captain Bliss had ill treated should have borne their burthen [sic] on their own shoulders, and not have subjected the first young men in the academy to the mortification of being arrested and suspended or of being dismissed, together with . . . losing so much time, which is irreparable at their time of life." [Sagely, Browse added,] "I am sorry to see you are so obstinately bent on disliking the professors. It seems that they return you good for evil, in giving you a very good character. Remember that your future success will depend, in some measure, on the figure you make at that seminary."[10] Trist took these stern and loving words to heart. He swallowed his pride and settled down to serious study, finishing his first year at the top of his class.

Browse, a faithful correspondent, served as his brother's main source of information concerning the Tournillons, Randolphs, grandmother Elizabeth, and Mr. Jefferson. Always a worrier, Nicholas was uneasy about the unresolved state of his relationship with Virginia. However much the two mothers may have hoped that the undeclared romance would fade, they were doomed to disappointment, for absence only made Nicholas's love grow stronger. Reports from Browse were reassuring. "I think Miss V. appeared somewhat affected the day after your departure," Browse wrote.[11] He became increasingly enthusiastic about the affair, writing, "I hope to see you united to Miss V. for whom I feel real affection, considering her one of the most amiable and sensible girls in existence."[12] He was somewhat less complimentary about Nicholas: ". . . you have already . . . every qualification except prudence and economy. . . ."[13] Prudence and economy—those words would linger like a prophecy. Later his encouragement was tinged with pessimism and scolding: "I fancy you are as much thought of now . . . by a certain person as ever you were . . . I think your chances are very good . . . but really, it passes my comprehension how you are to support a wife."[14]

Andrew Jackson Donelson, nephew as well as namesake of the famous frontier fighter and emerging Tennessee politician, was a classmate and close friend of Trist's. He would greatly influence his career in a few years, when both would serve on Jackson's presidential staff. The young men who entered the academy were then, as now, from all parts of the country. Some were "green as grass," presenting their instructors with challenges that tested their patience almost beyond human limits. One hot June day, a lanky Kentuckian named Henderson K. Yoakum toiled up the steep hill, entered the administration office and flung himself down, panting and sweating, alongside the superintendent, at whom he stared curiously. "Old man," he demanded, "are you Colonel or Captain or whatever-you-call-um Thayer?" Thayer, now advanced in rank, replied calmly, "I am Colonel Thayer, sir." "Wal, now, look-a-yere, Kern," drawled Yoakum, "this yere hill o' yourn am a breather, if it ain't, damn me!" Yoakum survived the interview, went on to graduate, and eventually wrote a history of Texas.[15]

Some who came as cadets would make their names as faculty members at West Point. Joshua Baker achieved a reputation as a mathematical genius. Edward H. Courtenay, first in the Class of '21, became professor of natural and experimental philosophy (called physics today). Dennis Hart Mahon, who arrived on the Fourth of July, 1820, was an instructor in tactics for nearly forty years and wrote a treatise on the art of war that became a textbook for Stonewall Jackson and other Civil War generals.

After the departure of Captain Bliss, Superintendent Thayer created a new post, which he called "Commandant of Cadets." The officer so designated would not only teach cadets how to drill smartly but would also serve as an organic head of the corps, demonstrating by example all of the soldierly characteristics that an academy-trained officer should possess. The man chosen to fill this role was Brevet Maj. William J. Worth, 23d Infantry hero of Chappequa and Niagara in the War of 1812. (A brevet commission bestowed nominal rank higher than that for which the officer received pay. Worth's actual rank was captain.) "Haughty Bill" Worth, as the cadets dubbed him, made his predecessor look like a milksop, for in many ways he seemed a prototypical Prussian militarist. Of average height but strongly built, he carried himself at all times with rigidly martial bearing, his handsome features set like granite. His dark eyes flashed fire when he spotted a sloppy cadet. His vocabulary, though usually more elegant than his predecessor's, could "descend to scurrility sometimes," according to one cadet, who presumably spoke from painful experience.[16]

Determined to erase the widespread impression that West Point was a nursery for the pampered sons of the rich, Sylvanus Thayer established Spartan standards, which he enforced rigorously and with absolute fairness. He issued a regulation prohibiting receipt of money other than the ten dollars per month salary from the government. From this meager stipend the cadets were to purchase uniforms, swords, extra blankets if desired and all other necessities not provided on the post.

Doubtless this austere policy reflected a belief that, since absence from the grounds was permitted only under extremely limited conditions, there should be no need for extra spending money. Although Colonel Thayer was for the most part realistic, in this he deceived himself, for at a short distance from the post lay Gridley's Hotel. Although sternly declared off-limits to all post personnel, Gridley's exerted a magnetic attraction for the more adventurous cadets. Here could be obtained not only wines and spiritous liquors (which not all who came that way consumed) but also succulent ham, roast turkey dripping savory juices, biscuits floating in gravy, mince pie, plum pudding, and sundry other delicacies. When the West Point mess hall fare proved unappetizing or unbearably meager, those who were in funds and bold enough to "run it" to Gridley's found warm food and genial hospitality. For eight years, until Gridley sold his establishment, Thayer was unable to discourage this breach of discipline.

Although no record reveals that Trist frequented Gridley's Hotel, he was certainly among those who could not subsist on ten dollars a month. In fact, he was four-hundred dollars in debt when he arrived at the academy, and more expenses were incurred soon thereafter. Ignoring regulations, he sought relief from his stepfather, using Browse as an intermediary. Although Tournillon's finances were at low ebb due to a severe depression in cotton prices, he sent what he could afford. In time Trist paid off his debts, but his need for supplemental income did not abate, nor would it in the future. "You lack only prudence and economy," Browse had written. Sage words from one so young.

Superintendent Thayer labored unceasingly to establish a perception of West Point as a vital element in the nation's defenses. For the few who were able to examine the evidence, the facts spoke for themselves. Yet many persisted in the notion that a healthy militia was all the defense America needed, and a school for the training of officers was a foolish extravagance. In early March 1820, ex-Cadet Ragland and his four co-insurrectionists were still intriguing in Washington. At the same time, Congress was drafting a resolution to abolish the academy. Thayer promptly launched a public relations campaign. Ordering Commandant Worth to institute extra drill and spit-and-polish, he arranged for the first of two summer exhibition tours. On a bright June morning, the entire cadet corps boarded steamboats, which carried them down the Hudson to land at Staten Island. Through New York, New Jersey, and many towns and villages in Pennsylvania, the young men of West Point paraded smartly. The tour climaxed in Philadelphia with a dazzling precision drill. Everywhere, audiences went wild with enthusiasm. The five disgruntled cadets subsided and were heard of no more; neither was the congressional resolution.

Meanwhile, Cadet Trist continued to excel in his studies and to find little satisfaction in other areas of his life. True to his promise to Mrs. Randolph, he wrote only occasionally to Virginia and in those few letters expressed little more than polite neighborly sentiments. Her responses were even fewer and cooler than his own tepid offerings. His mother wrote of money problems ("cotton is now selling from 13 to 15 cents and is believed will fall to 10 cents as soon as the river rises") and of her concern for his health, which remained surprisingly good.[17] He initiated correspondence with Virginia's father, Thomas Mann Randolph, whom he had barely known while at Monticello and who was by this time governor of Virginia. The governor seemed pleased to receive his letters, and the exchange continued. His boyhood friend Lewis Livingston writing about life in New Orleans, offered the army his opinion that hammocks should be used in the field (apparently expecting Trist to pass the idea along to the quartermaster) and expressed shocked amusement at his friend's intention to pursue a military career. "In this country," he declared, "I think no man that can pursue any other vocation ought to adopt a military life. Our wars are so 'few and far between' that no one can calculate ever with any degree of probability upon having an opportunity to display his talents."[18]

Aside from Browse, Grandmother Elizabeth was his most faithful correspondent. She assured him that nothing was more important to her "than the good opinion that is entertained of my grandsons and which I hope they will always be emulous to preserve." After lamenting his apparent lack of reciprocal feeling, she noted, "Mr. Tournillon finds it difficult to [pay] bills these are distressing times and money has been so scarce as not to be obtained." Then she came squarely to the matter that was pressing upon her heart:

> I hope you will never take up arms but in defence of your Country. I would as soon hear of you turning highwayman as to join an army from ambitious motives. War is at best a horrid calamity and those who wage war for the purpose of subjugating nations to their will are guilty of a heinous crime so my Dear Nicholas when the hour arrives that you must quit this World let not your conscience upbraid you with having done anything to dishonor humanity . . . the very reflection of having assisted to destroy [life] is a poignant stab . . . remember what your father Phil suffered in having taken the life of a fellow being tho he did it in justification of his own honor . . . yet it prey'd upon his mind what must be the reflection of those . . .

instrumental in heaping misery upon thousands, how many widows and orphans are thrown into the world destitute and wretched. I should glory in seeing you at the plough tail rather than hearing of your being a general in a foreign service.[19]

This final sentence was in response to a vague hint from Trist that he was considering offering his services to Colombia, where, according to cadet scuttlebutt, even an undergraduate West Pointer would be welcomed with a major's rank.

His services to Professor Crozet had led to friendship, and as friendship grew, Crozet confided to Trist that he was not satisfied with his situation at the academy. He hoped for a more congenial teaching post, but his recent arrival in America and his continuing struggles with the English language did not encourage this hope. Trist told him of the planned University of Virginia and, with a hint of self-importance, of his own relationship with its founder. When Crozet showed interest, Trist offered to advance his candidacy with Jefferson. He addressed a glowing recommendation to Jefferson and included it in a letter to Browse in which he asked Browse to deliver it in person and add his own endorsement. Browse's description of the interview is illuminating:

Obeying your directions, I carried your letter relating to Mr. Crozet to Mr. Jefferson & having told him the subject was saluted with a 'poh, poh? (or something like it), it is all needless, sir, we shall not engage professors for at least a year, all our endeavors will be used to get Mr. Bodwich, should we not succeed in procuring him, Mr. (I forget his name) has . . . the next best claim to the chair.' . . . Your letter was not read, so you see there is but little chance for Mr. Crozet. The university no doubt, will be ready for our progeny, but not for us. . . . the treasurer, Mr. Preston, as it seems made use of the public money, & there is a deficit of from eighty to 100,000$. It will therefore be useless for you to think any more about it. . . . for god's sake do not give me any more commissions to the old Patriarch.[20]

Despite Browse's pessimism, the story has a happy ending. When the university opened, the faculty included Claudius Crozet.

The voluminous exchange of correspondence between the brothers already reflected the extraordinary degree of affection, trust, and mutual dependence that would be evident throughout their lives. Requests for money or other assistance were accommodated whenever possible with dispatch and good spirit, but the best of their letters dealt with their plans, dreams, fears, and fancies. On one occasion Browse wrote from Philadelphia, where he had gone for needed dental repair and to pursue his seemingly hopeless search for affordable education. It was a gloomy, introspective letter, lamenting a persistent cold that had kept him in bed for a week. "I used to think," he wrote miserably, "that I was strong and active and possessed a hardy constitution, but the woeful truth is, that I have a very delicate frame that is likely to be shaken . . . by every wind that blows, and if exposed to storms will soon be wrecked, so care must be given to it." This susceptibility, shared with his brother, he blamed on "that cursed Louisiana what I would not give if my boyhood at least, had passed far from its fetid and polluted atmosphere." Both Trists may have acquired this susceptibility, as Browse suspected, in Louisiana during early childhood. Now both were returning there, albeit reluctantly. Browse's letter continued in the same melancholy vein: "If you have any expectations about my future eminence you may lay them aside, I have not the talents requisite for . . . a public speaker. . . . I must be content to jog through this dull world like the rest."[21]

Once after Nicholas received a letter from their mother expressing concern for his moral welfare, he confided to Browse: ". . . her suspicions however are groundless not that I am too good to [engage] in those follies, but that opportunities do not thrust themselves in my way, and I do not seek them. I have no licentious companion to allure me into the temples of Venus and from some cause or other I am not bold enough to introduce myself. I can say for myself that I have never been in a brothel in my life."[22]

His devoted grandmother continued to write, although her words squiggled and her lines wandered, the result of developing arthritis. She wrote: "I can't expect to live much longer nor do I wish it if I am to suffer as much pain as I have the last two or three days."[23]

As he approached the completion of his third year, Trist knew he would soon be eligible for his first furlough. In a letter to Thomas Mann Randolph, he put forth some hints that could hardly be called subtle. He was at pains to disabuse the governor of any impression that the choice of a military career was a settled matter. "Other thoughts," he wrote, "have occupied me since my residence here; I have long been convinced that happiness was to be enjoyed by me, if at all, as a married man, and I have therefore cherished every feeling with which I set off for this place three years since; they . . . will, I hope, be productive of much happiness to myself as well as to others." There was more of the same, which he hoped would preserve the spirit of his promise while putting Virginia's parents on notice.[24]

In the summer of 1821, the cadet corps went on tour again, even more elaborately and with more grandiose effect than in the preceding year. After traveling by steamboat to Albany, they marched through Lenox, Springfield, Liecester, Worcester, Framingham, Roxbury, and finally Boston, at every stop dazzling the townsfolk with their precision drilling and every evening thrilling the local damsels with their dancing. From Boston they went on to Providence, New London, New Haven, and New York, where a reception was held at city hall. Only in late September did the weary cadets return to the academy.[25]

Cadet Nicholas Philip Trist was not among them. He arrived at Monticello in early June and did not return to West Point in the fall.

CHAPTER 3

La Fourche

Love is hard to keep secret, especially when the "secret" is shared by several people over three years. Virginia was aware of Nicholas's intentions when the tall, slim young man returned. He was no longer a youth but now nearly a stranger, and the undeclared nature of his love put them both under a strain. Trist had first to obtain her parents' permission to unlock the secret, which proved simple enough, for his evident maturity coupled with the favorable impression they had gained from his frequent letters confirmed what they had already decided. Martha, speaking for both, happily released the impatient suitor, but the next step proved more difficult.

The sudden release of his pent-up yearning induced in Trist a nervousness bordering on panic. He dispatched a servant with an unsigned note inviting Virginia to meet him for a private conversation. To his dismay, she responded with a cool refusal, but his course was set and there could be no turning back. He poured out his feelings in a page-long letter, this time boldly signed "Nicholas Philip Trist." Its language was painfully stilted but its sincerity unmistakable. He explained that the invitation had been extended for "the purpose of making a declaration of passion which . . . you must have read in [my eye]. Since my return, I have been in a state of suspense which, if I have the smallest corner of your heart, you will be anxious to remove and which, if I have been doomed to adore a woman without return of Love, it is your duty to remove."[1]

This torrent of emotion swept away her resistance, which, one suspects, was at most only a token. She confessed to a longing that his three-year absence had intensified, and soon they were betrothed. Pressing his advantage, Nicholas begged for an early wedding date, but again his hopes were dashed. Both Virginia and her mother were uneasy about his abandonment of a military career. How did he now propose to support the two of them? The question echoed one that Browse had posed a year earlier: "I wish you to tell me candidly . . . what you propose doing for yourself in the world. As you inherit no fortune that I know of, you will have to struggle like others to support yourself."[2] Upon learning of the engagement, Browse, who had by this time returned to Louisiana, restated his misgivings: "When I read your letter, I was . . . thrown into a kind of melancholy reverie. . . . I felt how hard it would be that two beings whose lives have passed as yours have in affluence . . . & ease should . . . begin the world anew resting entirely on your exertions for a support." In a burst of candor he added, "There was I dare say a little selfishness mingled with my feelings, for . . . [now your] affection is concentrated on one object; other ties are soon relaxed & weakened 'till at last a Brother becomes a mere acquaintance." He closed on a note of regret over Nicholas's decision not to return to West Point and summed up with: "You must place all these feelings in their true light; they were the natural consequence of the deep interest I take in all that concerns you."[3] As always, Browse placed his brother's fortunes above his own.

What are you going to do, Nicholas? The question would dog him at frequent intervals until his dying day.

Nicholas was not indifferent to this problem, and now that Virginia had accepted him, somewhat conditionally, he was forced to face it squarely. His tentative decision was to study and eventually practice law. His introduction to the legal profession by Edward Livingston had awakened a keen interest in its abstract principles, but later observation of its everyday practice had repelled him. This ambivalence was not yet clear even to himself. He had, after all, made a quite respectable beginning that he did not care to discard unfinished, especially after so recently abandoning another promising career. With a show of enthusiasm that satisfied his ladylove without wholly convincing himself, he declared his intention to become a lawyer.

The Virginia bar was his obvious preference, but the perennial surplus of lawyers that had driven his father to the frontier and another occupation remained a formidable obstacle. On the other hand, lawyers were needed in Louisiana, and he was already partially trained in the emerging laws of that new state. He would have given a great deal to remain at Monticello and study under Thomas Jefferson, who had extended the offer, but common sense dictated Louisiana.

Reason and necessity were driving Nicholas away, while sentiment and responsibility were holding Virginia captive at Monticello. In temperament as well as looks she resembled her mother, who was a feminine replica of Thomas Jefferson and the one closest to the old man's heart, especially since the death at age twenty-five of her sister Maria. For many years, Thomas Jefferson had expected Martha to run his household, a duty she had willingly embraced even to the point of leaving her own home and bringing her large family with her.[4] Her responsibilities as hostess of Monticello (to be described in detail later) had increased steadily as Jefferson's fame grew, eventually to the point where she relied heavily on Virginia's help, a dependency she would never escape. Reluctantly, Virginia bade her fiancé farewell. She agreed to marry him when he completed his legal training. They parted, dissatisfied and unhappy, in September 1821.

Nicholas traveled north by stage, joining Browse in Washington, then both took a riverboat to Louisiana. Arriving at the Tournillon plantation on Bayou La Fourche, the brothers embraced their parents, whom Nicholas had not seen for nearly four years. Mary had been in an agony of apprehension for two weeks, unrelieved by her husband's reassurances, for she knew that the great rivers, like the Gulf of Mexico, swarmed with pirates. Grandmother Brown, now returned to Louisiana after residing for several years at her old home in Charlottesville, was confined to her bed with a heavy cold but rejoiced to be again with her adored grandsons. Their baby sister Mary had heard much about Browse and Nicholas; she warmed to them readily enough but looked apprehensively for her mother's approval when Nicholas ceremoniously dubbed her "My little Queen of Hearts."[5] St. Julien Tournillon bade them welcome to stay in his house as long as they pleased. The younger Julien, a mere lad at the time of their departure, was now nearly as tall as Browse.

Nicholas accepted his stepfather's offer with the understanding that he would reside with the Livingstons in New Orleans whenever Mr. Livingston could make time to tutor him, as he had offered to do. Although Browse's plans were less definite, he still hoped to advance his education when finances permitted. Meanwhile, he would study at home.

While waiting for a summons from New Orleans, Nicholas launched a stream of letters to Virginia that revealed many facets of his developing character. Covering many pages in a firm, regular hand, he wrote of the things that lay on his heart. Health was even more of a concern then than today, and one that revealed in Trist a trace of eccentricity, a trait that would become more pronounced over time. He considered bear's oil an effective treatment for sore throats and congested lungs; however, one jar he had intended to send had lain so long in the post office that it had become rancid. He recommended tea made from sassafras root as a stimulant for perspiration and an inhibitor of bleeding, describing it as "one of the most aromatic and pleasantly tasted woods in the world."[6] His growing interest in nature cures and alternative medicine is understandable when one considers the primitive and often dangerous treatment then commonly practiced by doctors. In some of his health habits he was far ahead of his time; for example, he made it a weekly practice to floss his teeth.

Not surprisingly, Trist's letters made frequent mention of Thomas Jefferson. "Every moment of your grandfather's society that I lose, is irreparable," he wrote.[7] The compliment to her grandfather scarcely flattered Virginia, but his impatience was significant. He had already chosen Thomas Jefferson as his role model, and he was painfully aware that Jefferson was then approaching his seventy-ninth birthday.

Nicholas also exchanged letters with other members of the family he so ardently desired to make his own. Of the daughters other than his fiancée, Ellen was his most faithful correspondent, and between them a warm and lasting friendship grew. He also continued writing to both of Virginia's parents and to receive letters from them. Their "favors" told him nothing of the turbulent Randolph history, a story that would have discouraged many a suitor. He would have to learn that from other sources.

Governor Randolph, despite appearances of domestic happiness and a successful career, was a troubled man. A mysterious mental disturbance had twice incapacitated him for long periods, and the panic of 1819 had driven him to the verge of bankruptcy. In spite of his malady and the unremitting stress upon his wife as mistress of Monticello, Martha bore him thirteen children, eleven of whom lived to adulthood. Charles, the youngest, was born during the Trist brothers' visit in 1818. Loyal wife and mother though she was, Martha made no secret of the fact that her role as her father's housekeeper took precedence over everything else in her life. Perhaps for that reason, her husband, despite long periods of apparent stability, remained deeply insecure and unhappy. Jefferson, no doubt guiltily aware that his demands on Martha were destabilizing her marriage, did all that he could to help and encourage his son-in-law.[8]

Two of the Randolph children, Anne and Jeff, were already married. Anne was the wife of a violent, drunken wretch named Charles Bankhead, who in 1819 nearly killed her brother Thomas Jefferson (Jeff) Randolph. Jeff learned of an insult to his wife by Bankhead and went seeking an apology. Instead, Bankhead sprang upon him, stabbed him several times and doubtless would have killed him but for the intervention of Thomas Jefferson's farm manager, Edmund Bacon. Although night had fallen by the time Thomas Jefferson received news of the incident, he flung himself on his horse and galloped several miles in pitch darkness to Charlottesville, where his grandson lay heavily bandaged on a pile of blankets. Seeing his seventy-six-year-old grandfather kneeling beside him, weeping inconsolably, unnerved young Jeff, he later confessed. He survived to replace Bacon and later to achieve some distinction in politics but considered himself permanently maimed by the assault.[9]

The family's anger against Bankhead was expressed by Martha, who declared it would be in their best interest to hire a bodyguard for Bankhead who would protect the family from him while allowing the brute to drink himself to death. When Bankhead fled to avoid prosecution, Anne joined him, bringing upon herself more criticism than sympathy. *What kind of woman would stay with such a scoundrel?* the neighbors wondered, knowing she was terrified of her spouse, and with excellent reason.

One of Trist's letters comments mysteriously that "The return of Mr. B. is a source of *great* uneasiness to me. I consider him . . . a curse entailed on all of us . . . whose weight will be felt so long as his hand can hold a Knife or his finger pull a trigger." This undoubtedly refers to Charles Bankhead, who returned to Albemarle County after the death of his wife Anne. This dark subject reminded Trist of a related concern: his fiancée's reiterated opposition to his ownership of a pair of dueling pistols. "You need not feel so much animosity against the pistols, as I have given them to Browse, who I trust will never be under the necessity of using them, . . . though it is an instrument which . . . every gentleman who can, ought to have."[10]

His use of the word "gentleman" in the context of dueling reveals his opinion of himself as well as of that popular mark of gentility, which he defended so staunchly. A new age was dawning when most of his fellow Americans showed no interest in class distinctions; but to Trist, gentility was all-important. A gentleman would never send a second to "call out" a social inferior; instead he might cane such an unworthy enemy in some tavern. But if both offender and offended happened to be "gentlemen," at least in their own eyes, redress could never be sought but by approved weapons, usually pistols. Many quarrels were settled nonviolently through intermediaries, although pride might dictate that the charade be carried out as though in earnest, usually after the adversaries had secretly agreed that no harm would be done. The custom of dueling lingered long after being outlawed in all states, and few high-spirited men of prominence escaped at least the threat of a challenge at some time.[11]

The Randolph children still under parental care consisted of four older girls—Ellen, Cornelia, Virginia, and Mary—followed closely by three boys: James Madison, Benjamin Franklin, and Meriwether Lewis (who was generally called Lewis by the family; he was given his name in honor of the coleader of the Lewis and Clark expedition, formerly President Jefferson's private secretary). At the end of the line came little Septimia, nicknamed "Tim," and the toddler George Wythe.[12] Nicholas loved them all, and they returned his affection in full measure. Virginia wrote long, encouraging, increasingly affectionate letters, each of which he reread avidly until the next arrived.

While waiting to begin his law studies under Edward Livingston, Trist decided to inspect the land in Mississippi that he and Browse would inherit upon their mother's death, the same land their father had inherited from his father before the turn of the century.

Although less than three months had passed since he and Browse had made the long voyage downstream, Nicholas welcomed the chance to be alone and to enjoy the slowly passing scene as the steamboat churned sedately up the broad, meandering Mississippi. Along the banks, majestic cypress, veiled in Spanish moss, guarded motionless black bayous, silent except for the occasional shrill *ker-loo!* of a whooping crane or the splash of an alligator. Rounding a bend, they came upon fields of cotton and cane where slaves paused in their labor to stare curiously at the passing vessel. Then a forest of live oaks materialized, opening on a vast meadow where buffalo grazed at the water's edge, heedless of shouts from the passengers. The dark current swept by hypnotically, bearing logs, stumps, boards, and other flotsam downstream. Occasionally snags from submerged trees imperiled progress and challenged the skill of the pilot.[13]

Nicholas was an infant at the time of his father's lonely exile in Mississippi and was, therefore, unaware of the elder Trist's impression of Natchez. Otherwise, he would have been prepared for the shock most travelers experienced in that lawless riverfront hell. As it was he disembarked, all innocence, and looked about with interest at a place of considerable charm situated partly on a bluff overlooking a bend in the river and partly on flatland barely above the water. The lower part of town he soon discovered was the notorious "Natchez under the Hill," famous, as he informed Virginia, "in the annals of vice and profligacy, and deservedly so, from all

I *hear* (for I have only passed through it) for I conclude that there is not another place on Earth where these monsters have dared to show themselves in the unblushing nakedness that they here exhibit. There is scarcely a square yard in the place, but has been the theatre of some murder and instances innumerable of swindling, and scarcely a house, with the exception of one or two warehouses, but is the receptacle of vice in its lowest, and most odious form."[14]

Unnerved but unshaken in purpose, Trist took lodging at a tavern where he found himself "surrounded by black legs [card cheats], horse racers and cock fighters." During a stay of two weeks at this sinister place, he sought refuge in writing long letters to Virginia when he was not scouring the countryside for the legacy that would one day be his and Browse's. He engaged the most likely looking of available citizens to help him in his quest but was disappointed even in that promising choice, for his guide proved "insouciant" and may have been guilty of intentional delay. He poured out his feelings in a letter that speaks as eloquently of his growing disenchantment with his career choice as with his immediate frustrations: "nature did by no means give me an inexhaustible stock of patience, however, and she will find this out before long. By the bye, she must have carved me out for a great misanthrope, for my contempt for my fellow-man increases exactly with my knowledge of him; the highest point of honor with three fourths of mankind is to refrain from actually stealing; and as for the finer feelings that constitute an *honorable* man, nine tenths have no more idea of *them* than the icelander can have of the charms of an Italian moonlight. The profession I have lighted upon is exactly the one that will bring me most frequently into contact with the 'herd.' "[15]

In this we glimpse the fastidious young idealist, repelled by humanity in its cruder forms. Disgusted, he gave up his search and returned to La Fourche, having gained nothing more than a general acquaintance with the region.

Soon after this adventure, as spring began to color the bayou country with an astonishing display of blossoming shrubs and trees, Mr. Livingston sent word that he was at last available to tutor Nicholas. More than four years had passed since he had seen the Livingstons, though he and Lewis had exchanged frequent letters. The two friends embraced joyfully, then stood back to inspect each other critically. Mere boys at the time they parted, both were now mature young men. Lewis, whom Trist had once described to his grandmother as "one of the finest boys I have ever known," was the same loyal friend who had written him at West Point, "I take a lively interest in all that concerns you." This interest was mutual and would bind their friendship throughout their lives.

Mr. Livingston proved far more demanding than he had been during their earlier association. In accordance with the long-standing method of training candidates for the legal profession, he assigned voluminous quantities of cases to be read and, when his own schedule allowed, examined his apprentice's retention and comprehension thereof. Trist discovered to his considerable chagrin that he had developed some poor study habits. With exaggerated self-pity, he confessed to Virginia: "I never *studied* anything; because I never knew *how*. The books that were put in my hands, I ran over, if they interested me, or slept over, and waded through if they did not." In fact, the musty law books and tedious briefs, which were actually rather lengthy, bored him. On a more hopeful note, he remarked that Locke's essay on the conduct of understanding had "lighted up my intellect a little."[16] If he lacked concentration, however, he did not want for self-discipline. Doggedly, he plodded on toward his goal.

As always, correspondence from loved ones gave him his greatest pleasure. His grandmother wrote from Charlottesville: "I enclose a letter from V___ R___ which you must keep I shall never do the like again."[17] And in reply to a letter from that young lady herself, he wrote with reference to a lecture she had attended: "The gentleman from South Carolina, like all dealers in hyperbole, overshot his mark, and reduced what he said to about nothing at all. You must content yourself with being the *equal* of men in point of talent and capacity . . . as you are superior to them in virtue. . . ." In another mysterious reference he added: "Leave, my dearest love, to Madame de Genlis and her tribe the idea that you must not show your husband the whole extent of your affection, and other *rules* of the 'art' of preserving love. Make him the repository of all that is in your 'heart and mind' and leave it to your unsophisticated nature, those virtues which you sucked with your mother's milk and have since been strengthened by her precept and example."[18] These florid phrases sound strangely like those of his father twenty years earlier.

As the years of separation dragged on endlessly, his longing intensified and his letters grew more poignant. "How dearly do I love you, my own Virginia!" he wrote, and begged her to send her portrait, insisting however, "I do not want a daub."[19] Slowly the warmth of his protestations thawed her cool responses until at last she signed off "with Love" and once, ashamed of what she had written, "If you love me, burn this *scratch,* which is a disgrace to a lady's name."[20] When she learned from other sources that he had taken a brief respite from his studies to appear in New Orleans society, and had even been seen in the company of a young lady, the "chillness" returned to her letters and she made icy and repeated reference to his "interests." "Will this song never end?" he protested, then contritely promised to return to his law books and eschew feminine society.

Browse, meanwhile, was grudgingly surrendering his last hope for a scholarly vocation. At least his brother's equal intellectually, he nevertheless lacked Nicholas's confidence and suffered the pangs of perfectionism. "You want me to skim too lightly over the surface of science," he had complained to Nicholas; "a superficial knowledge of anything is hardly worth having."[21] Reluctantly, he began to involve himself in the operation of his stepfather's plantations, which were beginning to recover from the recent depression. Tournillon, exploring sugar as an alternative to the steadily declining cotton, saw bright prospects ahead and was happy to note his stepson's emerging interest, however slight. He managed, however, to keep both brothers in a humiliating state of dependency, brusquely dismissing their increasingly persistent requests for clear title to their inheritance.

In the spring of 1823, Trist paid one of his infrequent visits to La Fourche, where his mother was soon to be delivered of another child. He found her in high spirits, not at all daunted at the prospect of having a baby in midlife. One evening as he was in his room writing a letter to Virginia's mother, his attention was aroused by the hurrying footsteps of his stepfather downstairs. He rushed to investigate and found his mother in bed and Tournillon attempting to give her a glass of water, which she appeared unable to accept. Hurrying to the bedside, Nicholas threw back the mosquito net while Browse and Mr. Tournillon supported Mary, attempting to get her to stand, for she was having difficulty breathing while lying down. She advanced two steps and slumped limp in their grasp. A moment later her mother, attracted by the noise and exclamations, hurried into the room, arriving to find her only child dying in Nicholas's arms.

Pouring out his grief in a letter to Virginia, he wrote: "When will I ever again repose any trust in Providence?" As it happened, his mother's death in its brutal suddenness destroyed permanently whatever religious faith he had formerly possessed. In closing he sent "an affectionate embrace for *my only* Mother and all her children."[22]

Early in 1823, the sale of a two-hundred-acre tract provided the brothers with twelve-hundred dollars each and a modest balance to be paid in three annual installments. This legacy, though not enough to afford long-term security, gave them a temporary measure of independence. Soon it would be needed, for the death of Mary Tournillon revealed that she had been the stabilizing force in the family. Within two months her sons were threatening to bring a lawsuit against their stepfather.[23]

At the time of her third marriage, Mary owned a number of valuable slaves left to her by her second husband, Philip Jones. Tournillon, who was at the time heavily in debt, persuaded his bride to sell the slaves to relieve his financial problems, promising in exchange to do all in his power to pay for educating the two boys, which he knew to be Mary's primary concern. His plan was carried out to the satisfaction of all, excluding the slaves of course. The sale quickly repaired Tournillon's fortunes; the brothers received the finest education that any private academy could provide, for which they were properly grateful; and their mother was relieved of her anxiety. Even so, there was a fly in the ointment.

By Louisiana law, now second nature to Trist, the property Mary had inherited from her first and second husbands remained in her name until her death. Then, half was to go to her sons and the other half to her spouse. The Trist brothers were understandably hesitant to bring up the matter immediately, assuming that when all funeral expenses and other debts associated with the estate were settled, Tournillon would make the necessary settlement with them. When nothing of the sort happened, they mentioned it as tactfully as possible. Their stepfather brushed them aside with his usual assurance that at any time they required money they needed only to ask for it. They countered by proposing a partnership, the terms of which they knew to be more generous than the law required. When he agreed to consider the matter, "reasons of delicacy" restrained them from pressing their demand. Once more an unsatisfactory silence followed. In early June 1823, Nicholas and Browse formally offered Tournillon a choice: either the partnership earlier proposed or a legal division of property. Property, of course, included both slaves and land.

Tournillon's reaction was astonishing. Let Trist himself report the conversation that followed:

"What does this mean?"

"Our meaning is very clear (and I repeated the substance of the above plans)."

"Well, I do not think you have any claims upon me, and I will not admit any."

"We pretend no claims against you but only the share of my mother's property which the Law gives us!"

"I do not admit this claim. I have taken advice upon the subject; and I will charge against you the $15,000 which your education has cost!"[24]

The Trists knew the actual sum to be a little above eight thousand, but whatever the sum, it had no bearing on the question at hand. Tournillon allowed his wrath to drive him to intemperate language, which Nicholas interrupted to remark that a case at law would show their indebtedness for their education to be owed only to their mother. He then coolly handed his stepfather a copy of the applicable civil code, which Tournillon refused to read. Nicholas asked, "Are you resolved to drive us to an action?" "Yes!" roared the older man. With that the brothers retired with more dignity than their agitated stepfather was able to muster.

For the time being, Trist rested his case, secure in the certainty that Louisiana law would protect the brothers' interests; however, he took little satisfaction in holding the stronger hand, for tension within the house of Tournillon was becoming unbearable. There was evidence that Mr. Tournillon was suffering even more acutely than his stepsons. "The violence of his passion increases every day," Nicholas wrote Virginia; "not a day passes at the plantation without one or more negroes being severely flogged."[25]

As he was again waiting on Mr. Livingston's availability, and having in hand part of the receipts of their recent land sale, he and Browse took temporary lodgings with a pair of young lawyers and their meals at a tavern. He wrote Virginia that little Mary was growing up undisciplined and at ten was already displaying "a boldness not to be daunted." His grandmother Brown shared his apprehensions. Uncomfortable in the deteriorating household, she longed to return to Virginia but her limited finances would not allow it.

Trist was increasingly unhappy about his long separation from his fiancée. A letter from Martha informed him that Captain Crozet had taken a teaching position at Richmond with a handsome salary of "$3,000 or $3,500" and was eager to have Nicholas for his assistant.[26] This news was both enticing and disturbing, for he could not leave Louisiana with his inheritance unresolved.

The brothers held firm in their standoff with their stepfather, certain that Tournillon's fulminations were not only gross exaggerations but also the final throes of a dying resistance. Actually the planter's fortunes, always rising or falling, were on the upswing, and the partnership offered advantages not lost on his shrewd mind. Abruptly, he capitulated. Once the agreement was drawn up and signed, family relations resumed an astonishing and lasting cordiality. Thereafter, during periods of absence from Louisiana, Nicholas received, as he had before, long letters in French addressed to "mon cher Trist." There was one notable difference. Never again did Nicholas or Browse call Tournillon "Father." From that day on he was known as "Mr. T."

At this time many religious folk were again locked in the ancient quarrel between liberal and conservative theologies. Trist had little interest in such squabbles, especially in the aftermath of his mother's death. Virginia, who under her mother's influence held moderate-to-orthodox views, sought to console him but only succeeded in antagonizing him by resorting to conventional religious condolences. (In an age when death struck haphazardly and with little or no warning, it was commonly accepted as "God's will.") Nicholas brushed aside her sympathy, writing: "I will defer our argument about divine will until we meet. To bear with fortitude and equanimity the evils to which we are liable, it is not necessary however to refer each of them to divine will. Without going beyond our earthly crust, we can discover the necessity of this resignation, to our happiness. For my part I believe that a man who had never even determined satisfactorily to himself the existence or non-existence of a divine providence may be as perfect in this virtue as the most devout Christian."[27]

In January, 1824, Virginia wrote of a "scandalous" Unitarian preacher named Whitaker who was shocking the community with his heresies. She confessed in a letter that "my curiosity is extreme."[28] Before his mother's death, Nicholas would have passed over this as an item of small interest but in the heat of his quarrel with God he reacted strongly. Savagely he wrote: "I give you all warning not to indulge too much in going to church for the privation will only be the greater when I get among you, as I intend to wage open war against any man . . . who would use his influence to prevail on you to catch a cold for the sake of having 'Jesus preached up.'"[29]

CHAPTER 4

Monticello

In the spring of 1824, Thomas Jefferson was acutely aware of his eighty-one years. His numerous ailments constantly reminded him that the last grains of sand were running out in the glass, and he still had much work to do. Although few suspected it, he was constantly dogged by guilt and anxiety. Guilt because of the mountain of debts he would soon leave for his daughter Martha to clear up, assuming that such an Augean task could be done at all. Anxiety about the long delay in opening the university, which he had hoped to see flourishing by this time, not bogged down in bureaucratic red tape and construction delays.[1] And he was especially anxious about the legacy he would soon leave to the world, for he possessed a strong sense of history and an insatiable appetite for public approval. He decided that he needed help.

Jefferson had been quietly tracking the activities of Nicholas Trist since the two brothers first came to Monticello some six years earlier. The West Point experiment had not turned out as he had hoped at the time, yet in a curious way Trist's decision not to return to the academy after completing three years had not been a great disappointment, for it reflected independence. He also appreciated the fact that the young man's devotion to his favorite granddaughter Virginia had survived six years of painful separation, broken only by a single brief visit in 1821. Such perseverance spoke volumes in Trist's favor. The old patriarch scratched a note to Martha, suggesting that another invitation be extended.

Virginia, perhaps with the encouragement of her grandfather, had already begun to reconsider the rigorous conditions she had imposed upon her fiancé. The time-consuming legal wrangle with Tournillon had not been anticipated, and the irregularity of his apprenticeship with Mr. Livingston left Nicholas still distant from his goal. It was beginning to look as if, under the original arrangement, they might never wed. She wrote to inform him that Mr. Jefferson (modestly, she made no mention of herself) wanted Nicholas to occupy rooms in the North Pavilion and to finish his law study under the old gentleman's guidance.[2] The recipient of this welcome news needed no urging. He packed at once and arrived at Monticello in late July.

Nicholas and Virginia were married at Monticello on September 11, 1824, the Reverend F. W. Hatch officiating. Family, relatives, neighbors, and friends from near and far beamed approval as Governor Randolph and his tall daughter approached the improvised altar where the groom and minister waited. After the ceremony a splendid banquet was held in the large dining hall, then festivities continued far into the night. At nine o'clock Mr. Jefferson excused himself, smiling and nodding goodnight to this one and that as he made his exit.

Within a few days after the wedding Trist plunged into the study program that Jefferson outlined for him, which reflected in breadth and liberality its author's attachment to nineteenth-century Enlightenment philosophy. It included fourteen hours of daily reading, relieved occasionally by a few hours of conversation to allow the mentor to evaluate his pupil's progress. On a typical day Trist read physical science, ethics, religion, and natural law before eight o'clock each morning; theory of law in at least three languages from eight to noon; politics and history in the afternoon; poetry, criticism, rhetoric, and oratory from dusk to bedtime.[3] Jefferson believed that a lawyer needed more than a head full of legal precepts; rather, he should be fully versed in classical, philosophical, and scientific knowledge; in short, he should be a Renaissance man.

In New Orleans, Trist had wearied of the endless legal case studies, opinions, and precedents. History, he once complained to Virginia, put him to sleep. Now there was no boredom; everything he read was vital, for his awareness of the necessity to be ready without notice for examination by Jefferson challenged him and stimulated his interest. His intellect was being honed to a keen edge. Each day was a new adventure.

Although their living quarters in the recently constructed North Pavilion were not spacious, Nicholas and Virginia were much too busy and lost in love to notice. The usual gay whirl of social events occupied what little time they could spare, Nicholas from his studies and Virginia from domestic duties. In addition to the regulars—family, relatives, and neighbors—there was the usual stream of visitors, many of them perfect strangers, demanding a chance to pay respects to the famous old revolutionary. Jefferson was ever the gracious host, even to those he did not know or care to meet. When it became evident that these hordes of intruders—frequently numbering twenty or thirty and at least once no fewer than fifty[4]—expected to be put up for the night, the resourceful Martha had to find ways to accommodate them, even when it meant sending appeals to neighbors for extra bedding. Edmund Bacon, indignant at the bad manners of these arrant freeloaders, directed that their horses be given only half the normal feed ration, but Jefferson learned of this action and countermanded the order.[5]

Obviously, the cost of entertaining such multitudes was enormous. Today, retiring presidents receive a generous pension to cover these and other expenses, but in Jefferson's time an annual salary of twenty-five thousand dollars during his term of service was the executive's only reward. Not a few early presidents returned to private life to find themselves undone by their own fame, especially Thomas Jefferson, whose debts, even without this new financial drain, had grown steadily over the years. Naturally Martha had to deal with his creditors, who soon came to recognize the improbability of ever collecting their bills.

Compounding Jefferson's financial troubles was a generous but unwise accommodation he had extended years earlier to his friend and neighbor ex-Governor Wilson Carey Nicholas, who had asked him to endorse a note for twenty-thousand dollars. In a series of subsequent reverses, Nicholas was wiped out. In due course the holder of the note called for its payment, and Jefferson was obliged to make good. He never recovered from this blow.[6]

In 1824, Lafayette paid a visit to the United States.[7] For the better part of a year, as he toured the new nation he had helped liberate, the aging marquis, symbol of France's friendship and support for America during the Revolutionary War, was met by wildly cheering throngs wherever he appeared. He was unfailingly gracious in accepting lavish tributes and zealous in looking up old friends, but, like a child saving his most cherished Christmas gift to the last, he delayed visiting Jefferson. When their meeting, which had been widely heralded in the newspapers, finally occurred, it was witnessed by a throng of curious onlookers. Arriving at Monticello, Lafayette descended stiffly from his carriage. Aged beyond his sixty-seven years by long imprisonment during the French Revolution, his body bent and his pallid face grooved and gaunt, he bore little resemblance to the dashing young general of the Revolution. As he waited, smiling an acknowledgment to the spectators, the front door of the great house opened and Thomas Jefferson stepped out. Like his guest, he showed alarming signs of age. Gone were the gun-barrel-straight posture and flashing eye so well remembered by his neighbors. Stooped and thin, he blinked dazedly against the light.

The two old men stood for a moment gazing upon each other. The crowd watched, hushed and expectant. Then Lafayette cried out hoarsely, "Ah, Jefferson!" and stumbled forward, bony arms outstretched. Jefferson echoed, "Ah, Lafayette!" and rushed to embrace his old comrade. They fell into each other's arms, pummeling, weeping, and laughing at the same time. A great cheer broke from the crowd, and tears flowed freely.

Lafayette and his small entourage remained at Monticello for two weeks while the old friends caught up on each other's news and discussed current international affairs. Trist was invited to attend some of these meetings, for by this time he was serving as part-time private secretary to Jefferson as well as pursuing his studies.[8] He considered these occasions no less beneficial than the shelves of books with which he wrestled daily.

In his new role as unofficial private secretary, Trist proved a valuable aid to the elderly sage, for Jefferson's right wrist, broken many years earlier and never properly mended,[9] was becoming arthritic and of limited use in writing, while his correspondence remained as voluminous as ever. As their relationship took on new aspects, their friendship grew. Trist sometimes accompanied the old man on his daily rides, which remained his principal exercise as his health declined. As they toured the several sprawling farms, inspecting fields and shops as they rode, their conversations ranged over many topics. Jefferson appreciated the young man's quick mind and articulate speech. To add spice to the game, the old gentleman would switch to French or Spanish, and always Trist responded easily and fluently in the same language. Jefferson noted with approval that young Trist was unfailingly respectful without being obsequious.

A favorite topic, and one in which the two were in close agreement, had to do with government by "aristocracy." This term had been an explosive one in Jefferson's political years, for his enemies, the Federalists, passionately believed that government should always be controlled by the upper tier of society, whereas Jefferson, the founder of democracy, hated this idea. Still, he readily conceded the existence of what he liked to call a "natural aristocracy," referring to those of outstanding talent and exemplary character. He believed that persons thus favorably endowed by nature and training should hold the reins of government, not those whose claim to leadership came merely from wealth, land, and social position.[10] He acknowledged, however, that the two conditions frequently coincided, and he firmly believed that Virginians, more than other Americans, possessed this natural aristocracy. Trist recognized in this reasoning the theme that had nearly gotten him expelled from West Point. Unlike many persons of philosophical bent, Jefferson loved detail, and when he observed that his protégé shared this trait he began judiciously shifting the paperwork of Monticello to Nicholas Trist.

At this time another young man was being groomed as Jefferson's farm manager. Jeff Randolph, eight years older than Trist, had accepted this responsibility when Edmund Bacon departed for the West, not long after Jeff's terrible wounding at the hands of Charles Bankhead in 1819. Jeff had learned his vocation well from his father, Thomas Mann Randolph, whom Jefferson considered "a man of science, sense, virtue, and competence" and who had taught Jefferson the benefits of contour plowing.[11] In his four plantations in and around Albemarle County, Jefferson owned some eleven-thousand acres, most of it in uncultivated woodland. Even the originally arable land was now nearly worn out by earlier overproduction of corn and tobacco and by gross mishandling from a series of overseers during the years when Jefferson was preoccupied with matters of state. Now, with the farms under the management of his trusted grandson, who was more closely attuned to his own thinking, Jefferson hoped for a revival.

Jefferson not only experimented with crop rotation,[12] fertilization, soil conservation, and other advanced agricultural concepts, but also attempted to establish the diversified, self-contained farmstead that he hoped would become a model for America. His labor force, at one time numbering more than a hundred slaves, was now reduced to something less.[13] These he used not only in simple farm labor, as did his neighbors: slaves who exhibited talent and interest were employed in the various crafts and trades needed to operate Jefferson's many enterprises. Among the men were carpenters, cabinetmakers, masons, bricklayers, blacksmiths, and coopers. Women and girls were engaged in spinning, weaving, sewing, candlemaking, cooking, and housekeeping. Some of the younger children were put to work in Jefferson's nail factory.

In the third decade of the nineteenth century, agriculture in Virginia was on the decline. Tobacco had depleted the soil and, as the industry declined, left a surplus of slaves to work fewer productive farms.[14] A sinister new commerce emerged from this condition: the sale and transport of slaves to the rapidly opening frontiers of the Deep South and West. From this trade came many mournful songs and stories of slave families broken when some of its members were, quite literally, "sold down the river." Thus far Jefferson had resisted selling his "people," as he called them. From his youth, he had detested slavery and in his prime he had even tried, albeit ineffectually, to limit the evil; yet he had never found a way to rid himself of his own dependency on the "peculiar institution." In his debt-ridden old age, a considerable portion of his remaining worth was in the form of human property. Aside from allowing a few favorites to escape, the author of the immortal phrase "all men are born Free" did nothing to free himself from his moral dilemma. It was another problem for Martha to resolve after his departure.

Nicholas was astonished to learn that the long-planned university that he and Browse had dreamed of entering more than six years before was still little more than a plan. To be sure, an impressive collection of buildings waited to be put to use, but no professors had been hired and no students enrolled. Jefferson was firmly of the opinion that suitable instructors could not be found among native Americans but would have to be imported from Europe, which, of course, meant from England. There had been no stampede of applicants from the mother country; moreover, some of the regents resented the founder's insistence on foreign instructors. By far the most controversial candidate was the freethinking Dr. Thomas Cooper, whom Jefferson considered the most gifted scholar in North America.[15] Cooper, who made no secret of his enmity toward all organized religion, offended pious board members, and Jefferson made matters worse by trying to spirit him onto the faculty in the face of growing opposition. Eventually Cooper broke away in disgust to take another position, leaving the Virginians out by the sum Jefferson had advanced to secure Cooper's services. The ill will left from this fiasco slowed progress still further.

In the spring of 1825, the University of Virginia finally opened its doors. Five professors, imported from England, had at last arrived after a delay of several months due to continuous Atlantic storms. Waiting for them were sixty young men, newly enrolled and eager to learn. The board of regents included three former presidents of the United States: Thomas Jefferson, James Madison, and the newly retired James Monroe, Virginians all and surely the most distinguished group to launch a public institution.

Inauguration of the university was Jefferson's final public appearance.

His health was deteriorating alarmingly, and over his objections Martha put him under the care of a physician. Dr. Robley Dunglison, a twenty-six-year-old Scot, was one of the imported professors at the university.[16] Highly qualified for his post as professor of anatomy and medicine, he was already on the way to international fame. His studies at four major European universities had included philosophy and general literature as well as medicine, so it was inevitable that the young doctor and his aged patient would become close friends. Dunglison's most valuable service came in the form of good conversation, for both men well understood that the case at hand was terminal and the best science in the world would be no match for mortality. Jefferson was a docile patient, for in spite of his low opinion of most medicine,[17] he was determined to spare his family unnecessary worry on his account. Fortunately, Dunglison was not a strong believer in the more violent practices favored by most of his colleagues. With his patient's grateful concurrence, he limited his ministrations to the judicious prescription of laudanum and bed rest.

Trist also became a friend and admirer of Robley Dunglison. Over the years Dunglison served as the Trist family's physician when proximity permitted and, when it did not, as consultant, advisor, and correspondent.

Dunglison was appalled by the relentless swarms of people who still flocked to Monticello expecting a couple of meals and a night's lodging as well as a glimpse of the expiring statesman. Later he wrote: "In Mr. Jefferson's embarrassed circumstances in the evening of life, the immense influx of visitors could not fail to be attended with much inconvenience. . . . I have no sympathy with the feeling of economy—political or social—which denies the ex-President a retiring allowance."[18]

In March 1826, the rapidly failing sage drew up a new will. Poplar Forest, one of his four farms, he left to his grandson Francis Eppes; the remainder of the real property he bequeathed in trust to Martha. Each of his grandchildren was to receive a watch, and his gold-headed cane he left to James Madison. Five of his slaves, whom he judged to possess skills sufficient to support themselves, were given their freedom. Jeff Randolph, Nicholas Trist, and Alexander Garrett, bursar of the university, were named to administer his will.[19] Most troubling of the dying man's reflections was his concern for Martha, his only living child. He summoned Jeff and asked for his promise never to leave his mother, a promise which young Jeff most willingly gave.

Jefferson's fertile brain continued to grapple with the problem of the overwhelming debt that he knew would soon envelop his loved ones. One morning he woke with the stunning conviction that a solution was indeed possible. Hastily, he sent for Nicholas and Jeff and outlined his plan. Although never a gambler himself and on one occasion an outspoken opponent of government lotteries, Jefferson now rationalized that a lottery of all his belongings, including Monticello itself, would be of universal benefit to its participants and a lifeline to solvency for himself and his family.[20] He was, of course, counting on his own celebrity to provide the bait that would ensure success. One difficulty presented itself: his earlier opposition had resulted in a state law prohibiting such an enterprise. It would be necessary to obtain an exception before advertising the lottery. Jeff was given the unenviable assignment of persuading the Virginia legislature to enact such a waiver, and he set about the task with energy and conviction. Jefferson well understood that he was in a race, for his death would mean the end of his scheme.

From time to time the dying patriarch rallied enough to join the family. Thus it was that in May, when Virginia presented him with the only great-grandchild he would live to see and hold, he was able to enjoy this honor as he had few others in a long and celebrated lifetime.[21] Nicholas and Virginia named their baby girl Martha and nicknamed her Patty, both names in honor of her grandmother. Thomas Jefferson lavished attention on this new member of his family.

In the early summer of 1826, as the fiftieth anniversary of the signing of the Declaration of Independence approached, newspapers all across America feverishly called attention to the impending demise of liberty's two great architects: Thomas Jefferson and John Adams. The two old men—who had started as warm friends, later become enemies, and finally recovered their friendship—had written to each other in these latter years at length on many subjects. Each knew he had not long to live, and both ardently wished to see the great semicentennial. To the public it seemed that the two old revolutionaries were locked in a race, each stubbornly clinging to life by sheer will power.

As Jefferson lapsed into the final stages of his slow decline, he retained his mental and vocal faculties until the very end, though he often drifted in and out of shallow sleep. Trist and Jeff Randolph agreed to spell each other at sitting up with the patient. In the waning evening of July 3, he inquired sleepily, "Is it the Fourth?" Trist, unwilling to lie and even less willing to disappoint his beloved mentor, compromised with a silent nod.[22] Satisfied, Jefferson drifted off to sleep again. At four in the morning on the Fourth, the old statesman roused purposefully and asked to see the household servants. As they filed in, snuffling and weeping, he bid fare-well to each. When offered laudanum he declined, saying "No more."

In the late afternoon of July 4, 1826, in Braintree, Massachusetts, ninety-year-old John Adams murmured, "Thomas Jefferson still lives," and died. But he was wrong. Jefferson had preceded him in death by about five hours.

While the nation mourned the loss of its two greatest patriots, the financial catastrophe that Jefferson had foreseen was not long in coming. Through Jeff's heroic efforts, the lottery bill had finally passed the legislature by the slimmest of margins. Too late. In the absence of its famous promoter the shares did not sell. Jeff had also obtained substantial pledges from leading citizens in New York, Baltimore, and Philadelphia—sufficient, in fact, to allow Jefferson to die thinking that his home had been saved, but alas! the pledges were never honored. The lottery scheme simply collapsed.[23]

Jefferson's long-suffering creditors now became noticeably brusque in placing their demands for payment and markedly resistant to the extension of any further credit. Even the Reverend Hatch, who had married the Trists, submitted a belated and whimsically diffident request for a bit of "the root of all evil." Others were not as coy. Some months earlier Nicholas had appealed to Browse, who was unwillingly giving ground in his struggle to escape the farmer's vocation, for such funds as their jointly owned enterprises might afford. Although cotton was still cheap and expenses high, Browse did his best to oblige, and his occasional bank drafts at least put food on the table.

Browse's letters, though erudite as always, were becoming gloomy and at times even misanthropic for a young man in his early twenties. He sought solace in books and declared that "Hume's system or the sceptical philosophy . . . has made a deep impression upon me."[24] He was continuing his legal studies, saying, "I am determined to give myself exclusively to the law, so that I may go to the bar next winter. I want to support myself without having recourse to the plantation." Increasingly, he viewed himself as a drone, commenting resignedly that, "I must arm myself with patience and plod along as well as I can."[25]

In late April, Browse reported that little Mary and young Julien had been christened, and Mr. Tournillon, financially embarrassed to the point of being "obliged to consult economy even where it is most repugnant to his feelings," was placing Mary in a New Orleans boarding school and sending Julien off to a Catholic seminary in Kentucky. This left only Browse and the hapless Grandmother Brown in the Tournillon household, and neither was there by choice. Browse wrote: "I dread the effect of [the children's] separation upon grandmother B's feelings. . . . Consider a woman at the verge of life, with a constitution shattered by age & misfortune, whose mental faculties, never of a firm texture, are going to decay, who cannot resort to books for a remedy against the tedium of life, who has not the strength for any active occupation, for whom the past is a scene of unhappiness & gloom, & the present contains no cheering prospect— consider this situation aggravated by exclusion from society & by being shut up in the house with the man she detests. Such is the picture of grandmother's situation. . . . I shall be under the necessity of residing at Mr. T's to keep her company."[26]

At Monticello no time was lost in setting to the perusal of Mr. Jefferson's will. The three trustees named to administer the estate met hurriedly, and soon their number dwindled to one. Mr. Garrett, the university bursar, excused himself apologetically, citing the pressure of his duties. Jeff had already shown exemplary loyalty to his grandfather, but he was burdened by dual responsibilities as farm manager of his grandfather's estate and of his own plantation. Trist had no choice but to shoulder the task alone.[27]

But, as it turned out, not entirely alone after all. Martha Randolph had managed her father's household for more than thirty years, and she knew every spoon and candlestick in the house, plus a great deal of the outdoor inventory as well. Trist, who loved her by now as he had his own mother, quickly formed with her an efficient, smoothly operating partnership. Had the times or her late father accepted the revolutionary notion of a woman in business, she could have handled the entire matter well enough alone. As it was, she acknowledged Trist "master of the house" and quietly gave him directions—as any sensible mother-in-law would do.

To meet the most urgent demands, they decided to auction at once such domestic furnishings as could be disposed of without undue hardship. The auction was widely advertised and well attended and the bidding, after a cautious start, enthusiastic. Inconspicuously positioned, Trist observed the proceedings with satisfaction. When the auctioneer called up Jefferson's handsome old grandfather's clock, Trist signaled a bid. Instantly the bid was raised, and he realized presently that he was locked in competition with a single rival. Considering the family's financial straits, he should not have made even an opening bid, but he was acting under specific instructions. Grimly, he hung on, and presently the clock was his. Later his mysterious opponent identified himself: Robley Dunglison! The doctor apologized profusely for forcing the bidding beyond prudence, explaining that he had always admired the old clock and had not realized that he was bidding against a family member. His astonishment must have been great when the clock was delivered to his house. Martha, knowing of his fondness for the old piece, had directed Trist to purchase it at any price as a gift to the doctor for his kindness to her father.

Realizing that his duties as executor would soon preempt all of his time and energy, Trist in a supreme closing effort completed his law studies, as assigned by Jefferson, and passed the Virginia bar just four months after his mentor's death. It was a notable achievement and one motivated by a need for money, yet one that would contribute almost nothing to his purse. There exists only one recorded instance of his actually bringing a case to court. Nevertheless, he did not immediately abandon his plan to become a lawyer. After convincing himself that the perennial surplus of lawyers still prevailed in Virginia, he turned his attention elsewhere. The result was not encouraging. Joseph Coolidge, recently married to Ellen Randolph, wrote from Boston to inform him that the entire state of Massachusetts was overrun with lawyers.[28] The same discouraging word came from other northern cities, and in any event he was not disposed to practice his profession in the chilly north. Soon more immediate responsibilities forced him to suspend his search.

Having inventoried the Jefferson library while assisting its owner, Trist was ideally equipped to administer its disposal. Although most of the original collection of more than twenty-thousand volumes had been sold to Congress (and subsequently destroyed when the British burned Washington in 1814), Jefferson's insatiable thirst for knowledge had resulted in its substantial rebuilding. The problem before the executor lay in realizing as much of the value as possible. Trist arranged auctions in various major cities, attending them when possible and occasionally placing a bid, for he had discovered that this quiet stirring of the pot usually turned apathy into interest.[29] In time he disposed of the entire collection, which considerably reduced the estate's indebtedness.

As household furnishings, farm implements, objets d'art, and fine books disappeared under the relentless gavel of the auctioneer, even more painful dispositions remained to be made. Although farmland was still hard to sell because of the general decline of Virginia's agriculture, every acre would eventually have to be sold, probably at far less than its true value. In the meantime, creditors were still howling and valuable slaves—always in demand—were eating them out of house and home. Martha shuddered as she contemplated the choices she faced—and put them off for the time being.

In the summer of 1827, Martha took her two youngest children, twelve-year-old Septimia and eight-year-old George, for an extended stay with her daughter, Ellen Coolidge, in Boston. From nearby Cambridge she wrote a remarkable letter to Trist.[30] In it she dealt with several business matters, instructing her son-in-law to forward any papers that required her signature, and after reiterating her complete confidence in him, addressed forthrightly her deepest concern: her husband. After displaying marked self-possession at her father's funeral, he had slipped again into a deep depression. Part of this may have been due, she hinted, to his jealousy of Trist for his exalted position as sole trustee of the estate and of herself for her *ex officio* role, which derived naturally from her long-held position as mistress of Monticello and the fact that she was principal heir to Jefferson's estate.

In his darker moments Randolph had suffered mightily in the long shadow of his father-in-law, and his suffering had not been alleviated by frequent introductions as "Governor Randolph, Mr. Jefferson's son-in-law."[31] Death had not removed the shadow; if anything, Randolph's condition had worsened. He had even threatened to kill his son Jeff and had given every sign that he meant to carry out his threat. Fear for the lives of her younger children had obliged Martha to bring them with her. Nevertheless, she declared, a sense of duty impelled her, and should impel her children, to "treat him with *kindness* and *respect*." She continued: "I never can feel myself absolved from affording him support as long as I have a shilling in this world." On a practical note she added, "His antisocial habits and the necessary restraints of a civilized life would I believe make him prefer a little establishment of his own in some sequestered spot of Monticello, where he could keep a woman to cook for him and perhaps some one to cut his wood feed his horse and cultivate a little garden with the power of joining the family whenever his inclination prompts it. That I believe is the best arrangement we can make for him." Unable to leave the subject, she went on to its most painful aspect: "But a separation is out of the question. I am inclined to think he will not seek it, and I *ought not*. Besides the control that the law gives him over George puts me completely in his power. I sincerely believe his taking that child would be my death warrant, and if pushed too much . . . I should be the victim as through my breast only could he stab [George]."

The following spring Trist received a letter from the ex-governor humbly requesting that he be allowed to make his lodgings at Monticello.[32] Plainly, poverty had taken precedence over pride. Randolph made it clear that he wanted to live alone and take no part in the family activities. Trist replied immediately, putting the North Pavilion at his father-in-law's disposal on the terms specified. He wrote again the following day: "Virginia has had the Pavillion scoured out today and it will be dry as well as clean for your reception. . . . Your determination to live secluded is a matter of deep regret to us, but we shall receive you in the hope that being restored to former scenes you will soon come to your former habits."[33]

Three months later, at age sixty, Thomas Mann Randolph died quietly.

Not long after this sad event, Trist made the hard decision to sell the slaves at the annual Charlottesville auction. It was a time of immeasurable sorrow for both races of the Jefferson enclave, for their relationships extended in some cases through several generations. Their emotions were sharply in contrast with the cold pragmatism of the buyers. Joshua Baker, a friend from Trist's West Point days, wrote from Richmond, enclosing a draft for $2,500 and instructions to "lay it out in the best manner you can. Be careful that none of the negroes have leg sores or other defects. Buy none but men unless you see a good bargain in a woman or two or a very likely young girl that would make a good nurse. Buy Capt. Miller's [slave] at $450 if you can, his mulato boy is no great thing so I do not care much about him. See that the titles are good."[34]

So much has been written about the presumed liaison between Thomas Jefferson and the beautiful Sally Hemings that no more need be added here. It is nevertheless relevant to note that Trist was scrupulous in carrying out the wishes of the sage in arranging for the emancipation of Sally's grown children, most of whom had already "escaped" with their owner's tacit permission. In the case of Sally, who was at the time in her midfifties, Trist was careful to document her consent to the arrangements he made for her future. She was not given her outright freedom because Virginia law at that time would have forced her to leave the state within one year, whereas she chose to remain with her "family," the Randolphs, for the time being. She later moved to Ohio, where she lived with two of her sons. Her death came in 1835.[35]

Part of Trist's duties as estate executor touched on the operations of the new university, for which Jefferson had served as rector of the board of visitors. The new rector was James Madison, who requested and was gratified to receive aid, especially in raising funds to meet operating expenses. Trist also assisted in the search for a successor to Thomas Hewitt Key, professor of mathematics, who had resigned. These activities produced two benefits: a warm and enduring friendship with ex-President

Madison and a small annual stipend as secretary to the board of visitors.[36]

In 1828, Nicholas and Virginia rejoiced in the birth of a second child, a boy whom they naturally named Thomas Jefferson Trist, then promptly shortened to Jeff, thus honoring both uncle and great-grandfather. Little Jeff was a happy, healthy baby who would grow into a handsome lad, but his parents were heartbroken to discover that he was deaf and dumb.

Even during his Louisiana years, Trist had entertained thoughts of trying his hand at journalism, and when his duties as executor began to wind down this possibility returned to mind. He had been in contact with Thomas Walker Gilmer, editor of the *Virginia Advocate,* since Thomas Jefferson's funeral, at which time he had been asked to furnish a statement describing Jefferson's last activities. He was also urged to publish what he knew of Jefferson's views on current political subjects. Requests of this nature soon came from many sources, and out of respect for Jefferson's memory Trist was reluctant (and highly selective) in obliging. Henry Lee, son of "Lighthorse Harry" Lee of Revolutionary War fame, received a polite refusal when he asked to publish some of Jefferson's correspondence, for the elder Lee, an ardent Federalist, had attacked Jefferson savagely during his presidency. Dr. Thomas Cooper made a similar request and received no answer at all. Henry Lee tried again, this time desiring some statement of Jefferson's opinion of Andrew Jackson, who was then seeking the Democratic nomination for the presidency. Although Trist believed that his mentor would have mildly favored Jackson, he did not think Jefferson would have been sufficiently enthusiastic to make a public declaration in favor of Old Hickory and, for that reason, decided he should not presume to speak for him. Pressure was applied, but Trist stood fast.[37]

In March 1828, at the urging of Professor J.A.G. Davis at the university, Trist purchased a half interest in the *Virginia Advocate.* Davis assured him that he should realize a profit of five- or six-hundred dollars a year, which, though not a great sum, would be of significant help to the financially strapped household. In any case, the role of publisher might advance his name and perhaps lead in time to better things. The outlay of $1,560 for the half interest was a risk that drew a cautionary comment from Browse: "I hope your editorial venture may succeed. There is only one objection to it—the expense is present, the profit future."[38]

Professor Davis's predictions proved optimistic and Browse's precaution, as usual, prophetic. Expenses preceded profits, which, when they finally came, were disappointingly small. There was a problem in engaging a qualified printer. With the help of brother-in-law Joseph Coolidge, Trist hired a man from Boston, who promptly refused the job when he learned that the *Advocate* was a pro-Jackson paper. Another Bostonian, either a Democrat—rare at the time in New England—or a political neuter, finally accepted the job but only after precious months had passed. Advertising proved hard to sell; circulation was sluggish; subscribers were touchy and quarrelsome. Grimly, Trist stayed the course, scratching out pro-Jackson editorials and striving mightily to capture elusive profits.

Browse's know-it-all letters became insufferable. He urged his brother to come to Louisiana, where his own fortunes were improving as a result of forming still another partnership. Mr. Penney, Browse wrote, was a paragon of planters. He was engaged in some interesting experiments on a sugar refining process and moving away from cotton in the direction of sugar. Besides being an experienced planter and ingenious inventor, Penney was a shrewd speculator in real estate and slaves; through his influence the Trists acquired interest in Willow Island, which Browse soon declared the finest sugar plantation in Louisiana. Still, most of the earnings had to be plowed back into the venture, and what little came to Monticello was never enough to meet the need. Trist resolved to sell his interest in the newspaper and seek his fortune outside the Charlottesville area.

A relative by marriage, Burwell S. Randolph, who was navy commissioner in Washington, responded to an inquiry from Trist with the offer of a position in the Navy Department, but the niggardly annual salary of six-hundred to eight-hundred dollars failed to entice. Randolph, however, out of sympathy for his relatives and especially for Martha, whom he knew to be dependent on her son-in-law, took the matter before Henry Clay, secretary of state in the John Quincy Adams administration. Clay wrote to Trist, extending an offer of a clerkship in the State Department at fourteen-hundred dollars a year. His letter contained one sentence that must have deflated the candidate's ego: "A strong motive . . . in tendering you this appointment is that I have reason to believe it may contribute to the personal comfort of Mrs. Randolph, your mother-in-law."[39]

Mr. Clay's motive in making the offer was the only one that moved Trist to consider it. He was not strongly inclined to serve an administration whose policies he had strenuously criticized; moreover, he was not sure he could handle the duties. On the latter point he sought the counsel of James Madison, who would offer no opinion other than his "pleasure that an option is afforded." Still undecided, Trist put the same question to

Burwell Randolph. The navy commissioner, no more tactful than the secretary of state, brushed aside Trist's concerns, writing, "Mr. Clay attends to and performs with his own hands all the *important duties* the clerks have nothing more to do than follow his instructions."[40] With misgivings, Trist concluded the sale of his interest in the *Advocate* and prepared to move to Washington. He would occupy single quarters until he could find suitable lodgings for his family.

CHAPTER 5

Washington Arrival

In late November 1828, Trist arrived at the nation's capital, a raw, unkempt, rural town a long way from becoming a dignified seat of government. The muddy road over which the stage had carried him continued unchanged into the city, where pigs and cows ambled undisturbed across its submerged ruts. Most of the scattered dwellings were cabins rather than houses, and the cluster of official buildings were obviously either unfinished or still undergoing repair from the ravages committed by the British in 1814. The charred timbers of the executive mansion had been covered hastily with white paint, causing it to stand out so conspicuously that people had taken to calling it "the white house." At each of its four corners stood a plain brick building; these were the departments of state, treasury, war, and navy. Only the Capitol building, newly finished in 1824 after a series of architects had successfully modified the original plan, promised the grandeur to come. Otherwise, Washington was an object of ridicule, a "City of Magnificent Intentions,"[1] "a village in the midst of the woods," "a capital without a city."

After establishing temporary residence at a boarding house, Trist went to the State Department and reported to its chief clerk, an elderly man named Brent. Aside from his three years as a cadet—when he was at least nominally an employee of the government—this was his first experience as a paid worker, and he regarded it with mingled feelings of relief and uneasiness. Throughout his life, he considered himself as good as any man; he was ever ready to serve, but never ready to accept a posture of servility. It soon became evident that there was no need for concern. Mr. Brent proved a gentleman in every sense and soon became a warm friend, as did most people once they got to know Nicholas Trist.

His duties soon proved as modest as Burwell Randolph had predicted, for Secretary Clay was indeed reluctant to delegate any of his important work, even to the seasoned Brent. A horde of younger men numbering four or five hundred droned away each day at menial tasks chiefly concerned with correspondence: copying, filing, and mailing letters. Convention called for official letters to be written in a fine hand and addressed in script of a quality that today would be considered calligraphy. Trist's beautiful penmanship surely must have captured the appreciation of his superiors, but that alone could not allay the boredom of such menial tasks. Infrequently the secretary made use of Trist's command of Spanish or French when translation was needed for international matters, but these requirements were few, and he chafed under the relentless tedium of his work.

Poverty, loneliness, and impending winter severely restricted Trist's early recreational opportunities. Aside from reading, his sole diversion was exchanging correspondence with his loved ones. Letters from his wife were now immeasurably more precious than those from his fiancée had been, even though both were from the same beloved Virginia. Now there was the cozy warmth of their shared lives, with vital news about their babies and the innumerable Randolphs. Virginia notified her husband of deaths and marriages in the community, mentioned visitors, and even teased him with coy intimacies, as when she replied to his first letter: "I did not expect that you would *turn bachelor* in a week. We shall see how it is a year *hence*."[2] Delicate in health, she could never disguise her mood; when she felt well she wrote joyfully, at times almost poetically, but when she was indisposed her letters were doleful. Best of all to him was the sincere and boundless love that flowed from every sentence.

Virginia's second letter, dated only a week after her first, brought devastating news. During the night of December 9, Trist's grandmother Elizabeth had died from a respiratory infection, probably pneumonia. This venerable woman, mentioned in many histories and praised by Jefferson as "a rare pattern of goodness, prudence, and good sense," was second only to the sage himself as an influence on the life of Nicholas Trist. In the space of four years he had lost his mother and both grandmothers.

As usual, Browse found little to applaud in his brother's latest career move, for Trist's acceptance of the post had barely preceded the election of Andrew Jackson to the presidency. Browse pointed out that Nicholas, while he was publisher of the *Virginia Advocate,* had established a reputation as a "prominent Jacksonian." Accepting a job from the opposition during the last few months of the Adams administration would not stand him in good stead with the incoming Democrats. This thought had not escaped Nicholas, but his was a case where beggars could not be choosers. Income from Louisiana had again dwindled to a trickle due to the capricious market and a dry season, and his meager salary, plus the small residue from the sale of the *Advocate,* would have to meet the expenses of two households until he could bring his family to Washington. He spent his spare time house hunting but found nothing within his means. Life was indeed bleak.

He did not, however, allow himself the luxury of despair, for he realized that opportunities lay all around him and that diligent effort would bring them within his grasp. He wrote a letter to James Madison and another to Edward Livingston, his tutor and benefactor at New Orleans, requesting introductions to well-placed leading citizens in Washington.[3] Both gentlemen responded promptly and enthusiastically. Madison wrote to Albert Gallatin, his old secretary of state (as well as Jefferson's), and Gallatin presented Trist to Martin Van Buren, the current secretary of state (who could hardly have realized at the time that a certain Trist was one of his subordinates), as well as other Washington notables. Mr. Livingston commended Trist to Secretary of the Treasury Ingham as one worthy of sponsorship, both social and political. There were unsolicited testimonials as well. Without being prompted, William Cabell Rives, a Virginia member of the House of Representatives, helped the cause by pointing out to Van Buren that Trist, as editor of the *Virginia Advocate,* had stumped for Jackson.[4] Each of these actions had its effect; soon his name was known around town. Within two years of his arrival, he would be a minor celebrity.

In January 1829, just two months after Trist's departure, Monticello was placed on the market. Virginia and her two babies went to live at nearby Everetteville with the family of her brother Jeff, where they were warmly received. Her husband's search for suitable family lodgings was proceeding at a snail's pace due to few rentals being available within their means, and she was in no hurry to leave familiar surroundings in any case, for she was by nature a nesting creature.

Soon Trist began making congenial friends, both within his own department and elsewhere, and although he still pinched pennies, he allowed himself one Saturday evening to be persuaded by some jolly companions to spend a dollar to attend a highly advertised play, Sheridan's *The School for Scandal*. By the time the gentlemen arrived at the theater, the lobby was jammed and the only seats to be found were in the gallery, or "loft," notoriously favored by prostitutes and their clients for the evening. Unwilling to pass up what promised to be an entertaining performance, Trist and his friends "mounted to the upper regions, where [they] found an abundance of respectable men to keep [them] in countenance." They took seats near the front of the gallery. Presently two "Cyprian dames" arrived and created a scene, complaining loudly because all seats had been taken, whereupon two dignified gentlemen seated next to Trist rose and departed. He started to do likewise but was dissuaded by his companions. The two "very handsome women" promptly occupied the vacated seats and soon began to flaunt their bejeweled fingers, which Nicholas admitted in his letter to Virginia "flashed in my eyes quite splendidly." However, the play did not hold their interest, and failing to capture that of their neighbors, the ladies soon departed. Trist returned to his dreary lodgings stimulated by this "adventure," though disappointed in the play.[5]

With the inauguration of Andrew Jackson, life began to brighten for the newcomer. He survived the political changing of the guard, though many of his colleagues did not. It was a desperate time to be thrown out of work, and many of those who lost their positions were devastated. One committed suicide and another went mad, but patronage was a fact of American politics that would brutalize its victims for generations to come. Eventually, significant civil service reforms began to appear during the Hayes administration in the 1880s, but traces of the "spoils system," which many historians say began with Andrew Jackson, remain to this day. Whether Jackson originated the practice or not, he unquestionably employed it as enthusiastically as any American president ever has. He brought with him his nephew and namesake, Andrew Jackson Donelson, Trist's closest friend at West Point, to be his private secretary. One day soon after the inauguration Donelson introduced Trist to his uncle.

With the passing of Thomas Jefferson, Andrew Jackson had become the most recognizable name and face in America. His stunning triumph at New Orleans, the only major land victory in the War of 1812, catapulted him into national prominence, and his every public act thereafter added to his fame. His indomitable will, frequently expressed in a defiance of authority that sometimes bordered on treason, only endeared him the more to ordinary folk, who regarded it as rugged frontier independence and him as the embodiment of the American spirit. Although limited in education and political experience, plagued by ill health and tortured by two pistol balls still festering in his thin frame, he radiated a charisma that attracted widespread admiration which, if not universal, was at least sufficient to make him the leading political figure of his time.

At six-feet one-inches tall and 145 pounds, the president was an inch taller and fifteen pounds heavier than Trist, though both men were spare to the point of emaciation. A stiff thatch of gray hair crowned his long, white face. Deep-set, hawklike eyes that missed nothing and revealed nothing studied the young Virginian, who in his twenty-ninth year was something less than half his own age. Through his nephew Donelson, Jackson was of course aware of Trist's former intimate association with Thomas Jefferson. If he also recalled that Trist had once politely turned down a request for an assessment of Jefferson's views on the Jackson candidacy,[6] he counted it an honorable act and, being a true gentleman, nursed no grudge. Many years ago Jefferson had allegedly described him as a barbarian scarcely able to spell his own name. But that had been long ago, and by the end of Jefferson's life their differences had narrowed, for both were true democrats and both revered the Union. He wished to know more about the sage, but on this occasion limited himself to pleasantries and, with a nod, returned to his duties.

With improved social life came temptations. Nicholas confessed to Virginia that he had fallen from his vow to eschew smoking; the aroma of fine cigars around him, combined with the stimulation of good talk and the excitement of a game of cards, proved too much for his resolve. When she reminded him of his promise to wear a piece of oil cloth around his wrist as a reminder,[7] he renewed his vow and with it pledged to "avoid going into rooms where smoking & playing are going on." He described his astonishment when, having accepted a casual invitation to "take pot luck" with a Mr. Ringgold, he found that "the table groaned under a profusion of... turkey, partridges, oysters, canvasbacks, cold fowl, ... dessert—ginger, limes, figs, etc., etc.—porter, cider, wine, toddy." His amazement only increased with the realization that this was "evidently not a set dinner" (that it really was pot luck) and the discovery that his host was currently undergoing his third bankruptcy![8]

Diligent house hunting finally showed some promise of success. A place not far from the White House, advertised for rent at four-hundred dollars a year, came highly recommended by knowledgeable friends. Notifying his wife of this discovery, Trist was at pains to explain that its fortuitous availability was due to "the owner being obliged to break up housekeeping, his wife having gone out of her head (the result of Presbyterianism)."[9] In the interest of domestic harmony, he would have done well to omit this explanation. Two weeks later he was still interested but unwilling to make a firm offer, being unable to examine the interior because the owner's "crazy wife is still in it. . . . He is going to take her either into the country or to the lunatic asylum in Baltimore; which last would be the more judicious course, as, under proper treatment, she might be recovered; whereas if left within reach of the priests, her mind will be kept afloat."[10] It was another gratuitous comment soon to rebound.

A month later he was allowed to tour the inside of the house and declared himself delighted. In addition to the outside attractions that had originally caught his notice—a handsome exterior and pleasant yard and garden—he found two comfortable parlors and four rooms with fireplaces, plus other desirable features. Strongly tempted but mindful that a number of in-laws, as well as his own growing family, would have to be accommodated, he included a sketch with his letter to Virginia, then offered the owner, Mr. James Handy, a year's lease contingent on the construction of specified additions and modifications. Handy was cool toward the offer but promised to consider it. Still afraid that he would lose a superb opportunity, Trist put forth an interesting proposal: four-month occupancy at an annual rate of three-hundred dollars and, thereafter, a three-year lease at four-hundred dollars a year, with the owner to add an office at the renter's expense only if found necessary during the trial period. The offer was accepted, the contract signed, and a loan from the bank initiated. Trist's friends were impressed with his bargain and even more with his canny bargaining; next day, the advertisement appeared in the paper and Mr. Handy, already moving out, informed his new renter ruefully that he could have rented a dozen such houses if he had them.

Virginia was overjoyed at the prospect of finally joining her husband, but less than pleased with his snide and needless reference to "Presbyterianism." Though it had been disguised as an explanation for the favorable rental opportunity, she recognized it as another thrust at her religious faith. She remonstrated gently, and in doing so provoked a serious spat that flared for several weeks. His retort, dated June 10, 1829, reveals Trist at his worst: "I never can be of your mind on this subject. . . . There cannot be a retrograde from the convictions and insights into these matters which result from the cool, dispassionate exercise of pure reason. . . . This being the case, the more play you give to those propensities and the more steps you take into what I conceive to be the region of pure *imagination,* the more you lessen those sympathies on which affection depends. Besides, the deeper you stray into these regions, the more you diverge from the path of cold reason, in which I deem it my *duty* to endeavor to lead our children to the best of my abilities. To use the language of religioners, Providence—through the agency of lawgivers—has made *me* the ultimate arbiter of the manner in which they are to be brought up."[11]

How this must have grieved her sensitive spirit! Not only did he brutally and arbitrarily impose his own "cold reason" over her "pure imagination" (at least he refrained from calling it superstition), but he even invoked the very "language of religioners," by which he meant scripture, as the authority for his superior legal position!

Virginia, replying at once to his letter, acknowledged that "my hand trembles with agitation in answering it." Read in the light of modern values, her words seem conciliatory, even excessively so, but in the context of her time they bordered on open defiance.

> With regard to what you say of the education of our children, my dear husband, I have never thought for one moment of diverting from your plan . . . and as far as the circumstances in which I am placed will allow it, I pursue it steadily, *sometimes* against *my own* judgement but still feeling confidence in its being right. . . . It is because [we] have not the same insight . . . that I differ from your opinion. In observing a silence on religious subjects I make a great sacrifice, but . . . it will be adhered to . . . but I should wish to teach our children what *I* believe *true,* and what is perfectly true and adapted to all ages and understandings, setting aside the fabulous [miraculous?] parts and not meddling with *doctrinal* points. . . . Perhaps I can make you understand me better by repeating a question from Patty—one day she asked me, "Mother, is God a bad word?" I was afraid to reply, as I did not know what you would have answered. I simply said no and began to talk of something else. . . . It *is* making a sacrifice *not* to give my children instruction . . . tending (more than what you call the path of *cold reason*) to their happiness here & hereafter. Besides, I believe that I should be teaching them what is *true.*[12]

So the argument ended in a draw. Both had had their say; neither changed views. Fortunately, their love was strong enough to stand the test and their lives full enough to distract them from the brief quarrel. Browse came on a rare visit, bringing good news: their esteemed partner Mr. Penney had acquired for them fifty acres of the finest Creole cane at a bargain price, and all the local planters envied their Willow Island plantation. The occasion for the visit was twofold: Browse's much-needed dental repair, there being no "scientific dentist" anywhere in Louisiana, and the possibility of a permanent change of scene.[13] Nicholas had approached Mr. Van Buren about a clerkship for Browse and had gained a promise that an existing vacancy would be held open long enough to receive an expression from Browse as to his interest. Nothing came of this, however; Browse was by this time making a commitment to the planter's life while also serving in the Louisiana legislature. He assured Nicholas that soon he would be sending regular amounts from their profits in Louisiana.

In the late fall of 1829, a promotional opportunity of some importance seemed imminent in the State Department. Old Mr. Brent, the chief clerk, fell desperately ill and was not expected to recover. Speculation arose immediately as to the succession, and among other candidates, Trist's name was mentioned. The position carried an annual salary of two-thousand dollars and somewhat more prestige than the title indicated, for the chief clerk was second in rank in the department and was sometimes required to act for the secretary in the latter's absence. Josias King, Aaron Vail, and William Waddell were also under consideration. All three were senior to Trist, but none had risen as rapidly in the administration's esteem. Trist, however, was at first not interested in the position. He was on good terms with the other three men and especially friendly with Vail, but he held a very low opinion of some of the clerks, having observed dishonesty among many. Supervisory responsibility therefore held little appeal. As time passed, however, and the matter remained unsettled, he began to think otherwise. By all accounts he could expect nothing more than his present salary for a long time. Perhaps . . . but stout old Mr. Brent rallied, recovered, and returned to work, his grip on the reins as firm as ever. The speculation quickly died.[14]

Virginia's poise and warmth made her a universal favorite at Washington parties, and Nicholas, always at his best in society, charmed the ladies and entertained the men. As a frequent guest at such levees, President Jackson favored Virginia with old-fashioned gallantry and took the opportunity to draw on Trist's recollections of Jeffersonian political philosophy. In December, the Trists received an invitation to dinner at the White House, the first of many more to come. Invariably the name of Thomas Jefferson came up in the after-dinner conversation, for Jackson seemed obsessed with him, and Trist enjoyed nothing so much as talking about his beloved mentor. More than one historian has credited these talks with forging a mystic friendship between two presidents who had scarcely met, linked by Nicholas Trist.

In the spring of 1830, preparations were initiated for a banquet in celebration of Thomas Jefferson's birthday, to be held on April 13. Sen. Robert Y. Hayne of South Carolina, chair of the festivities committee, arranged for toasts and speeches by Washington notables. Hayne called on Trist to look over the guest list and suggest appropriate changes or additions.[15] Foremost among the honored guests, of course, were President Jackson and Vice Pres. John C. Calhoun. This seemingly harmonious event was to ignite a spark of hostility between the two men that would outlast them both and set the nation ablaze.

"Nullification" was the incendiary word of the day, and John C. Calhoun was its foremost firebrand. The term simply meant that any state taking exception to a federally enacted law could, by action of its legislature, declare that law null and void within its boundaries. Such a concept assumed that the several states were, as the thirteen colonies had been before the Revolution, a loose federation of autonomous entities. The applicable pronoun for the United States of America was "them," not "it." Such a notion was anathema to the patriotic Andrew Jackson, who, while respecting states' rights, revered the Union. Washington was still reverberating from a debate between Senators Hayne and Daniel Webster just two months earlier, but no one was expecting the issue to be raised at the Jefferson banquet. No one, that is, except John C. Calhoun and a few of his cohorts—among them Sen. Robert Y. Hayne.

In an effort to trap President Jackson into an unguarded endorsement of their position, Hayne and Calhoun had arranged for several toasts to precede the president's, each exalting nullification, in the hope that he would feel obliged to do the same. This awkward and unrealistic strategy failed utterly, for Jackson immediately saw their purpose. When his turn came, he rose with great dignity, turned and looked Calhoun full in the eye and, holding his glass high, cried out, "Our Federal Union—it *must* be preserved!"

Calhoun turned pale and drank the toast with a trembling hand. Visibly nervous when his turn came, he nevertheless offered a challenge of his own: "The Union—next to our liberty, the most dear!"[16]

Following this Olympian exchange, the toast to Jefferson came almost as an anticlimax. Nevertheless, Trist, having been granted the honor in recognition of his membership in Jefferson's family, managed it with commendable aplomb, and the festivities resumed, if slightly subdued.

The break between Jackson and his vice president had been in the making since their inauguration in 1829, when Jackson had announced his intention to limit his presidency to a single term. Age, ill health, and a deep sadness over the recent death of his beloved wife Rachel were his reasons. Calhoun, one of the most ambitious politicians in our history, immediately began making plans to succeed Old Hickory, believing he could expect Jackson's support. His hopes were to be frustrated by a minor scandal that today would hardly make the tabloids. At the time, however, due in large part to the personality of the president, it turned Washington upside down and changed the course of history. It also had a direct effect on the fortunes of Nicholas Trist.

A man with a dangerous temper in his younger days, Andrew Jackson remained touchy and thin-skinned throughout his life. His enemies had made much over his wife's presumed bigamy—actually her mistaken belief that her first husband had long since divorced her at the time of her marriage to Jackson—and the poor woman died broken-hearted by years of malicious slander. Jackson, always gallant toward women and chivalrous in their defense, brought to the White House an extreme sensitivity about gossip involving "the fair," as he liked to call the ladies. One of the men who helped get him elected was fellow-Tennessean John Eaton, whom Jackson appointed secretary of war. Eaton promptly started carrying on with an attractive young married woman named Peggy O'Neale, whose husband was away at sea. When it presently came to light that the husband had died suddenly, the secretary made haste to marry her, some said at Jackson's insistence. The marriage did not stop the wagging tongues of Washington's society ladies, foremost of whom was Mrs. John C. Calhoun. Mrs. Calhoun refused to receive the new Mrs. Eaton at social affairs, and presently other cabinet wives followed suit. The chill in the Washington air became unbearable when Emily Donelson, wife of the president's nephew/secretary and herself official White House hostess for the widower president, joined the clique.

The crisis came at the president's birthday ball in January 1830. Peggy was ignored by all the ladies present, causing the famous Jackson temper to reach the boiling point. He called a special cabinet meeting to settle the matter and declared Peggy Eaton "as chaste as a virgin." This led to much ribald humor, some snide newspaper cartoons, and a new disease called

"Eaton malaria" because of the highly contagious nature of the gossip. (Malaria was then erroneously believed to be communicable.) Secretary of State Van Buren, who nourished ambitions of his own and enjoyed the trust of the president, played on the situation until Jackson came to believe that Calhoun had put his wife up to her back-stabbing. Relations between the president and vice president quickly deteriorated. All cabinet members were forced out and a new cabinet was formed. Jackson, determined to frustrate Calhoun's hopes for the presidency, reversed himself and announced he would run again, whereupon Calhoun, convinced that his chances for national power were extinguished (at least for the present), openly embraced the separatist sentiments of his rebellious South Carolina. Thus the seeds of secession were sown.[17]

How did this tempest in a teapot affect Nicholas Trist? The president's displeasure with Emily Donelson made her life in the White House so miserable that in early summer she took herself off to Tennessee, where she did not have to answer to the crotchety chief executive. Contrite, Jackson tried to persuade her to return, but she would have none of it. Her husband stayed on as the president's secretary for a time, but presently loyalty to Emily called him home as well. Jackson, needing a secretary, turned to Trist: ". . . All for the lack of a horseshoe nail."[18]

The president was in the habit of summoning Trist at various times, even in the late evening, to discuss not only his continuing interest in Jefferson but also to hear his aide's views on contemporary issues, which the young man did not hesitate to provide. These interviews took place over time and changed in character so gradually that Trist was uncertain as to the exact time when he became the president's secretary. Officially, he never really did, for Jackson, who valued his nephew's services, consciously or unconsciously held the position open for Donelson's return. At the bottom of a note Jackson handed him on May 19, 1831, Trist noted, "This, (or the note of April 12th, I forgot which) was to invite me to become his private secretary."[19]

As had been the case in his services to Jefferson, Trist quickly proved invaluable to the president. Although his intelligence has never been questioned, Andrew Jackson was almost entirely self-taught, having educated himself at a time and place where resources were few and more pressing matters usually intervened. Jefferson had been unjust in calling him a barbarian but had not been far off the mark in sneering that Jackson could hardly spell his own name. Trist, on the other hand, possessed a classical education of rare quality and unusual fluency of tongue and pen as well.

There was, of course, no difficulty about his absence from his regular desk, but as the new arrangement continued, the question of remuneration awkwardly raised its head. With pressing domestic expenses and a constantly varying number of in-laws to support, Trist was never free of financial cares, and at his State Department salary of sixteen-hundred dollars a year (two-hundred dollars more than his starting rate), he was aware that his earnings were much less than his present duties merited. Moreover, he was in line for promotion within the State Department but would almost certainly be overlooked if he continued as the president's aide. He remained silent on the matter, and in time Jackson brought it up himself, remarking obliquely that Trist would suffer no financial loss from the unusual arrangement. Later he handed Trist an envelope containing a check for three-hundred dollars and repeated his assurance.[20]

Trist was beginning to make himself known, not only by virtue of his highly visible position but also because he was writing articles for several publications in which he expressed his views on matters of current moment, such as the proposed federal protective tariff and the related nullification issue. He was developing a polemic style that would characterize his later writings and profoundly affect his career. Robert Drexler astutely noted that Trist's many State Department writings "have a sharp, adversarial tone. In commenting on views held by other persons with whom he did not agree, Trist had a tendency to go for the jugular. He mercilessly exposed their non-sequitors, raged against their inconsistencies, highlighted minor omissions and magnified mere slips of the pen which others had committed."[21] Although this criticism applied more accurately to his later writings than to those of his early Washington years, the tendency was already evident, and in an age of intensely adversarial politics, aggressive writing attracted popular attention and admiration.

Soon Trist became something of a presence in Washington. Seekers after presidential favor solicited his advocacy. His writings were increasingly in demand, and out of consideration for the president he customarily used a pen name. He published a scathing series of articles in the *Richmond Enquirer* excoriating Calhoun by name, thus further ingratiating himself with Jackson. In the summer of 1831, he was asked to deliver the keynote speech at the fifty-fifth anniversary celebration of the signing of the Declaration of Independence but was forced by pressing executive office duties to decline.

In 1831, Alexis de Tocqueville, that indefatigable tourist and observer of American folkways, began a visit to the United States in Boston. He was for a time the house guest of Joseph and Ellen Coolidge, whose knowledge of the region was as helpful to him as their hospitality. Joseph gave the young Frenchman a letter of introduction to Nicholas Trist. When de Tocqueville arrived in Washington, Trist also put himself out to be helpful, and the two young men seem to have formed an immediate friendship based on intellectual compatibility. Trist spoke at length about a subject that troubled him greatly at the time: the fading influence of the earlier leaders—specifically Jefferson and Madison—and the growing trivialization of their part in the nation's history. De Tocqueville listened with interest and reflected some of Trist's views in his writings.[22]

Sudden notoriety has turned the heads of humbler men than Nicholas Trist, who, it must be admitted, already entertained a rather high opinion of himself. Now he was given a room at the White House (a convenience to the president more than a perquisite) and was often asked to travel with Jackson and other notables in the presidential retinue. Trist found it all intoxicating, but Virginia, pregnant again, was less enthusiastic. Bills were as pressing as ever, and the capacity of their house was strained by a steadily growing number of occupants. In the summer of 1831, Trist was asked to accompany the president on a two-month vacation at Old Point Comfort. While Jackson relaxed in the fresh salt air and sunshine with members of his "Kitchen Cabinet," his overworked aide stayed indoors and struggled to gain ground on a mountain of correspondence. Virginia wrote that in Washington every day brought rain, rain, rain. Somewhat enviously she noted, "I was delighted to hear that you had fine weather. . . . I hope it will continue till you return home, even if you should find that the clouds here have not exhausted themselves."[23]

At about this time Jeff Randolph, acting for his mother, accepted an offer for Monticello from a Mr. Barclay. As it turned out, negotiations would continue until the following January. Proceeds from the sale were hardly sufficient to pay off the remaining debts, some of which no doubt had been written off. In the following years Monticello passed through numerous hands, each time falling deeper into decay. At length, on July 4, 1926, the centennial of its designer's death, the grand hilltop mansion that had once been called the finest example of architecture in America was acquired by a group of appreciative Virginia ladies who turned it into a national shrine. Today its halls, gardens, and paths are trod by thousands, but in former times it was neglected.

While Trist was at Old Point Comfort with the president, Virginia accepted an invitation for a fall visit to Jeff's family in Edgehill. Her departure barely preceded his return, obliging Nicholas to resume bachelor living. A major factor in the timing of this trip was a desire to see her mother, who had completed a stay in Boston with her daughter Ellen and was residing temporarily at her son Jeff's farm at Edgehill before joining the Trists in Washington. Martha's straitened circumstances now caused her to move about frequently, paying long visits to first one and then another of her married children and hoping—needlessly—that by so doing she would not wear out her welcome at any one location. Ever the conscientious matriarch, she had written apologetically to Virginia, who was clearly her favorite daughter, saying that when she next came to Washington she felt obliged to bring with her a grandson, Willie, who had been orphaned by the death of her eldest daughter, Anne Carey Bankhead, and was now destitute of any other means of support. Her letter betrayed the excruciating embarrassment that her impoverished condition, due solely to her self-sacrificing loyalty to her debt-ridden father, had imposed upon her.[24] Virginia, wanting desperately to reassure her mother, decided to meet and conduct her to Washington with every display of loving hospitality.

As late as 1833, there remained lingering details of Thomas Jefferson's estate to clear up, and the partnership of Martha Randolph and Nicholas Trist dealt with each as opportunities arose. Most painful to Martha was the disposition of the slaves, some of whom continued in the service of others as rental property for a number of years after their master's death. Eventually Israel, for some time a baker in the kitchen of Mrs. Grey, had to be sold. Martha's letter to Trist clearly reveals her agony over the fate of her father's "people": "I could not reconcile it to my conscience to tear a human creature from his wife and children and send him off to a distance where he would never again see or hear of them. Nor do I think it right to . . . [put] him under an overseer and a strange master. I am truly sorry that I possess such property. If I could afford it I would liberate every one of them, in the meantime I [am] bound by the most sacred of all duties: to protect and guard them from the misfortunes incident to their situation."[25] Unfortunately, there is no record of Israel's fate.

Martha Randolph, as the only living child of Thomas Jefferson, had immediately become a notable presence in the nation's capital during her first visit there in 1829. Fifty-seven years of age, she bore a remarkable resemblance to her father during his presidency, a likeness made even more striking by her stature, for her six-foot frame was only two inches below that of "Tall Tom." Moreover, Washington's knowledgeable insiders admired the quiet dignity, efficiency, and dedication with which she had sacrificed her own interests to liquidate her father's debts. Soon she began to receive invitations, and these of course included her daughter and son-in-law.

Andrew Jackson, who was always gallant toward ladies and especially so in the case of Thomas Jefferson's daughter, made it his yearly practice to call on Martha Randolph, usually accompanied by Secretary of State Van Buren. Mrs. Randolph cherished these attentions, and the Trists put forth their best efforts to entertain their distinguished guests. This was no mere toadying on Trist's part, for he was developing a genuine affection for the president comparable to his devotion to Thomas Jefferson. That Jackson warmly returned his feelings is evident from the words of James Parton, a respected biographer, who wrote in 1864 that "among the young men who surrounded General Jackson during the early years of his presidency, there was none who enjoyed more of his affection and none more worthy of it than Mr. Nicholas Philip Trist of Virginia." Parton added that Trist "was one of those happily constituted men who see clearly and lovingly the nobler traits of a friend and are blind to the less worthy ones."[26] Or, if not blind, at least reluctant to acknowledge them.

Trist was not hesitant to put himself forward for advancement, for despite his rapid and impressive progress, he felt well qualified for better work than either his clerical job in the State Department or his secretarial services to the president required. He made his ambitions known to Old Hickory, and Jackson took the hint in good spirit. He assured Trist that he had had the same thought in mind. His words, as nearly as Trist could recall them, were, "I will improve your situation; there will be an occasion before long, I believe." At the same time he pressed another envelope into Trist's hand; it contained another three-hundred dollar check.[27] Nevertheless, when Donelson returned to his interrupted post, sending Trist back to his humble desk at State, and as Jackson continued to call on him more frequently for assistance, a suspicion arose in his mind that he was more useful close at hand than he would be if promoted out of convenient reach.

If his abrupt return to clerical tedium was a disappointment, at least it was mitigated by a pleasant surprise when Edward Livingston was named secretary of state. His old friend and mentor, who would quickly distinguish himself in international affairs, made better use of Trist's talents than had his predecessor; nevertheless, Trist remained dissatisfied. After tasting strawberries, who could enjoy prunes?

As though their lives and their house were not already full, the Trists received a letter from Browse dated December 28, 1831, airily announcing that young Julien Tournillon "has consented to leave home for a year or two and wishes to put himself in your charge. His intellectual capacity is limited, and you must confine yourself to have him taught a competent knowledge if possible of the english and french and of arithmetic. It is also desirable to have him taught some accomplishment, music for instance, if he has the *organ*." Browse's letter concluded with a postscript: "No more, I pray you, about the money you get of me. If I had not bought a boy (about $600) to be paid at the end of the year I could afford to let you have more."[28]

The new year of 1832 brought a sudden upturn in the sugar market. Mr. Penney went on a land-buying spree, and the Trist brothers, willy-nilly, went with him: three thousand dollars laid out in February for one additional plantation and another tract acquired at a bargain price in April. The usually glum Browse exulted that "nothing can be foreseen that would prevent us from waxing rich." In February, Virginia gave birth to a healthy boy, whom his parents named Hore Browse Trist after his uncle.

In May, another letter from Donaldsville brought assurance that an earlier rumor of a slave uprising had been false. "Not a mouse stirring," Browse wrote. "There is no possibility of concert among them, and white agitators would, if detected, . . . be put to death without mercy."[29] This was not an isolated occurrence or an exaggerated report; the white citizens of the Deep South lived in constant dread of a slave insurrection.

In July, a cholera epidemic then sweeping the nation reached Washington. Virginia described it in a letter to her sister: "I believe we may consider ourselves safe even though it is raging here, they say, worse than any city in the United States. There is a population here that will be swept off very fast, among whom are the people brought here to work on Pennsylvania Avenue and on the Canal; the poor free coloured people too, are its unresisting victims. They generally refuse to be removed to the Hospitals where they would be perfectly well attended for fear of being *experimented* upon by the doctors, & frequently die in their houses without calling on medical aid. . . . Although no one can help a feeling of awe & melancholy when they see their fellow creatures dying around them of this dreadful epidemic, I believe the disease will [harm] very little among those who can take proper care of themselves."[30]

In November, Browse wrote that "a confederation of pestilences—Yellow fever cold plague . . . and the cholera are making sad havoc in the City. . . . So we are on the *qui-vive!*" Nearly two hundred, including Louisiana's secretary of state, had died and many more deaths were expected. A plaster of burgundy pitch applied to the abdomen was thought to make the wearer invulnerable. Camphor was selling in New Orleans for twenty dollars a pound.[31]

In the fall, Andrew Jackson made good his threat to run for reelection and won easily, despite advancing age and increasingly poor health. Trist was so certain of the outcome that he expressed surprise that the margin of victory was not greater. If anything, the president's reliance on his assistance increased.

Little Pat was suffering from a chronic sore throat, which Trist insisted on treating with frequent swabs of alum. The child hated the treatment, and her throat only grew worse. In desperation her father took her to Philadelphia to be treated by the famous Dr. Physic, who diagnosed the condition as tonsillitis and prescribed a gentler treatment. While he was in the city, Trist visited its respected school for the deaf and dumb and assured himself that its high reputation was well deserved.

In the spring of 1833, the American consulate at Havana was vacated by the retirement of the current official. The vacancy attracted an immediate scramble of applicants, for the post was considered quite a political plum. A New Yorker named John Hefferman, well qualified and superbly connected, had secured the backing of Van Buren and a powerful group of bankers and politicians from his own state and seemed to have the job locked up. But Andrew Jackson was impervious to pressure. On one occasion he declared, "I care nothing about clamors, sir, mark me! I do precisely what is just and right." Now he recognized an opportunity to pay a long-standing debt.

On the 24th of April, 1833, Nicholas Trist was commissioned American consul to the Cuban port of Havana.[32]

CHAPTER 6

Havana

The appointment generated widespread interest and some apprehension among Nicholas's relatives, friends, and acquaintances. James Madison sent a congratulatory letter and begged a visit before the new consul's departure. Browse wrote, "It seems you have made an excellent bargain for once in your life." Then, bewilderingly, he scolded his brother for putting his life at risk, declaring it "outrageous and criminal folly in you to waste the little stock of health you possess."[1] Of the same mind, Virginia, no doubt influenced by nervous friends, thought that going to live in Cuba was almost an act of suicide. Someone identified only as Uncle William sent word that he was sure Nicholas was "in the way of making a fortune, for I consider the place of Consul at Havana as one of the most lucrative" of government appointments.[2] The ambitious Mr. Hefferman, evidently of the same opinion as Uncle William, offered Trist a monetary consideration if he would refuse the post and recommend Hefferman in his place. Trist politely rejected the bribe.

He did not, however, accept the appointment at once or without misgivings of his own. For many reasons, the family would have to remain in Washington, at least for a time, and he did not look forward to another long separation from his loved ones. And as always, anxiety about his health and dread of the tropics weighed on his mind. But all things considered, the advantages—most of which were financial—far outweighed the disadvantages.

An annual salary of two-thousand dollars, he was assured, would amount to less than half the total emoluments of the consulship. As official representative of the government, responsible for the protection of American commercial interests in Cuba, he would occasionally be required to act as a notary, for which service he would be permitted to charge and keep a sizable fee. An even more attractive perquisite was an unusual banking arrangement. In those times even American banks were suspect, and foreign banks were considered impossibly risky. Americans doing business in Cuba customarily entrusted their funds to the American consul, allowing him to invest them and keep the interest as his commission, requiring only that he return the original deposit on demand.[3] These attractive perquisites of the consular service—not limited to the Havana office—would, not surprisingly, undergo severe criticism and eventual reform in the next decade.[4]

As he was preparing to depart, Trist received an unexpected order that considerably altered his plans. President Jackson had decided to tour the northern states to speak against nullification, and he wanted his favorite aide to accompany him. Presidential requests being not easily refused, Trist did not object, partly because midsummer was near and he did not look forward to arriving at his tropical post during the hottest time of the year.

Just then a fortuitous message arrived. Vice-Consul Cleveland wrote from Havana proposing to discharge all the duties of consul until the following spring for half the total emoluments accruing to the consul, thus allowing Nicholas to delay his arrival until that time. The opportunity to remain with his family until early 1834 was irresistible, and Trist accepted despite a warning from Ellen Coolidge. Having heard unfavorable reports about Cleveland, she felt sure he would try to steal Trist's position or harm him in some other way.

The president's tour was a notable success. Cheering throngs greeted him everywhere, and his fiery indictment of nullification was well received. However, the many required appearances, social as well as political, placed too great a strain on his failing health, and he was forced to cut short his scheduled itinerary and return to Washington. As he slowly recovered, he found other work for his favorite aide. On a convalescent vacation to Old Point Comfort, he brought along his Kitchen Cabinet to keep him company while he sunned himself on the beach, leaving Trist at his vacation headquarters to deal with a mountain of correspondence.

Eventually Old Hickory released Trist, allowing him to direct his attention to a myriad of closing details. First he broke away for a fall vacation with Virginia at White Sulpher Springs, the last carefree moments the two would enjoy alone together for a very long time. Then the entire family went on a round of visits, spending time with their many relatives in Virginia. Finally in late fall, intending to make a short visit to Louisiana before sailing to Cuba, Trist bid a sad farewell to his family.

The river steamer *Henry Clay* was a vessel of oceangoing size. Its cavernous hull was laden with three-hundred tons of freight, which, added to its own weight, made for tricky navigation because unusually dry weather had lowered the water depth. Moreover, the meandering river system was infested by countless submerged logs, snags, and sandbars. Instead of the rapid and comfortable trip he had expected, Trist found himself disembarking with the other passengers at all hours of the day and night to lighten the *Henry Clay* enough to clear hidden obstacles. An Irish laborer, employed to help haul the vessel through the Ohio River locks and over Mississippi shoals, swore, "Oi've bin a Clay man for siven years, but damn me if Oi iver vote for him again!"[5]

Arriving at last just before Christmas, Nicholas had a joyful reunion with Browse. The Tournillon family also made him welcome. Touring the plantations with Browse and Mr. Penney, he quickly came to share Browse's enthusiasm for their new partner. He wrote to Virginia: "You may rely upon his friendship for you, as well as upon his integrity and his good management."[6]

For once it was Virginia who complained of the infrequency of mail. She wrote that she was resolved to make no calculations about the time of receiving letters. Nevertheless, she shared her own news from Edgehill, where she and little Browse and Patty were staying with her brother Jeff. Jeff's icehouse would not be filled unless the pond ice should freeze thicker. Her mother would not return to Washington until fall, because of "the great embarrassment she is under for money." The banks had begun to discount money, causing immense distress among the populace. Nicholas had rented the Trist house in Washington to the family of Sen. William Rives—who had been recently appointed minister to France—and they moved in. Virginia enlightened Mrs. Rives by mail concerning a slave soon to be set free; Ellen, the house servant; 'Mrs. Suk,' the family cow; various household furnishings and utensils; Washington society in general; and the much-preferred friends of the Trist family in particular.[7] In late January, she wrote with deep sadness of the sudden death of her brother James, the quiet, decent Randolph who was so easily overlooked in life and now so grievously missed. "This world was no place for him," she wrote. A slave was heard to say, "Master James would share his last crust with a black man."[8]

Another brother, Meriwether Lewis Randolph, an official in the Treasury Department, wrote to Virginia of the president's shocking appearance and depressed state of mind. At a recent White House dinner party, Jackson had declared that he was tired of life and, if his enemies would cease to molest him, he would lie down and die quietly. Lewis informed her that the Rives family had removed to Paris, leaving the Trist house vacant. He would attempt to find new renters. The gay, carefree bachelor added a message for younger sister Septimia: "Tell Tim the City is so full of belles that some of them . . . are sighing like high-pressure steamboats after my whiskers, the envy of all the men and the admiration of the ladies."[9] James and Lewis were as different as night and day.

In early March, Trist said his farewells once more and, after several lonely days and nights in New Orleans, where he waited for a ship bound for Havana, wrote miserably to Virginia of his longing for home and family. He concluded: "I never before felt the force of this world."[10]

On March 26, after a disagreeable voyage of six days from the mouth of the Mississippi, the little brig *Rapid* came within sight of the mountains of Cuba. Though land still lay many miles to the south, the sweet perfume of orange blossoms, magically wafting on the trade wind, cheered the weary passengers. Later, as they entered the harbor and dropped anchor, a barge approached and an official boarded the brig. He was the captain of the port come to inspect the passenger list, and when he discovered that it included the new American consul, he insisted that Trist accompany him ashore. Upon being conducted to the consular office, where he was received "with all kindness" by the staff, he was informed that Mr. Cleveland, the vice-consul, was away in the country for a few days. An elderly gentleman named Smith acquainted him with the affairs of the consulate and answered his questions courteously and with commendable knowledge. Determined to make health his first concern, Trist ordered a warm bath and retired to the comfortable quarters that had been prepared for him nearby.

Trist had, of course, already acquainted himself with the basic duties of an American consul, which, according to *Consular Regulations,* consisted of (1) endeavoring to create a situation favorable to the importation and sale of American goods, (2) submitting frequent reports on commercial and other economic subjects, (3) replying to private inquiries of American citizens touching commercial and industrial matters, and (4) lending aid and service to American citizens doing or contemplating doing business within his jurisdiction. There were also associated duties, such as protecting the rights and interests of American seamen.[11] The social obligations of the position were considerable. In a pretelegraphic era, when ready access to higher authority was impossible, the position called for tact, judgment, and resourcefulness. Obviously, the consul must possess the full confidence of the administration.

The international community at Havana lost no time in welcoming its newest member. A splendid levee at Government House, hosted by the British commissioner, was attended by the bishop, the governor general, a phalanx of local government functionaries, and the officers of the armies and navies of three nations, plus their ladies. The civilians were in formal attire and the military ablaze in a variety of dress uniforms. Trist was at his most charming as he conversed in three languages, accepted as many invitations as possible and did his best to remember names. When one dowager remarked to another that the new American consul was the handsomest man present, the compliment was passed along to him, and in his next letter home he made certain to mention it.

Acutely homesick and longing to have his family near, Trist set about finding a suitable home for them. He immediately rejected the city because of its crowded, noisy streets and fetid odors. In a rented *volante* (carriage), he scoured the surrounding countryside and soon found a delightful house on a hilltop, formerly owned by a wealthy merchant, that seemed perfect. The sea breezes cooled the house when the windows were left open, and a pleasant stream flowed through the garden. In glowing terms he described this find and assured Virginia that the Cuban climate was more hospitable than he had expected. Unfortunately, his offer on the house was refused, and he was obliged to continue his search.

Although much about the city was repugnant, he was enchanted by the markets with their profusion of fruits, vegetables, flowers, and handcrafts. Because of his preoccupation with health, he had always favored a diet of raw fruit, and the marvelous flavors, abundant variety and novelty of the Cuban species delighted him. He began shipping crates and barrels of his favorites home for the enjoyment of his family and his Washington associates and friends. With his customary exactness, he gave Virginia precise instructions: a dozen oranges to the president, six grapefruit to Mr. Van Buren, a box of guava marmalade (a special favorite of his) to Henry Clay, so many "pines" (pineapples to the uninitiated) to this one and so many limes to that. Virginia faithfully carried out his instructions, and the gifts were happily received. He also sent shipments to Louisiana, where the results were less fortunate. Browse wrote that, of a barrel of oranges, nearly one-third were rotten. With his usual practicality, he advised against further shipments.

Relations with his deputy were less than agreeable. Cleveland took his time returning from his trip to the country, then showed no disposition to leave, as he had supposedly intended. His patronizing air suggested that Trist would be adrift without his assistance and, therefore, he would postpone his own plans in the interest of the consulate. He gave no indication when he might leave, and Trist, having accepted his offer, felt himself in a poor position to push the man out in favor of a more agreeable associate. The situation became increasingly uncomfortable, and more than a year passed before Cleveland finally departed.

Letters from relatives, friends, and family sustained the lonely consul. Browse, now thirty-two and long considered a confirmed bachelor, surprised his brother with the announcement of his engagement to Rosella Bringuer, "one of the many children of a rich sugar planter." Virginia described farm life at Edgehill and reported on the progress of the children. Little Jeff, now in his sixth year, presented a major obstacle to her plan to come to Cuba, for Jeff would soon need special instruction. Eugene Vail, a family friend, had visited a school for deaf and dumb children in New York and spoke in its favor. She had heard of another such school in Paris, but Dr. Livingston, who had kindly investigated the place, gave an unfavorable report. Meanwhile, Jeff was doing well on his own; he had developed a sign language the others could understand and even used it to spell out simple words. Trist felt a special tenderness for his afflicted son and refused to accept the permanence of his condition. There was, he insisted, a cure for every ailment, if only it could be found. He frequently wrote hopefully of the "restoration" of Jeff's speech and hearing, as though they had once existed.

Even after taking up his duties, Trist was not committed to permanence in his position. Although the spring weather was surprisingly pleasant, he was nervous about the onset of summer, and his old dread of the tropics haunted him. He found a solution to this problem more easily than he could have expected. On May 1 he wrote asking Donelson to seek permission for him to take a long leave each summer. He was prepared to resign if the request should be denied, but Secretary Livingston agreed after querying the president. On June 22, he again boarded the brig *Rapid* and sailed for New York.

The summer was a happy blend of work and play. Jeff Randolph was enlarging his holdings and soon moved his family to Everettsville, taking the Trists with him. Nicholas and Jeff, always the best of friends, spent much time organizing the Jefferson manuscripts for preservation. They continued to receive requests for the Jefferson letters, most of which they refused. Trist made several trips to Washington, where Andrew Jackson made use of his services and even arranged for his temporary lodging at the White House. There were social engagements as well, and at these he received warm expressions of gratitude for the gifts of fruit he had sent and many questions about life at Havana. In speaking of Cuba, he was aware of his own ambivalence, for he detested the long months of steaming heat; yet he was at pains to quiet Virginia's apprehensions in order to persuade her to join him there. He confided to Madison that he feared he had made a mistake in accepting the post and was considering resigning the following spring after a brief return to arrange for his departure. His first leave extended through November.

From Louisiana Browse, the former misanthrope, wrote in a mood of unprecedented contentment. His weight had risen to 130 pounds, the most ever. Of his marriage he wrote, "I have certainly drawn a prize in the matrimonial lottery. Rosella is an angel in disposition . . . no cloud ever comes over it . . . not even the vexations which the negro servants never fail to occasion."[12]

With Lewis's failure to rent the Washington house, Virginia and the children returned there, where they were joined from time to time by various family members. In December, three of her four sisters—Ellen, Cornelia, and Mary—were with her, and all four sisters enrolled in a Spanish class. When the capital was plunged into one of the coldest winters in memory, she began to think more favorably of Havana as she wrote of their "canada winter," with the mercury falling to -15°F and lower, while ice formed on the wash basins in the bedrooms. In January, a chimney fire started from a blaze in Ellen's bedroom, launching a geyser of sparks onto the roof. Fortunately a blanket of snow on the roof prevented a wider conflagration.[13] News of this incident did not settle Nicholas's nerves.

The Washington weather moderated in February, and the residents resumed interrupted social activities. A certain Captain Levi, taking note of the presence in Washington of a bevy of Jefferson granddaughters, began calling in the afternoons. He entertained the ladies with stories of Parisian society and informed Cornelia, with a certain look in his eye, that common French gossip held that no man could be a true Jeffersonian unless he married a descendant of Thomas Jefferson.[14]

In Havana Trist began feeling more optimistic about his situation. He wrote about the "divine" weather and, aware that his wife's hesitation to join him was largely due to her mother's unsettled situation, he added, "Mother must make up her mind to come if it be but for one season."[15] The administration's indulgence in allowing him to take long annual leaves helped allay his reservations. Another factor was the substantial income he was already receiving, far more than he had ever earned, and his prospects for the future were even brighter. He began campaigning through Browse to bring Mr. Penney to Cuba with a view to employing his proven genius in a sugar venture. Browse dutifully conveyed the suggestion to Penney but soon informed his brother that their partner already had too many irons in the fire and was not likely to "take your bait."

Trist began house hunting in earnest and found a promising place in nearby Guanabacoa, though he was disappointed in the single-level architecture prevalent in Cuba. "I want to live upstairs," he complained, "being convinced that it is healthier and more pleasant every way."[16] In this he betrayed one of his many health idiosyncrasies as well as a determination to live by his own terms. Often he would say, "I never forget that my health is the *first* and *governing* consideration, to which all others must count as nothing."

In Washington Captain Levi made another of his afternoon calls on the way home from his government post. In casual conversation he informed Cornelia that he had in his pocket a newspaper clipping reporting complaints of some Yankee ship captains about the difficulties they had experienced in trying to see the American consul at Havana. Upon going to the consulate specifically for that purpose, they were intercepted by an agent who informed them that he, the agent, "sufficed." Even as these frustrating conversations were in progress, the visitors sometimes saw "a handsome young man in black curled whiskers," who they supposed was the consul, "sauntering through" the office. The arrival of some other visitors interrupted Captain Levi, and he left without showing the clipping.[17] His report of this trivial affair was somehow ominous, like the first snowflake that heralds a blizzard.

In Louisiana Browse and Rosella had become parents, and they were thinking of naming the baby boy after his Uncle Nicholas. Browse's newfound domestic happiness was dimmed somewhat by the discovery of "shooting chest pains" and a sense of suffocation while falling asleep. "More ties attach me now to life than ever," he wrote despondently, "and death would be rather unpalatable."[18] His relatives were thrown into panic at this news, but on consultation Dr. Harris wryly advised Cornelia that the case sounded like hypochondria. His long-distance diagnosis proved astute; soon Browse reported feeling fine, boasting, "I have vanquished the King of Terrors." The family breathed again.

When his second summer vacation was delayed by the serious illness of Mr. Smith, Trist was obliged to await the coming of his new deputy, Mr. Mortland, until late July. Shortly before he arrived in Washington, a bizarre event occurred there that rattled the nerves of the citizens. The young male servant of a certain Mrs. Thornton burst into her bedroom in the dead of night brandishing a pair of pistols and raving that she must pay with her life for the crime of owning him. The woman was frightened out of her wits and doubtless would have been murdered in her bed but for the fact that another slave, the intruder's own mother, was sleeping in the same room and leaped up to intervene. During the ensuing struggle, Mrs. Thornton rushed from the room and cried the alarm. When two neighbor men came to investigate, they found the young man locked out and hammering on the door, howling threats and daring them to take him. Since he was still armed, the rescuers prudently waited for the constable, who arrived too late; the would-be assassin had escaped.

Much discussion followed this event and its tone and speculations were indicative of the times: since the young man had been raised from birth and always kindly treated by Mrs. Thornton, why—unless he was insane or drunk or both—would he wish to harm her? Also, his ravings about "his natural right to freedom" sounded like something planted in his mind by abolitionists, not the spontaneous utterance of an "ignorant" house servant. After this incident, the abolitionists were more detested than ever.[19]

Again Trist was asked to devote a portion of his leave to the president. He also made a hurried visit to Montpelier, where he found his old friend James Madison failing rapidly but happy to see him. During the time he was able to spend with his family, he and Virginia discussed plans for the future. She longed to join him in Cuba but still felt constrained by her mother's circumstances and even more so by the question of Jeff's education.

Their persistent search had convinced them that the Institution for the Deaf and Dumb in Philadelphia was the finest facility of its kind; even so, it was with great reluctance that they decided to enroll their son there. To ease the transition, Virginia would take temporary lodgings in Philadelphia. The Trists' Washington house was put on the market, and luckily a buyer was quickly found in the person of Secretary of the Navy Dickinson, who agreed to a price of seven-thousand dollars.

When Trist departed in early December, Virginia, by now settled in a small Philadelphia apartment, began paying frequent calls on her Aunt Hackley. Taking Jeff with her, she made frequent and seemingly casual stops at the institution. The kindly director, Mr. Hutton, greeted them warmly at each visit and conducted them to classrooms where they observed teachers and pupils at their silent studies. Keenly interested, Jeff quickly interpreted the signs and by degrees became more a participant than a spectator. Virginia played the game with patience, love, and skill. When one day in late December she bade her son good-bye at the gates of the institution, it was she who most keenly felt the pangs of separation.[20]

Before his departure, Trist, still bent on "restoring" Jeff's hearing, learned about a Dr. Togno, who claimed miraculous results with similar cases. There being insufficient time to investigate for himself, he left written instructions for his wife to do so. He was particularly insistent because, while watching Jeff play with his watch, he saw the boy hold it to his head, then react in a way that led him to believe Jeff might be made to hear.

With Jeff accompanying her, Virginia visited Dr. Togno, who examined the boy and pronounced the case an interesting one. He spoke learnedly of two alternative procedures, one performed by operating on the eustachian tube and the other by piercing the tympanum. He expressed a desire to spend some time getting acquainted with the boy in order to "ingratiate" himself with the prospective patient. Virginia was appalled by the descriptions of both operations and wisely sought counsel from the familiar and trusted Drs. Patterson, Harris, and Dunglison. They promised to investigate and did so, but were unable to respond immediately. Meanwhile, from Havana, the impatient father was pressing for action: "I would without grudge pay him thousands could I afford it . . . should he restore [Jeff] to hearing at all."[21] Dr. Harris's response when it came was anything but reassuring. Togno had been telling people that he expected to operate on a descendent of Thomas Jefferson, boasting that such a coup would secure his reputation and make him a rich man. Virginia indignantly informed her husband that she would never allow such an unconscionable charlatan to experiment on their son.

Trist conceived another ingenious idea concerning Jeff, a crass scheme quite out of character and one that does him no credit. He fell to thinking of a wealthy cousin in Philadelphia named Sally Thompson, "a kind-hearted old maid" who had taken a fancy to Jeff and once said she would like to adopt him. In a letter to Virginia, Nicholas assured her that he had no intention of giving Jeff to Cousin Sally, but as "she is as likely to leave her money to me as to anyone else," it would not be amiss to let her know that Virginia and the children were now living in the same city and would like to have Sally pay a visit. He urged her to take care of this matter straight-away.[22]

A better side of Trist is revealed in another family incident. Virginia's brother Lewis, the devil-may-care bachelor (so everyone supposed), sud-denly left his post in Washington and disappeared into Tennessee Terri-tory, where he presently emerged a married man, father, and aide to the territorial governor. In a letter to Virginia announcing the birth of his son, Lewis said apologetically that he was thinking of naming the boy after Andrew Jackson and hoped the family would not suppose he was slight-ing the memory of Thomas Jefferson, who had a considerable number of descendants named for him already. No more letters followed until the family received the shocking news of Lewis's sudden death and the disap-pearance of his wife and infant son, the latter believed to be dangerously ill. The Trists appealed to Andrew Jackson, by then retired to his Tennes-see home, to help locate the missing mother and child, whom they pro-posed taking into their already crowded household.[23] Fortunately, not long thereafter, another relative wrote to inform them that the widow had re-turned to her parents' home, and she and the baby were both well.

As noted earlier, one of Trist's duties entailed the submittal of reports on the activities of the consulate. To this responsibility he brought a zeal that became the misfortune of those whose duty it was to read his mes-sages. He was, in the words of historian Louis Sears, "the slave of his pen," belaboring all subjects, minor and major, with maddening prolixity.[24] Thirty or forty pages seemed to him hardly sufficient to cover the most routine matter. In this he reflected the laborious training he had received in the study of law and his own extraordinary analytical ability and concern for justice. Lawyerlike, he was convinced that if a subject lacked clarity, more words would help, and if they did not, more still perhaps would do the trick.

When his emotions were involved the ink flowed even more copiously, for when angry he seemed able to relieve his feelings only by the exercise of his pen. The inclination revealed in his earlier writing toward adversarial prose was becoming even more pronounced with his greater authority and the backing of a supportive administration. He was by now firmly in the habit of handling disagreeable situations by written rather than face-to-face communication.

Virginia's hesitation to join her husband in Cuba continued to derive from her mother's increasingly grievous physical and financial circumstances. Martha Randolph was sixty-four years old, destitute but for the assistance of her children, and saddened by the loss of the five she had outlived. A deepening resignation had settled over her, and despite her treatment as a celebrity because she was Thomas Jefferson's lone surviving child, life itself had lost its savor. She declared that she was perfectly surrendered "to his will who has hitherto guided me with the hand of a father." On October 10, 1836, her surrender was accepted. The family was plunged into grief, and the nation mourned a vanished symbol of its early glory. In late November 1836, Nicholas, Virginia, Patty, little Browse, and a young household servant named Lavinia sailed for Cuba.

Trist had purchased a house two miles outside the city. Situated on a low hill facing a semicircular bay, it commanded a pretty view of the sea, where every day ships could be seen majestically entering and leaving the harbor. Because of its location, the place was called *El Cerro* (the hill). Virginia was pleasantly surprised to discover that her husband had not exaggerated the charms of Cuba, though she found the house in need of a thorough cleaning, an opinion not shared by the servants, whose "Spanish indolence" exasperated her. The children were enchanted by it all. Every late afternoon, when the sun lowered and the heat of the day was broken, the two parents took canvas chairs to the beach to watch Browse's kite climb in the steady trade wind and soar far out over the blue-green bay. Close by, Patty sketched and painted or waded in the warm shallows collecting shells. To Trist, having his family with him at last was balm to his soul.

Though all mourned her passing, Martha's death had devastated her five daughters to varying degrees. Ellen and Virginia, being married, drew comfort from their own families, while Mary and Cornelia especially, and young Septimia to a lesser degree, felt emotionally marooned. For a time Cornelia was acutely depressed, declaring herself a useless burden and a misfit. She announced her intention to become a governess, an occupation for which the others considered her hopelessly unfit. There was a palpable air of relief when she eventually stopped speaking of this plan. Nicholas and Virginia urged all of the Randolph sisters to pay them a long visit, and all but Ellen, who was leaving on an extended voyage to the Orient with her husband Joseph, accepted the invitation.

Patty was approaching eleven and Browse was nearly five when they arrived in Cuba; thus, the subject of their education frequently occupied the thoughts of their parents. Trist was of much the same mind as his grandfather-in-law, who had been convinced that a first-rate education was not to be obtained in the United States. Virginia shared that view: her mother, who was Jefferson's daughter, had, after all, received most of her education in a Paris convent, though it had terminated abruptly when she asked for her father's permission to adopt the Catholic faith.[25] They agreed, however, that the time was not ripe; the children were not old enough to be sent abroad. Instead, for the sake of having the whole family together if only for a time, Trist persuaded Mr. Hutton to grant Jeff a long absence from the institution. (At the time it was believed that the profoundly deaf should be isolated for their own good.) He arranged to have Jeff escorted to Havana by a trusted skipper.

Jeff was now nine, tall for his age, handsome, and amiable. His personality was, as his Uncle Browse said, "charmingly naive." Little Browse was still a rosy-cheeked cherub not yet rid of his baby fat and, though given to bursts of temper, strongly inclined to please his parents, a trait that sustained him through horrific medical and dental trials. Preadolescent Patty possessed the high-strung temperament that so often accompanies artistic ability. All three were apt students. Affectionate toward each other, they seldom quarreled.

In the summer of 1837, Jeff was returned to the Philadelphia "asylum." Trist sailed a short distance with him to quiet the boy's anxiety, but when Jeff became interested in the working of the vessel and in watching passing whales, his father bade him farewell and returned by launch. The devoted Aunt Hackley met Jeff in New York harbor and arranged his trip to Philadelphia. Some time later Patty also returned and entered school in New Brighton under the guidance of the same accommodating aunt. Patty wrote demanding that "father make me a good many pens, . . . for he makes them to suit me better than anyone else."[26]

In all matters pertaining to their children, Nicholas and Virginia consistently applied a policy of "disinterestedness." The term, more in vogue then than now, simply meant that the children's needs came before the parents' interests. At times this brought much heartache to both parents and children, but the Trists were unsparing in their commitment to the policy.

Septimia stayed on at Havana for some time after Mary and Cornelia returned to the Boston home of their sister Ellen Coolidge. She sometimes strolled on the beach with young Dr. Meikelham, but their relationship appeared more companionable than romantic and so was not taken seriously by the family. This fact was especially evident when Tim said her good-byes and returned to Boston to join Mary, Cornelia, and the Cool-idges, who had recently returned following a long stay in the Orient. In February 1838, however, Septimia dropped a bombshell by announcing her engagement to Dr. Meikelham. Mary, who had been counting on Tim to accompany her on a long ocean cruise, went into hysterics. Joseph, the proper Bostonian, who had planned a more suitable match for Tim with one of his Brahmin associates, pronounced her "a foolish, foolish girl." Nevertheless, the marriage was a happy and successful one and produced three sons.

In early 1839, after much discussion, Nicholas and Virginia decided it was time to implement their long-deferred plan for the European instruction of Browse and Patty. Still following the Jeffersonian model, they felt that a French education would be most beneficial. They realized that Paris would be impossibly expensive, but by all accounts very respectable schooling could be found at reasonable cost in some of the provinces. Virginia would accompany the children and remain with them as long as necessary. Another parting of indefinite duration faced Nicholas and Virginia. Mary and Cornelia were still despondent over their mother's death. Cornelia was especially melancholy, feeling useless and at loose ends following Septimia's marriage. With her usual sympathetic generosity, Virginia invited her two sisters to accompany her, and both readily accepted. Their destination was St. Servan, a village on the Brittany coast that was said to offer a fair climate and other advantages.

The party set sail in early March 1839. After a stormy twenty-nine-day passage, during which the two spinsters were almost continuously seasick, they arrived off the French coast. The weather was still so foul and fogbound that the captain deemed it necessary to put in at the English port of Dartmouth overnight before attempting a landing at Havre, which was finally successfully negotiated. For the last two nights of this wretched voyage, they all slept fully dressed with their life preservers on.[27]

Patty's thirteenth birthday, May 8, 1839, was celebrated in a modest and "rather shabby" cottage Virginia managed to rent in the village of St. Servan. Patty was promptly enrolled in a small school taught by three nuns. Virginia, doubtless thinking of her mother's crisis a half-century earlier, assured Nicholas that she considered it not very likely that their daughter would "turn Catholic." Reading this and remembering Thomas Jefferson's account of his daughter's attempted conversion, Nicholas must have shuddered. Virginia also engaged the services of a Spanish music teacher, who praised Patty's *"disposiciones"* for instruction and pronounced himself *"muy contento*" with her progress, cautioning only that she must learn *"paciencia."* Virginia was delighted to have Patty exposed to Spanish as well as French, and to learn music in the bargain.[28]

Up to this time, Virginia's domestic experience had been, for the most part, limited to the supervision of a staff of household servants. Now she must learn to cook, sew, and clean as well as shop for comestibles in a foreign market. There was, of course, some sharing of tasks among the sisters, but the main burden fell on Virginia's slender shoulders. The rental arrangement included use of a small vegetable garden and several fruit trees, which reduced living costs and added a measure of bucolic savor to their lives. The small lot on which the house was located faced the sea and was closely ringed by meadows and woods. Most of their neighbors were peasants and small farmers who, with rare exceptions, spoke only French.

On August 15, Virginia wrote to Nicholas, informing him that she had found a lady "of good family but in straitened circumstances" to instruct Patty in French. "She [the instructor] speaks the purest and most elegant french . . . where the lower classes speak the vilest patois, and the dialect of the higher circles even is not purely Parisian." Her letter betrays a touch of class consciousness strangely at odds with her warm and generous nature. She was "dissatisfied with the manners of the school [Browse's], the children of the tradespeople are received promiscuously with those of the upper classes." On a lighter note, she wrote glowingly of Browse: "I wish you could see him taking dancing lessons. He compresses his lips to keep from smiling, but the dimples in each cheek [reveal] his mirthful mood, as well as the laughing expression of the eyes, which [grow] darker and more expressive every day—more like one other person of my acquaintance in 'auld lang syne.'" As her thoughts came to bear on this "other person," she described a dream: "Last night, dearest, I dreamt of crossing a giddy height over a torrent on a narrow, slender plank with you for my guide, holding my hand and walking before me; I followed fearfully, then I was walking with you on a sandy Beach, where the water and sand sparkled in the bright sun. Then the scene changed, became confused, . . . but you were by my side, and my heart was *content.*"[29]

A frequent dreamer, Virginia possessed the ability to recall her dreams in sharp detail and to describe them vividly. Although dreams are said by some to be unfathomable, hers reveal a person of great sensitivity, a trait that is also apparent in her three children and may be the legacy of her grandfather.

Communication between Nicholas and Virginia was haphazard at best, for the delivery of a letter depended not only on wind and wave but also on ship captains of various degrees of reliability. They learned, painfully, that messages of special importance must be copied and the copies sent by several carriers. Even then six months might elapse between transmittal and receipt. A note attached to a packet of letters by a conscientious Havana postmaster is revealing: "Dear Sir: You will be surprised at receiving such a number of letters, and more so when you observe that, most of them are marked 'for barque Ellen.' I cannot account for your not receiving them earlier, as, when the Ellen arrived, I asked the Captain if he had brought any letters for you, his answer was 'no.' . . . I am afraid that [Captain Gordon] is not all right sometimes."[30]

Experiences of this kind may have been a factor in the developing tension between the consul and a number of Yankee skippers who frequently dropped anchor in Havana harbor. When possible, Nicholas and Virginia sent their letters by trusted transatlantic travelers.

Trist's letters made frequent mention of health. His reports on his own condition were often overly optimistic, for he sometimes declared himself "perfect" to Virginia at the same time he was querying Dr. Meikelham orally and Dr. Dunglison by lengthy letter concerning the advisability of his continuing to live in the tropics. Turning from his own condition, he urged his wife to "implant in our children a *living faith* . . . that health of body is the very first of worldly blessings."[31] He sent strange items advertised as possessing marvelous health-giving properties and added to the manufacturer's claims his own enthusiastic endorsement. A thick doughnut-shaped pillow called a Napoleon cushion was guaranteed to correct internal disorders. A horsehair mitten called a Renovator was certain to induce glowing health by vigorous chafing of the skin, and he directed Virginia to massage herself all over with this fearful object and do the same to both children. Hearing no response, he again urged its use, declaring that by combining a Renovator rub-down with his dumbbell exercises and a daily cold-water dousing, he was receiving wondrous results. At length Virginia confessed she was not able to inflict the Renovator on the children but had tried it herself with no apparent result other than a great deal of red and irritated skin.

If Nicholas's nostrums seem quaint, Virginia was encountering others that sound positively barbaric. Early in her stay she wrote that Browse had been ill, so "our good old Dr. Blachier applied a couple of leeches to the inner part of the thigh, . . . a hot foot bath with vinegar in it, a syrup for his cough, and the next day Calomel followed by purgative powder. . . . The Dr. is not of Mr. Duqueney's opinion about 'roughing him out of his delicacy.'"[32]

Nicholas had not abandoned the idea of recovering Jeff's hearing. He learned of a Dr. Turnbull in France who was credited with producing dramatic results and urged Virginia to investigate. She did so and replied that Dr. Turnbull was "a quack decidedly"; furthermore, Cornelia had read of two deaf patients who had died as a result of operations on their ears.[33] Undeterred, Nicholas wrote of another European practitioner who was reported to cure deafness with "magnetic and galvanic" treatments. Nothing came of this either.

Operation or no, Trist did not intend to deny his elder son the advantages enjoyed by his other two children. Virginia was planning to conclude her long stay in France with a visit to Paris, and Nicholas began devising a means of transporting Jeff there to join the family. The hazards inherent in this scheme were terrifying, yet by dint of much letter writing and with the help of trusted friends, Trist arranged to get Jeff transported across the Atlantic and escorted safely by coach in the care of one Captain Pell from Havre to Paris, where he rejoiced to find his mother, brother, sister, and two aunts waiting for him. Five months later, from the familiar institution in Philadelphia, Jeff rewarded his father with a remarkable journal of his adventure. He began, "I will now tell you the things I have seen . . . ," then proceeded to do so in minute detail. Mr. Hutton, who had expressed misgivings before Jeff's departure, reported to Trist that the boy remained in a "reverie" for two months after his return before finally refocusing on his surroundings.

In the summer of 1839, soon after Virginia's departure for France, the grievances of a group of Yankee skippers against the American consul at Havana blazed forth like spontaneous combustion. More or less simultaneously, their complaints began appearing in geographically scattered newspapers across the land. Charges of high-handedness, inefficiency, and failure to uphold American interests were leveled at Trist. So intense and sustained was this drumbeat of accusations that the *Charleston Courier* noted dryly in an editorial that "we shall be obliged to establish a standing head [regular column] for Consul Trist's delinquencies, if accounts of them continue to flow in upon us with as much rapidity as they have done for some weeks."[34]

The specific charges were too numerous and varied to be dealt with exhaustively here. However, four alleged offenses are representative.

    1. Captain Kendall of the brig *Kremlin* was said to have been

imprisoned without cause as a result of Trist's intervention when the captain withheld the wages of a drunken mate. According to the charge, the consul demanded three months' advance pay for the mate and, when refused, had the captain jailed.

2. Captain Straw of the brig *Sarah Ann Alley* was imprisoned—allegedly at the behest of the consul—when certain ship's funds entrusted to his care were at first missing and later discovered in his cabin under circumstances suggesting they may have been planted there by a crewman.

3. A nonviolent mutiny—in reality only a work stoppage—took place aboard the *William Engs* when the ship's destination was altered by the owner without regard for the concerns of the crew. When the affair escalated into a brawl between master and crew, a force of soldiers, allegedly acting on a request from the consul, removed the crew, who were then tried without counsel and sentenced to from two to four years of hard labor.

4. The purser of the *Boston,* on setting out by carriage for an evening at the theater, was stopped and allegedly assaulted at the city gate by a mounted guard. An appeal to the lieutenant governor received sympathetic consideration until Trist allegedly interceded, placing blame for the incident on the purser.

Other more general charges included insulting and oppressing American captains and favoring Spanish authorities over his fellow Americans. When one recalls that the official duties of the consul were basically limited to the promotion of American commercial interests, one is inclined to concede at least the appearance of straying from a strict interpretation of *Consular Regulations.* On the other hand, the number (over two hundred) and spontaneity of the charges tend to strain credulity. Although he disdained to engage in a "newspaper war" with his accusers, Trist insisted that he was the target of a conspiracy and grimly began documenting his defense. But if he would not defend himself in the newspapers, others were willing to do so on his behalf, and an impressive number of publishers, most with Democratic sympathies, stood behind him.

Then another crisis exploded. Incredibly, the British government began accusing the American consul at Havana of abetting the illegal slave trade. A recent treaty between England and Spain had outlawed maritime transportation of slaves. Soon after the agreement was signed, the Spanish decided they had gotten the worst of the bargain, suspecting it to be a device for undermining the Cuban sugar industry in favor of growers in the British West Indies.[35] But the British government, under intense pressure from abolitionists in Great Britain, was zealous in enforcement and even sent two of its representatives, who were also members of an Anglo-Spanish joint commission, to Havana to promote enforcement. The two, both abolitionists, did not limit their activities to goading the reluctant Spanish authorities but also set to work on the American consul, demanding that he use his influence to get his government to allow the boarding and inspection of ships flying the American flag and suspected of participating in slave traffic. Deeply offended on two counts, Trist refused to cooperate or even meet with the commissioners. As a Virginian with typical opinions about abolitionists,[36] he detested what he considered their fanaticism, hypocrisy, and apparent eagerness to put Southern lives at risk. And as a patriotic American old enough to recall the War of 1812, he violently opposed the forcible boarding of his country's ships by the British navy, all the more so because the United States was not a party to the treaty he was asked to support. The British commissioners responded to this latter point by insisting that ships engaged in slave-running, of whatever nation, often hoisted the American flag to escape inspection. They persisted in their demands until Trist's temper reached the boiling point. Resorting as usual to written counterattack, he fired off an intemperate blast that presently reached the office of Lord Palmerston, prime minister of Great Britain.

Much of this tirade was unassailable in logic, but as usual he could not let well enough alone. He started out reasonably by denying having knowingly issued ship's papers to American flag vessels engaged in the slave trade, pointing out that it would have been impossible for him to do so without military support from the Spanish authorities, who would have refused help. He noted that he had served his critics' cause by curbing the hiring of American seamen known to be destined for African ports. Then he began wandering far afield by outlining his own views on slavery and insisting that slaves were better off working on southern plantations in the United States than they would be if left in Africa. (This was probably thrown in to annoy the abolitionists.) He accused the commissioners of hypocrisy for demanding of him "miracles" of enforcement while doing nothing themselves to combat the open sale in Havana of English-made iron slave shackles. By this time, having lost all chance of a sympathetic reading, he finished with a salvo directed at the government of Great Britain in general and the House of Lords in particular. Today a copy of this astonishing document rests in the archives of the State Department, condensed in print to a mere 140 pages. It must have been much longer in its original handwritten form.

An official British protest was, of course, inevitable, but its reception by both the administration and Congress was lukewarm. A congressional committee was at the time reviewing the mariners' accusations, and to this body the Van Buren administration sent the official British complaint and Trist's voluminous letter to the two commissioners. In a defiant mood, he wrote Virginia: "You may have heard the rumor of my having been *ordered* to Wash. No such thing. And if I had been, I should not have gone."[37] Despite this defiant assertion (significant for its future portent if only vain posturing in the immediate circumstance), he began laboriously assembling proof of his innocence, and with this "camel load of documents," as his brother described it, returned voluntarily to Washington prepared to defend himself before the congressional investigating committee.

Because of the notoriety of his case, Trist's presence in the capital was naturally well publicized. He began receiving letters from Sarah Easton, an impoverished widow with whom the Trists were slightly acquainted. The burden of these messages was an agonizing lament at her hopeless state of poverty and an appeal for assistance. The third letter was delivered in person. Trist donned his coat and hat and accompanied the lady to his bank, where he withdrew one-hundred dollars in gold and handed it to her.[38]

Soon after this incident the Committee of Commerce of the House of Representatives announced that the evidence submitted to it did not "at all affect the character of Mr. Trist for integrity and honor." The committee was further of the unanimous opinion that no case had been submitted calling for congressional action.[39]

In December 1841, after a separation of nearly three years, the Trist family was reunited in Havana. The reunion was a joyful one even though the future seemed dismal, for Trist had lost his position after the Democrats were turned out of office in the presidential election of 1840. The blow came as no surprise, though he nourished a faint hope until the official notification arrived. He declared his intention to remain in Cuba and devote himself to agriculture and writing.

CHAPTER 7

Washington and Veracruz

When Andrew Jackson left Washington in 1837 and returned to his beloved Hermitage, he was not expected to survive more than a year or two in retirement. Few supposed he would ever again be a force in national politics, for he was broken in health and, seemingly, in spirit. But as long as an ember of life remained, the iron will of Old Hickory was strong as ever. As the critical election year of 1844 approached, with his party splintered by a fearful discord, he detected what he thought was the cause of Democratic fragmentation. The regional leaders of the party were pushing regional issues rather than the interests of the whole nation. It seemed clear to Jackson that expansion was the unifying theme, the most obvious example of which was the drive to immediately annex Texas. He even went so far as to put in writing that Texas was needed as a buffer for "the safety and protection of New Orleans" against the threat of British meddling.[1]

The Republic of Texas was eager to enter the Union as a new state, but many in the North feared it would tilt the delicate balance of power in favor of the Southern slavocracy.[2] So volatile was the issue that the apparent nominees—Van Buren for the Democrats and Clay for the Whigs—both decided to sidestep the Texas question during the campaign.[3] Van Buren was a Jackson favorite—had even followed him into the presidency—but his unwillingness to embrace annexation did not please his sponsor and eventually cost him Jackson's support. While Jackson was still unconvinced of Van Buren's apostasy, a neighbor, James K. Polk, began paying frequent visits to The Hermitage, and soon the general offered to support Polk in a campaign for the vice presidency.[4]

Neither the rapid escalation of public enthusiasm for expansion nor the general disarray of the Democratic Party was lost on the alert James K. Polk. Trimming his sails to the rising breeze, he abandoned his quest for the vice presidency and boldly went after the larger prize. As Andrew Jackson regretfully accepted the unmistakable fact of Van Buren's position against annexation, Polk moved quickly to claim the old warrior's favor, even declaring that Jackson was now definitely "of the opinion that Mr. V. B. ought to withdraw."[5]

There followed a period of intense turmoil during which various Democratic factions, each with its own agenda, sought to tie up the party's convention at Baltimore, but it was Polk, the dark horse, who emerged as the candidate, thanks to some nimble behind-the-scenes maneuvering by his close friend, Gideon Pillow. Polk's campaign slogan was frankly expansionist: "All of Texas and all of Oregon!" In a hard-fought election he defeated the better-known Henry Clay by 38,000 votes.

Mr. Polk was not such a political unknown as the Whig newspapers made him out to be. As a member of Congress, he had served as speaker of the House, and twice he had run unsuccessfully for the office of governor of Tennessee. He assumed the duties of his new office with a zeal that has seldom been equaled, but his personality did not match his capacity for work. His immobile features and cold gray eyes were well suited to a nature much inclined to favor his own counsel, an unfortunate trait that concealed large and important plans. His appropriation of the expansion issue was not political opportunism, for he sincerely believed that the nation's economic growth was tied to expanding world trade, which in turn would depend on acquiring deep-water harbors on the Pacific coast. He is thought by some historians to be the first chief executive to perceive maritime mercantile development and overland agrarian expansion as complementary rather than competitive forces.[6]

The nation—or at least its self-appointed fourth estate—felt a need to morally justify what was soon to occur, and the need was supplied by a journalist named John O'Sullivan, who in mid-1845 coined the convenient and oft-quoted term, "Manifest Destiny."[7] As O'Sullivan explained his catchphrase, God wanted the United States to "overspread the continent allotted by Providence for the free development of our yearly multiplying millions. . . ." That meant, at a minimum, annexing Texas, acquiring California from Mexico, and securing the Oregon Territory before Great Britain snatched it.

After the election Jackson made a request of his protégé: find a job for Nicholas Trist, preferably chief clerk of the State Department. After the Whig victory in 1840, it had been a foregone conclusion that the consulate at Havana would change hands; nevertheless, it was not until November 1841 that Trist had been required to turn his duties over to a successor and only then with assurances from President Tyler's Secretary of State Daniel Webster that "this resolution has been adopted [by Tyler] without his having formed any judgment of the charges which have been suggested against you."[8] Trist accepted his dismissal in good spirit and even sent a cordial message to the new president. Then, true to his stated intention, he settled in Cuba, intending to live out his life there. But it was not to be so, and what followed in the next four years, on being reported to Jackson, moved the old man to tears of pity.

The expected financial support from Browse failed to materialize because of "the disastrous state of pecuniary affairs" in Louisiana. Trist purchased a thirty-seven-acre farm outside of Havana, expecting to make at least a comfortable living from it, but—despite a beautiful view of the bay, where passing ships could be observed from every window—the anticipated profits were not forthcoming. One by one, the trappings of gentility had to be sacrificed, beginning with the two *volantes*. Soon the Trists were advertising rooms with board for single folk at one-hundred dollars a month, laundry included. Trist's literary plans resulted in the translation from French of a treatise on dairy cows, nothing more. A visitor in 1844 was shocked to discover the decline in the family's fortunes; he wrote to Andrew Jackson that "Trist has bronchitis and cannot live out of a southern clime and at Havana he lives by the sales of a market garden . . . Mrs. Trist is condemned to live in Cuba by pandering to the stomachs of rich Spaniards."[9] It was this heartwrenching account that caused Jackson to appeal to incoming President Polk.

In August 1845, the family returned to Washington, and Trist began his service as deputy to Secretary of State James Buchanan. As a member of the congressional committee that had investigated charges against Trist five years earlier, Buchanan had reason to remember his name, yet the memory was untainted by misgivings. He soon came to appreciate the businesslike way in which Trist addressed his duties and especially the experience gained from earlier service in the department. Soon he added more responsibilities to the chief clerk's position, even delegating to him the role of acting secretary during his own absence.

It was inevitable that both Nicholas and Virginia would be attracted to the courtly Buchanan, for he exuded the sort of innate gentility that meant so much to them. Tall and stately, invariably attired in a black suit with white stock framing his patrician features, the bachelor secretary regarded the world around him with calm blue eyes, his white silky hair impeccably brushed back from his high forehead. His bearing was erect and his manner stiffly formal. "Distinguished" was the word most often used to describe James Buchanan. Soon after the Trists arrived in Washington, Mr. Buchanan took to dropping in for afternoon tea, and before long he was their frequent Sunday dinner guest as well. Trist came to regard his superior as a close personal friend.

In a time before undersecretaries of state were known, the chief clerk bore the responsibilities of that office without the dignity of the title. He was also a channel of communication between the secretary and the several hundred clerks who performed the necessary tasks. Every scribbled directive from the secretary must be read and logged by the chief clerk, then assigned to a likely underling, and every letter drafted for the secretary's signature must be screened and possibly edited by the same official on the way to the top. The workload was frequently heavy, but its content was often stimulating.

Candidate Polk's slogan "All of Texas and all of Oregon!" ensured that President Polk would be a foreign policy president. On the Oregon question, the defiant cry of "Fifty-Four Forty or Fight!" referred to a wildly unattainable international boundary though the notion had many passionate adherents. But Polk soon decided to negotiate more realistically with the British, who appeared equally reluctant to go to war over the undeveloped Pacific Northwest.

Tyler had maneuvered the annexation of Texas through Congress by a joint resolution just three days before leaving office.[10] Now Polk *reannexed* it just to prove that his campaign promises meant what they said. Contrary to the widespread expectation, annexation was not immediately followed by war; nevertheless, Mexico refused to acknowledge that Texas had ever ceased to be part of Mexico and, in any case, disputed the American claim that the Rio Grande should be recognized as the international boundary.

This dispute over who owned Texas had arisen in the early years when

American settlers occupied what was to become the Republic of Texas. The settlers insisted that the Rio Grande, whereas Mexico considered the Nueces River to be the boundary of the state of Tamaulipas. When the argument reached an impasse, the territory between the rivers became a troubled no-man's-land,[11] which it still was at the time of annexation. Relations between the two neighbors had been deteriorating for decades; now the tension became palpable. Polk sent Gen. Zachary Taylor and the Army of the Southwest first to Galveston and later to the Rio Grande with ominous orders: "It is not designed in our present relations with Mexico that you should treat her as an enemy; but should she assume that character by a declaration of war, or any open act of hostility towards us, you will not act merely on the defensive, if your relative means enable you to do otherwise."[12]

In November 1845, thinking to make good on one of his objectives with minimum cost, effort and delay, Polk sent John Slidell to Mexico with an offer of twenty-five million dollars in cash for the purchase of California plus another five-million dollars for the vast but largely arid region called New Mexico. But the unfortunate emissary arrived in the midst of a revolution and was sent home empty-handed without the courtesy of an audience. Polk saw this as tantamount to a declaration of war, and the prospect of approaching conflict set Washington abuzz. War hawks saw no problem in taking on Great Britain and Mexico at the same time.[13] Embattled newspaper publishers, safely beyond fighting age, thundered "Who's afeerd [of England]?" Other jingoists clamored even more noisily for war with Mexico, calling her "a mongrel nation" and declaring that her citizens would only benefit by Yankee domination. But quieter and more rational voices, chiefly from New England and Ohio, argued with equal fervor against "Mr. Polk's war," as the Whig newspapers soon came to call it even before war was declared.

Early in 1846, the administration came to terms with Great Britain on the forty-ninth parallel as an international boundary to the north, and a treaty was signed on June 15. Hawkish expansionists still chanted "Fifty-Four Forty or Fight!" and grumbled that Polk had sold out too cheaply, but there was enough excitement along the Rio Grande to satisfy most, and soon there would be more. The impatient Polk wanted more pressure put on the Mexicans to encourage them to accept his offer, which he considered generous; moreover, he was prepared to go even higher should there be any sign of acquiescence on their part. When none was forthcoming he thought a declaration of war might make Mexico more tractable,[14] and he even drafted a war message, citing Mexican discourtesy to Slidell. But one member of his cabinet objected that the expulsion of an American diplomat would hardly be accepted by Congress as grounds for war. Even so, the cabinet supported his rather overstated complaint; then, fortuitously, a messenger dashed into the capital with news of a skirmish near the Rio Grande in which sixteen Americans had been killed or wounded.[15] Polk saw this as providential. He spent a busy Sabbath rewriting the war message, which he presented to Congress on May 11, 1846. In it he declared that "the cup of forebearance had been exhausted even before the recent information from the frontier of the Del Norte."[16] By the overwhelming vote of 174 to 14 that same day, the House supported the president. The Senate took a bit more time, with some doubts expressed about Polk's claim that Mexico had "shed American blood upon American soil." (These reservations referred to the disputed territory between the Nueces and the Rio Grande.) Still, on May 13, the Senate voted the war declaration 42 to 2. "Mr. Polk's War" was now a reality.

From its outbreak, the war went badly for the president despite an unbroken series of American military victories, some of which even the English admitted were brilliantly executed. There were many reasons for this but none more fundamental than President Polk's inability to deal realistically with Mexico. Polk did not understand the Mexican people and he had little respect for them. Although he had eagerly sought a war declaration, chiefly for its mobilizing effect, he had no intention of waging a vigorous war. He merely wished to pressure the stubborn Mexicans into selling land they seemed unwilling or unable to use for themselves. But his military posturing only succeeded in inflaming their hatred and stiffening their resistance. When American indignation arose against the war, he met it with secrecy and dissimulation,[17] causing the Whigs to label him "the mendacious Polk."

Although the war obliged them to work closely, Polk and Secretary of State Buchanan were not on the warmest personal terms. Polk suspected correctly that the secretary wished to be the next president,[18] and though he did not covet reelection for himself and had said so, Polk wished to help pick his successor—who would, of course, be a worthy Democrat—but not James Buchanan. The secretary sometimes acted as though the matter had already been settled in his favor, and his presumption irked Polk. Even though their differences had to be put aside in favor of duty, both men were aware of the tension. With difficulty, a semblance of harmony was achieved.

In Mexico, expressions of American and European sympathy were joyfully received. Some *gringos* were saying openly that by holding out, Mexico could eventually make "a brilliant treaty." Even the *yanqui presidente* had assured them that he wished Mexico to be strong, prosperous, and friendly; surely that meant he would not crowd their country too far. Repeated offers to negotiate were interpreted as evidence of lack of resolution, for if the *Norteamericanos* insisted on buying land, were they not admitting the inability to take it by force?

As the war that was expected to last only a few weeks dragged into its second year, even the obstinate President Polk was forced to acknowledge one disagreeable fact: the intransigence and chronic instability of the Mexican government offered little hope for a settlement.[19] As soon as one precarious regime showed the slightest signs of weakening, it was sure to be overthrown and replaced by a more bellicose successor. Even if an olive branch were waved by some peaceable faction, it would be snatched away before an American negotiating team could be rushed to the scene. The president and his secretary of state held many discouraging and inconclusive meetings on this problem. At last they came up with an idea that showed promise.

Why not send a qualified diplomat, clothed with necessary powers and guided by a firm set of directions, to accompany the army and, at a propitious moment however transitory, seek an agreement that could be ratified expeditiously by both governments? They discussed various candidates for the task, but for each they found some objection. No man of the first rank, such as a senator or ambassador, would go to Mexico and suffer the frustrations and humiliations that the Mexicans could be expected to impose.[20] Polk thought the secretary of state would be a natural choice, but Buchanan reacted coolly. For political reasons, he did not favor a prolonged absence from Washington, and the president knew it. The problems began to appear insurmountable.

Then, somewhat tentatively, Buchanan put forth the name of Nicholas Trist. When the president offered no immediate objection, the secretary pursued his suggestion more forcefully. Trist knew State Department protocol. He had traced the Mexican affair from its inception; indeed, he had drafted most of the correspondence to Slidell while that emissary was in Mexico while simultaneously taking care of personal business for Slidell during his absence. He was an experienced diplomat, fluent in Spanish. In appearance, bearing, and character, he was without flaw, and his education was universally admired. Best of all, he was a loyal Democrat. After extended discussion Polk called a brief cabinet meeting and quickly obtained unanimous affirmation of Trist's appointment. Consistent with the president's passion for secrecy, the cabinet was also unanimous in its opinion that Trist be appointed an "executive agent" to avoid the necessity of Senate confirmation. Trist then received his first knowledge of the plan in a private meeting with the president and Secretary Buchanan.

Having on several occasions served as acting secretary in Buchanan's absence, Trist was on reasonably cordial terms with the president, which was perhaps as much as anyone could claim. After scant preliminaries, Polk nodded a signal to Buchanan, who explained the purpose of the meeting. Trist listened silently. His impassive features revealed nothing of his reaction. He readily understood the concept, which seemed nicely tailored to the actual situation, and he appreciated the thoroughness with which it had been developed. At the same time, his heart sank at the prospect of another indefinite absence from his family and he dreaded another prolonged stay in the tropics. The two officials waited for his response, but before it came the president spoke.[21]

"Mr. Trist, if you can but succeed in restoring peace, you will render a great service to your country and acquire great distinction for yourself."

"The service shall be rendered, sir," Trist replied, "if it be possible for me to do it. But as for the distinction, I care nothing for that."

Polk obviously took this for an insincere disclaimer intended to make its author appear nobly disinterested, for his wintry smile was skeptical. He remarked that all men desire distinction. Offended but careful to conceal it, Trist commented that his ambition was limited to something on the order of an appointment as military storekeeper, where he might earn a modest living at a task that would make no great demands on his time. No record has been kept of the president's reaction to this curious rejoinder, but Polk then casually offered a suggestion that has baffled historians from that day to the present. It might be best, he said, to avoid troubling General Scott, the supreme field commander, with details of the diplomatic mission, since the general already had enough on his mind. Any necessary coordination with the army could be brought to the attention of General Pillow, who, as a lawyer and former associate of the president, would know what to do.[22]

Far from feeling slighted by this apparent belittlement of his mission, Trist was relieved. Everyone in Washington knew that Polk detested the pompous Whig, Winfield Scott. Indeed he had denied Scott the honor of field command for seven months following Scott's arrant insult to Polk and, even after reluctantly reinstating Scott, had tried to place over him a commander more in sympathy with the administration. Only the quiet counsel of Secretary of War William Marcy had convinced the irate Polk that competence was more important than good manners or acceptable politics, and that no other officer approached Scott in the matter of competence. Knowing only part of this, Trist, who had met Scott only once, felt certain that he disliked him and would like him no better on longer acquaintance. He was relieved to have the amiable Pillow as a contact.

With the essentials of the commission concluded, Polk dismissed his visitors with a brisk nod and turned to a mountain of waiting paperwork. Back in his own office, Buchanan reviewed the assignment, together with its limitations and available resources. Specific terms and conditions were painstakingly spelled out in a draft treaty, called a *projet*. A plain copy of this document was provided for Trist to study. An identical copy was impressively enclosed in a heavy envelope bearing the presidential seal in red wax and addressed to the Mexican minister of relations. A separate letter introduced the commissioner, affirmed his credentials, and announced his authority and readiness at all times to negotiate. There were also letters from the secretaries of war and navy to General Scott and Commodore Perry, respectively, concerning the mission. Trist was directed to have the sealed documents forwarded to the Mexican minister of relations. He was also *authorized* by Buchanan to show General Scott his own instructions. Unknown to him, Secretary Marcy used the word *directed* in his corresponding dispatch to Scott. The variation in language would make a world of difference.

The terms of the *projet* called for Mexico to relinquish all claims to Texas, acknowledge the Rio Grande as boundary, and cede to the United States all of upper California and the territory of New Mexico, which then included what are now Arizona, Nevada, Utah, and sizable portions of Colorado and Wyoming, as well as the present state of New Mexico. These requirements were firm; only the price was negotiable. Polk hoped to get the whole for twenty or twenty-five million dollars. Also desired but not mandated were lower California and a passageway across the Isthmus of Tehuantepec, to be the site of a canal joining the Gulf of Mexico and the Pacific Ocean. If these additional attractions could be obtained, Trist was authorized to raise the price to as much as thirty-million dollars.[23] If greater inducement should prove necessary, the president was willing to cancel certain long-standing claims by American citizens against the Republic of Mexico.

Satisfied at length that all had been covered, Buchanan followed Trist partway downstairs, still gripping his hand warmly. "If you succeed in this," he declared, "we shall have to take you up as our candidate for the Presidency."[24]

It was a startling remark but one that most would have dismissed as amiable hyperbole. Trist was immediately affronted, yet he did not consider the comment facetious or uncalculated. This was, he felt certain, a plainer offer of what Polk had hinted at, for it would have been unseemly for the president to extend such a prize himself. And what of Buchanan's own presidential ambitions? From remarks the secretary had shared with him privately, Trist supposed that Buchanan now considered the main chance lost, possibly because of Polk's growing animosity, and had lowered his goal to a position on the Supreme Court. Was he building his claim to a place on that august bench by grooming Trist to be the future executive who would appoint him? It was all quite fanciful and speculative, yet such was likely the state of his thoughts and emotions that anything must have seemed possible. *How far you are from understanding me,* he later reported having thought. As he turned away, the secretary's words must have rung in his ears. They were the last words he would ever hear from the lips of James Buchanan.[25]

What exactly were the commissioner's qualifications for his assignment? Historians pondering the question for a century and a half have arrived at widely diverse conclusions. Justin Smith, one of the more sympathetic, described Trist as a starry-eyed dreamer with an "ethereal" sense of destiny, comparing him to "the gazing astronomer who walked into the ditch."[26] Others have seen him as a conscientious, hardworking, loyal functionary, not likely to do much harm and having some prospect for success if carefully managed by his superiors. Jesse S. Reeves wrote somewhat disparagingly that Trist's selection was probably due to the president's underestimation of the difficulties involved. Recent historians have been both admiring and deprecatory; some have acknowledged Trist to be a suitable choice for the mission, while others have depicted him as a pompous minor official carried away by his own perceived importance.[27]

Trist's instructions were to maintain utmost secrecy about his mission and to proceed by water to Veracruz, a major Mexican port on the Gulf of Mexico. In early April, Veracruz had been invested and conquered by General Scott after receiving heavy damage and substantial casualties. From there, only four weeks before the commissioner's arrival, Scott's small army had plunged inland over the historic National Highway, headed for its destination and target: Mexico City. The road proceeded through low coastal terrain for a distance of fifty-five miles, then rose in a series of steps along lofty mountains to the capital, about 170 miles from Veracruz. Only a few days' march from the coast, in a narrow river gorge near a hill called Cerro Gordo, Gen. Santa Anna laid an ambush. But he misread both the terrain and the ingenuity of the Americans and consequently suffered a devastating defeat. These operations were unknown to the administration at the time of Trist's departure, for reports from the field sometimes required as much as a month to reach Washington. Indeed, the glacial pace of communication was a major cause of the problems that followed.

Secrecy was the watchword of the diplomatic mission. Trist's abrupt departure was explained as a visit to Louisiana to see his brother Browse, who was alleged to be ill. Both the State Department and the Trist family were solemnly committed to this fiction. Virginia stuck to it faithfully, but somewhere between the desk of a minor State Department clerk and the office of the president the story leaked, and before the secret envoy was five days at sea, a dozen newspapers carried the news of his mission.[28] A piece appeared in the *New York Herald* that was so accurate that Polk was certain it must have been obtained from an insider. Yet he could not be sure the insider was not himself, for he had confided in Thomas Ritchie, editor of the *Daily Union*. But any doubts he may have had about his own innocence did nothing to soothe his temper; he carefully listed in his diary all those who were in on the secret: his cabinet, Trist, and a clerk named Derrick, who swore fervently that he had revealed what he knew to "no human being."[29] Trist seemed in the clear because of his prompt departure, and Derrick's denial was convincing. Unwilling to blame himself, the president settled on his cabinet as the source of the leak, and within that body, the secretary of state seemed the likely suspect. Questions soon turned to accusations, and those brought counter accusations; soon the president and the secretary were involved in a blazing quarrel[30] that cooled only gradually and incompletely in the face of necessity.

Whatever reservations Trist may have felt on accepting his assignment, once it was actually under way he became a driven man, obsessed as with a holy crusade. Leaving Washington on April 14, he traveled incognito first by mail coach and then by a steamer that put in at Charleston, Mobile, and Augusta on its way to Louisiana, where he was delayed for several days. Dropped off unceremoniously at Lake Pontchartrain, he made his way to New Orleans, where he cautiously disguised himself as a French merchant traveling under the name of Dr. Tarro. Part of the elaborate scenario conceived by the administration to conceal his mission from the public included a secret voyage from New Orleans to Veracruz, to be arranged by the Louisiana collector of customs, one Denis Preur. Unaware that the secret was now shared by most of his fellow Americans, the commissioner engaged a closed carriage and scoured the city unsuccessfully searching for Mr. Preur. Finally, he was obliged to ask the aid of his coachman, who promptly drove to the customs house and brought Preur out to meet his mysterious caller. Preur quickly arranged for the newly built revenue cutter *Ewing* to deliver the passenger to Veracruz.[31]

Before embarking for his destination, Trist engaged as his personal servant a Catalan named Juan Gilpin to attend him in the event of illness and to assist, as he explained in a report to Buchanan, "whilst I shall be surrounded on all sides by the enemy." He also purchased a brace of pistols.

Some of these activities have cast the enterprise in a rather comic light and undoubtedly contributed to the ridicule later heaped upon the agent, but it should be recalled that he acted under the sternest orders of the president and without knowledge that the secret was already out. Also, the purchase of sidearms and the engagement of a bodyguard are not exaggerated precautions for one who is moving into a war zone with no assurance of protection and no exact knowledge of the whereabouts of the American military forces. In some respects, however, Trist behaved like the principal character in a melodramatic farce.

On May 6, after a stormy passage, the revenue cutter nosed into Veracruz harbor, passing under the frowning stone fortress of San Juan de Ulúa. Clearly visible, the snow-covered peak of 18,700-foot Mount Orizaba, seventy miles inland, glistened under brilliant sunlight. The city itself, roughly hexagonal in shape and some two miles in circumference, lay only slightly above the surrounding marshland. From the water, its high, white-walled buildings and sixteen gleaming domes revealed nothing of the damage wrought in the recent twenty-day bombardment. The day was hot and humid, and noting with apprehension the low, steamy terrain, Trist recalled the "fetid miasma" of Louisiana during his boyhood and the yellow fever that had taken his father when he was only four. He had been warned that Veracruz was a pesthole of the same deadly *vomito* from midspring to autumn, so he was eager to quit the place as soon as possible in favor of the healthier interior highlands.

The cutter cast anchor off the beach a mile or so south of the city, where the American garrison was encamped. Once ashore, Trist learned from the garrison commander that the main force had already departed and, after a bitter engagement at Cerro Gordo, was resting at Jalapa, seventy-four miles up the National Highway, awaiting supplies and reinforcements before proceeding to the capital. The garrison at Veracruz consisted mainly of a sizable quartermaster contingent left behind to provide logistic support to the advancing army. Supplies were sent forward only under strong escort, for the highway was infested with lurking guerrillas, known to prey savagely on small parties and stragglers. A portion of the expected reinforcements in the form of a thousand members of the Tennessee Dragoons was due to arrive in a few days and would serve as a powerful escort for the commissioner. In the meantime, he was provided with a tent and granted virtual freedom of movement.

After writing a long letter to Virginia, assuring her that his health was "perfect" and that his forthcoming trek would be made in "easy stages [with] every prospect of a delightful time of it,"[32] he toured the city in the company of an agreeable young civilian, a correspondent for the New Orleans *Delta* named James Freaner. Their association was to grow into another of the many significant friendships in the life of Nicholas Trist.

Seen from within its walls, damage to the city was considerably greater than had appeared from the sea. Many major buildings were either in ruins or heavily marked by the bombardment. By the most reliable report, a hundred or so military defenders and approximately as many civilians had been killed and an unknown number injured during the shelling. Under heavy criticism from Europe as well as the United States, Scott had refused to ease the pressure. He had even turned down an appeal from the city leaders to allow women and children to quit the city. For this he was roundly condemned as a barbarian. His reasons were plain, harsh, and irrefutable: Veracruz commanded the National Highway that led inland, away from the imminent threat of yellow fever, which would arrive in a matter of weeks and would surely reduce his troops to helplessness should it catch them still in the lowlands.

Desiring to put his task in motion and learning of a courier soon to depart for Jalapa, Trist dashed off a brief note to General Scott and gave it to the messenger along with the sealed *projet*. The note, which has not been preserved, presumably instructed the general to place the *projet* in the hands of the Mexican government. The author signed his name and, fatefully, his title.

CHAPTER 8

Jalapa

Gen. Winfield Scott was indignant to say the least. His massive frame seemed ready to burst his blue uniform, and his mouth, always the barometer of his emotions, was compressed in an inverted U. His fist slammed down on the cause of his annoyance: a curt note from a civilian, whom he barely knew as a minor State Department official, that *directed* him to deliver a sealed message to the Mexican government. As if that impertinence were not enough, a directive from Scott's immediate superior, Secretary of War William Marcy, forwarded from Veracruz in the same dispatch, gave him to understand that this lackey Trist could, on his own authority, decide to suspend military operations and require the supreme commander to implement that decision!

The message from the War Department was dated April 14, the day before the commissioner left Washington. In it, the secretary noted that Scott's signal successes to date encouraged the administration to expect an early peace overture from Mexico. If this compliment was intended to soothe the general's notoriously sensitive feelings, it failed in its purpose. With a rising temper, Scott read that Mr. Trist of the State Department had been sent to the army headquarters for the purpose of securing peace. Should the commissioner advise Scott that a contingency had been reached suggesting suspension of military operations, the General was "to regard such notice as a direction from the president."[1]

These words, like Polk's bland suggestion to Trist that he need not bother Scott with his diplomatic activities, reveal a breathtaking lack of comprehension by the administration of the real obstacles facing both the commander and the emissary. How could the president suppose that a civilian agent could somehow make contact with the enemy's government without the active participation of the commander? This stupendous blind spot in Polk's thinking seems to confirm Scott's suspicion that he faced one enemy in the field and another, his own government, at his back,[2] for it reveals—or at least suggests—that the administration was already looking past Scott to a successor.

To Scott's thinking, it was a double insult: one part from a deceitful, ungrateful administration, too far away and too obsessed with politics to learn the realities of the war, the other from a puffed-up, ink-stained *clerk*— a civilian clerk at that—who presumed to order the commander about! It was an indignity not to be borne. Without taking time to reflect, Scott followed his usual custom when piqued; he took up pen and paper.

The acrimony between Scott and Polk was not new. At sixty-one, Winfield Scott had been in the army all his adult life. He had become a major general during the War of 1812, a war in which he was one of only a few army officers to win distinction. As a member of an American diplomatic team, he had taken part in negotiating the Treaty of Ghent. As longtime supreme army commander, a notable public figure and a prominent Whig, he was an obvious presidential prospect, for military heroes have always been likely candidates for high political office. And therein lay the burr that galled James K. Polk.

The president held a generally low opinion of the military profession. He considered Scott excessively "visionary and scientific,"[3] and he especially resented Scott's insistence on elaborate preparation before taking the field. Most of all he hated the idea of grooming a man he disliked so intensely—and a Whig at that—to be the next occupant of the White House. He exerted himself to create a post superior to Scott's, one that he could fill with a trusted Democrat like Thomas Hart Benton; but he learned that such an action would require reactivating the rank of lieutenant general, vacated since George Washington had held it. Unfortunately for him, Congress balked at the idea.

While these machinations were in progress, Scott learned of them and penned an insulting note to Secretary Marcy—unfairly, as it turned out, because the long-suffering Marcy was at the time defending him. This was too much for Polk, who promptly ordered Scott to remain in Washington, thus dashing the general's hopes and expectations that he would receive overall command in the field. When Zachary Taylor unexpectedly halted operations in northern Mexico and all the Whig newspapermen in the country set up a howl over the war's cost and apparent stagnation, Marcy convinced Polk that the country could not afford to keep its best general idle. Reluctantly, Polk reactivated Scott and authorized a grand campaign: an all-out thrust at the heart of Mexico, the capital itself. Overjoyed to the point of tears, Scott promised the president that he would not use the war for personal political gain,[4] but Polk could not take the general at his word. En route to the marshaling area on the coast of the Gulf of Mexico, Scott learned that the president was again seeking to elevate Benton over him. As he assumed command of the campaign, bitter resentment of the administration continued to haunt him.

Now, the documents before him involving the civilian clerk confirmed his doubts. Straining his vocabulary for the most biting sarcasm, Scott penned a savage reply to the commissioner: "I see that the secretary of war proposes to degrade me by requiring that I, as commander-in-chief of this army, shall defer to you, the Chief Clerk in the Department of State the question of continuing or discontinuing hostilities. . . . if you are not clothed with military rank over me, as well as with diplomatic functions, I shall demand . . . that, in your negotiations, if the enemy should entertain your overtures, you refer that question [of an armistice] to me, and all the securities that belong to it."[5]

In somewhat calmer tone, Scott pointed out that, since no real government existed in Mexico at the time, it was impracticable to send the *projet* to Mexico City; therefore, he had not done so. Even these relatively moderate words dripped with the scorn he felt for the ill-informed Polk administration. He explained that President Santa Anna had taken command of the Mexican armies in the field and that Pedro Maria Anaya was acting in his stead; further, that recent decrees by the Mexican government made it a crime for any Mexican official to enter negotiations with the enemy, which cast doubt on the likelihood of any success coming, at least for the present, from getting the *projet* into the hands of the Mexican minister of relations. Should Trist decide to deliver the document despite this information, he added stiffly, he would provide an escort for that purpose. As a final thrust, he noted that the Mexicans would certainly require a guarantee from the army commander before agreeing to an armistice. In closing he promised Trist "the respect due a functionary of my government."[6]

As noted earlier, Trist was predisposed to think poorly of Scott, largely because his superiors disliked the general and perhaps also because of the adverse publicity that had attended Scott's seven-month suspension. It has also been noted that Trist, like Scott, had formed the habit of resorting hastily to his altogether-too-facile pen when faced with criticism or opposition. He read Scott's letter with incredulity and disgust, failing to detect that its biting sarcasm subsided after the opening outburst and that the message ended on an almost conciliatory note, even offering help to the newly arrived emissary. All that registered on Trist's mind was its pomposity, arrogance, and gratuitous insult. Outraged, oblivious to the reasons for its sender's animosity, and firm in the belief that his own position was unassailable, he could think of nothing but revenge. He chose the weapons of his enemy: pen and paper.

As always when writing in anger, Trist was incapable of brevity. He filled eighteen pages with sarcasm, invective, and infuriatingly one-sided logic, reviewing in scathing detail all that had happened since his arrival at Veracruz. No escort had been provided to conduct him to headquarters, so he was now cooling his heels on the coast and awaiting the arrival of military reinforcements, with whom he hoped to make his way safely to headquarters. (Scott was unaware of the secret mission until informed by Trist himself. In any case, his forces were spread so thin and the guerrilla threat was so menacing that he would have judged it hazardous to detach an escort any earlier, even had he known about the impatiently waiting agent.) Trist explained that the *projet* had been sealed not to hide its contents from the commander but to make its appearance impressive to the Mexicans. He pointed out with exasperating patience, like a teacher instructing a backward pupil, that his role was analogous to that of a military aide carrying a commander's orders to a subordinate officer, and that Scott should understand that instructions proceeding from Trist were to be taken as orders from the president himself. Then, as if the point had not been established with sufficient clarity, he added that Commodore Perry, upon receiving virtually identical instructions from the secretary of the navy, had found nothing remarkably offensive about them. He acknowledged that the president might have found a better representative to negotiate with the Mexicans, the best being "the gallant commander of our land forces in Mexico," but the fault was not his own, for he had not sought the post.[7]

This last point was not a shot in the dark, for Trist knew, as did every Washington insider, that Winfield Scott wanted not only to win the war but the peace as well and had nourished hopes of being its principal negotiator. He also knew (and knew that the president knew) that if Scott were permitted to accomplish both objectives he would be virtually unbeatable as a presidential candidate in 1848. Trist leaped to the conclusion that Scott was attempting, for political reasons, to thwart the government's objectives in Mexico, and he so reported in a letter to Buchanan.[8] Then, to calm his nerves, Nicholas wrote a long letter to Virginia in which he described General Scott as "utterly incompetent" and "decidedly the greatest imbecile I have ever met."[9] He resolved to avoid personal contact with the general regardless of the consequences.

A number of historians have recorded erroneously that Nicholas Trist became desperately ill as soon as he arrived at Veracruz and that this illness accounts for his ill-tempered exchange with Scott. In truth, although he feared illness and would encounter it soon enough, he was in excellent health during the early days of his mission. And fortunate it was for him, for already the saffron haze was appearing that invariably accompanied the onset of the yellow fever season, causing the natives to proclaim that "King Death in his yellow robe" had assumed his throne.

The dragoons arrived at last, and soon Trist was accompanying them up the highway. Aware that the supply train attached to the column carried specie as well as materiel, Trist kept his two pistols in his saddlebags until one of them disappeared. Thereafter he kept the remaining weapon stuck in his belt.

For some miles the road was level, or only slightly inclined, as it passed through plantations and lowland jungles where brightly colored vines spilled from tall trees. Monkeys chattered, and parrots and macaws screeched at the column. Arriving after several days at a narrow river canyon, they soon found grisly signs of the fierce fight at Cerro Gordo, now nearly a month past. A few bodies still remained by the roadside, unclaimed except by scavengers. Peasants foraging for shoes, weapons, and abandoned equipment stared expressionlessly at the passing troops. Most of the equipment had been dropped by the Americans, who had suffered intensely from the heat as their officers pressed them hard to overtake the fleeing Mexicans. After leaving this mournful scene, the highway proceeded at a noticeably steeper but still gentle grade between flowering hedges, where songbirds poured forth liquid melodies and blossoms of many kinds perfumed the clear, cool air. Soon huts and cornfields began to appear, and on May 14 they arrived at the charming little city of Jalapa.

Although no official welcome was extended—nor was any desired—General Scott, true to his promise, had made provision for the creature comforts of his unwelcome guest. Trist was assigned lodgings at the headquarters of Brig. Gen. Persifor Smith, an unassuming gentleman whose character and personality Nicholas soon came to appreciate. A Princeton graduate and later a Philadelphia lawyer, he had also practiced law at New Orleans and had some previous military experience in Florida.[10] The two men quickly discovered that they possessed mutual friends and held similar views, so the relationship was a cordial one from the beginning.

Finding his mission stalled at least for the moment, Trist took advantage of the opportunity to acquaint himself with his surroundings. He found Jalapa an exquisite little paradise, temperate in climate and pleasing to the eye. Every dwelling had its tropical garden of varicolored flowering blossoms, and from many a window drifted the music of a guitar. It soon became apparent that the good citizens of Jalapa found the presence of the *Norteamericano invasores* not entirely unwelcome.

Like most Americans newly arrived in Mexico, Trist was stunned by the number of churches and the opulence of their interior furnishings. His feelings about the trappings of religion, formed by the influence of Thomas Jefferson and intensified by his own later reflections, now rose in revulsion. Suffering martyrs with haunted eyes met the viewer at the twelve stations of the cross. A life-sized figure of the dying Christ hung crucified and bleeding realistically above each altar. Rich tapestries emblazoned with scenes of torment, agony, and death adorned every wall. Trist viewed these displays with distaste and soon formed a strong antipathy for the clerics who, in his opinion, imposed their fearful will upon an impressionable flock.[11] The words of Jefferson, familiar at the time to every grammar school student, came to mind: "I have sworn upon the altar of God eternal hostility against every form of tyranny over the mind of man." He reflected that there had never been any doubt about the kind of tyranny the old priest-hater had in mind.

Soon growing restless and eager to get on with his task, Trist wrote another long letter to Scott—actually, as he explained, a continuation of the earlier one. In it he sternly took the general to task for not forwarding the *projet* to the Mexican minister of relations as he had requested, adding that if he had not felt the matter to be urgent he would have hand-carried it to Scott's headquarters. Piling insult on insult, he observed that he had not come to Mexico to exchange correspondence with the commander but would do so willingly if that would return Scott's musings "from the lofty regions into which they have danced." He concluded with a warning against any interference with his mission, a warning he explained was intended to bring Scott to his senses.[12]

On the following day, May 21, General Scott took time from the war to answer the two bulky epistles from Trist. This time he soared to new heights of vituperation that made his earlier missive seem almost cordial: "My first impulse was to return the farrago in insolence, conceit and arrogance to the author; but, on reflection, I have determined to preserve the letters as a choice specimen of diplomatic literature and manners. The jacobin [sic] convention of France never sent, to one of its armies in the field, a more amiable and accomplished instrument. If you were but armed with an ambulatory guillotine, you would be the personification of Danton, Marat and St. Just, all in one." He also declared that he was happy to learn that he would not be expected to serve as a peace commissioner, for he would feel degraded to be placed on such a commission with Trist, who he doubted was capable of negotiating a treaty.[13]

Throughout these hostilities the combatants were at pains to keep their respective superiors informed of their exchanges; in fact, Trist provided Buchanan with copies of the Scott letters as evidence in support of his own belief that the general was trying to sabotage the government. Some of these he directed through Virginia to avoid widespread distribution and rumor. The administration was bemused, if not amused. The secretaries of war and state were summoned to the president's office to explain the unexplainable. Polk was in a state, and of course his wrath was directed more at Scott than at Trist, for he tended to agree with the commissioner's suspicions, and he was always ready to believe the worst of the Whig general. With difficulty Marcy headed off a court-martial of Scott; nevertheless, Polk asked the cabinet as a whole to advise him whether to recall both officials.[14]

The two secretaries returned to their offices to write official rebukes, telling their respective subordinates in no uncertain terms to cease their asinine behavior and get on with their work. Buchanan wrote two letters, a personal letter meant to lessen the sting of the other, more official letter, which informed Trist that he had acted with needless urgency in pressing Scott so hard; his duty was only to put the *projet* in Scott's hands, then wait until the Mexicans showed a willingness to negotiate. This must have taken the eager emissary somewhat by surprise. Marcy's letter to Scott was formal and rather gentle, considering that the administration regarded the general as the greater offender of the two. He expressed regret at having to write at all on so unpleasant a subject and offered his belief that the commander, on reflection, must also have regretted his own actions. He explained that all concerned in Washington had assumed that the dispatches would be delivered in person, allowing opportunity for explanation, and that Trist should be regarded as a bearer of dispatches, not to the Mexican government but to the American commander; for that reason Scott was at fault for refusing to forward the documents. (What he failed to say was that he, Marcy, had previously notified Scott that Trist was *directed* to show all of his instructions to the commander, whereas Buchanan had used the permissive word *authorized*, leaving the decision to share or not share their content with Scott more or less up to the messenger, Trist.) His closing words conveyed both a rebuke and a reassurance: ". . . you could not have wandered further from the true view of the case, than by supposing the president or myself has placed you in the condition of deferring to the Chief Clerk of the Department of State, the question of continuing or discontinuing of hostilities."[15]

Almost forgotten during the heated exchange between Trist and Scott was the purpose of the emissary's mission. Almost but not quite. Early in June it occurred to Trist to explore another avenue, the British legation headed by Charles Bankhead, minister to Mexico. He had reason to believe that Bankhead's government desired peace between the United States and Mexico. Trist and Bankhead undoubtedly knew each other slightly from the Jackson administration, when the British diplomat had been chargé d'affaires to the United States; later Bankhead had sought assistance from Trist when Trist was American consul at Havana. It proved a shrewd move; Bankhead was happy to cooperate. Best of all, he was in friendly contact with what precariously constituted the government of Mexico. An avenue of communication was established through Bankhead's subordinate, Chargé Edward Thornton, who promptly called on Trist. Soon thereafter Thornton delivered the American dispatch to its designated recipient, none other than Presidente and Generalissimo Antonio López de Santa Anna himself, who was encamped at nearby Puebla.[16]

Returning from Puebla a few days later, Thornton gave Trist the official response from Minister of Relations Ibarra to Secretary of State Buchanan, acknowledging receipt and promising to lay the communication before the Mexican Congress. He also brought unofficial word from Santa Anna: the wily dictator promised to use his influence to ensure favorable action by Congress and expressed the opinion that an American assault on the capital would be counterproductive for the cause of peace. The British legation was of the same mind.

Peace, personal if not international, came unexpectedly. (Seen from another perspective, perhaps it came in a most predictable way.) At about the same time, two normally amiable gentlemen began to feel foolish and then to behave like grown men. Trist was now in possession of information that was essential to the commander, and he passed it along in a civil and even brief note to Scott.[17] For his part, the general must have been impressed by Trist's skillful diplomatic maneuvering, which was evident from the content of the message, and he probably felt chagrined for having given so little support to the proceedings. He responded with a friendly acknowledgment.

Just when he was beginning to glimpse a faint ray of hope, Trist became violently ill. He was forced to take to his bed and to remain there for many days. Solicitously, General Smith saw to his care, but there was little to be done, for the patient had no appetite for food, company, or reading matter. Smith of course kept the commander informed, and Scott, who was not lacking in compassion, gave thought to how he might make his guest's convalescence more bearable. After rummaging about, he wrapped a small package and penned a note to General Smith: "My Dear Sir—Looking over my stores I find a box of guava marmalade which perhaps the physician may not consider improper to make part of the diet of your sick companion."[18]

The effect of the peace offering was astonishing. Of all the gifts that might have been chosen, none could have worked so powerfully to heal a sick body and mend a seemingly hopeless relationship. Guava marmalade!—to Nicholas the most treasured of all tropical sweets and the one surest to bring back fond memories of Cuba. Realizing that it could only have been a lucky choice, Trist nevertheless returned warm thanks to the sender. Scott's note he kept among his personal papers to the end of his days. The next day he reported to Buchanan: "I am now so decidedly convalescent that the improvement . . . is plainly perceptible to others as well as to myself. . . . With General Scott's reply to my letter I received a message from him evincing so much good feeling that it afforded me the sincerest pleasure to meet it, as I did, in a way which should at once preclude all restraint and embarrassment between us."[19]

Remembering the damning documentation—altogether speculative, to make matters worse—that he had placed in the files of the Department of State concerning that same commander, Trist wrote another letter pleading for its withdrawal. Scott wrote a similar letter to Secretary Marcy. Unfortunately, the damage done by the two in the heat of their anger was not to be easily repaired; in fact, their abrupt turnabout would lead to new misunderstandings and fresh condemnation of both Scott and Trist.

In the days that followed, while Trist was recovering, General Scott paid him several lengthy visits. It soon became obvious to Trist that his original appraisal of the general could not, in the colorful words of Secretary Marcy, "have wandered further from the true view of the case." His preconception of a crusty martinet of rigid mindset and limited cultural attainment soon gave way to admiration for a charming, scholarly esthete, a knowledgeable man of the world, a witty and articulate raconteur, and a good listener. They discovered many mutual friends, of whom the general spoke with warm affection. He was interested to learn that Trist had spent three years at West Point—a privilege the general himself had never enjoyed—and asked many questions about cadets and instructors during Trist's three-year stay. At the mention of Capt. William Worth, the fiery commandant of cadets, the old commander's blue eyes sparkled keenly. Mr. Trist might be interested to know that the same soldier, now Brigadier General Worth, was at the very moment serving as military governor of the occupied city of Puebla, forty miles up the highway.

CHAPTER 9

Mexico City

In the entire American invasion force in central Mexico, the man most interested in the Scott-Trist feud, other than themselves, was Maj. Gen. Gideon Pillow. The abrupt cessation of hostilities and establishment of friendly relations between the two men puzzled and at first dismayed General Pillow, who was second in command and considered himself a special agent for the president as well.

The president felt indebted to Pillow for successfully defending Polk's brother, who had shot a man, and for adroitly maneuvering the Democratic convention to ensure Polk's presidential nomination, as previously noted. Although somewhat lacking in formal education, the genial attorney made up for this deficiency with his handsome face, quick black eyes, trim physique, and facile tongue. To the president, who looked upon military leadership as a useful but hardly an exalted skill, these qualities, together with Pillow's impeccable Democratic credentials, easily qualified him for command. Soon after Pillow was sent to northern Mexico at the head of a division of volunteers, he finagled a long leave to return to Washington for reasons of personal promotion. Later he was one of a large company of officers and men who were transferred from Taylor's force in northern Mexico to the Veracruz campaign. Although Pillow's military accomplishments were modest, his ego was not. The enlisted men detested him and the officers barely tolerated him. One who served with him, in writing to Lt. (later Gen.) William T. Sherman, described Pillow as "a mass of vanity, conceit, ignorance, ambition and want of truth." But he possessed a surpassing advantage that no other soldier, even Winfield Scott, could claim: he enjoyed direct access to the president of the United States.

Despite having committed a number of ignominious blunders and more than one act of arrant cowardice, General Pillow coveted the position held by Winfield Scott.[1] He was not the only politician to go to Mexico with dreams of personal glory, but no one else was in such a favorable position to make those dreams come true. He cultivated the president's confidence by forwarding his own dispatches on the progress of the war to the White House. Noting that Mr. Polk seemed to appreciate and even act on his reports, he assumed increasingly the role of informant and critic of the execution of the campaign. Gradually and insidiously, he built a case against his superior.

Soon after the reconciliation of General Scott and Nicholas Trist, and coincident with the latter's recovery of health, a decision was made to move the army from Jalapa forward to Puebla, a much larger city—in fact, second in size in Mexico—where Gen. William Worth was acting as military governor. This consolidation of forces was to precede the final thrust at the enemy's capital. However, planned operations were interrupted by a crisis that set American generals to feuding and placed the invading army in peril.

Brigadier General Worth—the same "Haughty Bill" Worth whom Trist recalled as commandant of cadets during his West Point days—was a man whose ego matched that of General Pillow but who resembled him in no other way. Still at fifty the epitome of martial pride, he was gallant, decisive, and charismatic in battle, courtly and charming toward his peers and even so, as administrator, toward the enemy. In temperament, however, he was intense, high-strung, and at times unsteady. Before the battle of Monterrey he had declared it his purpose to win "a grade or a grave," and when his vital contribution to that great victory was rewarded with the promotion he so ardently sought, he gloated, "I am satisfied with myself." Worth was a lifelong friend of General Scott; so unstinting was his admiration for the older man that he had named his small son Winfield Scott Worth. The crisis at Puebla would destroy their friendship so completely that the lad's name would soon be officially changed.

When Worth, impatient for glory as always, claimed and won the honor of leading the army into Puebla, it was natural that he would also be appointed its military governor. Recognizing the hazards of holding with a force of four-thousand men a city of eighty-thousand people with a long religious history and a priestly hierarchy that had planted in the mind of every citizen a holy fear of the "demonic invaders," Worth was understandably desirous of allaying those fears. He virtually nullified General Scott's order placing Puebla under military law and, on his own authority, reinstated preexisting municipal statutes. Prowling guerrillas, common criminals, and patriots brave enough to risk their lives promptly took advantage of the situation, with the result that military stores were sacked and several American lives lost. Recoiling from his role as benevolent conqueror, Worth put out a poster accusing the populace of attempting to poison the American troops and threatening the harshest reprisals for any further lawless acts. His sweeping accusations and insulting characterization of all Mexicans were so offensive that Scott was obliged, for the safety of his army, to intervene. He ordered Worth to apologize and withdraw his circular. Worth refused, so Scott issued the countermanding communication himself. Furious at this blow to his pride, Worth demanded a hearing by his peers. On June 30, a court of inquiry consisting of Generals Twiggs, Quitman, and Persifor Smith strongly condemned the original circular and pronounced Worth deserving of a severe rebuke. Worth rejected the chastisement and from that day on was a mortal enemy of Winfield Scott, despite the commander's repeated attempts to restore good relations.[2]

These activities were duly reported to the president by his busy agent Pillow, always to the discredit of General Scott. The seemingly slow forward movement of the army was already a source of dissatisfaction to the administration, which apparently failed to understand that its own reluctance or inability to provide supplies and reinforcements left Scott with no choice but to wait until they arrived. When he did advance, the army's movements, according to Pillow, were ill-advised to the point of imbecility. The incident involving Worth was not overlooked by Pillow, who would eventually recruit Haughty Bill as an active coconspirator.

Meanwhile, Trist was still in close contact with the British legation whose access to the fragile Mexican government gave it information not available to the Americans. Edward Thornton offered the opinion, suspected by some to be Santa Anna's rather than his own, that business would never be done with the Mexican government without prior application of a "lubricant."[3] Trist discussed this interesting notion with Scott and found the general open-minded. Both men felt sure that a bribe was being solicited by the crafty Mexican and that any moral stigma attached thereto rested solely with the solicitor of the lubricant. Scott's consistent policy was to wage war in a way that would minimize loss of life—the enemy's as well as that of his own troops—and in a choice between spending money, even covertly, and spending lives, he came to a ready decision. Nevertheless, being aware of Pillow's secret surveillance, he wisely decided to take the matter up with his general staff. But first he advised Trist that, in his judgment, peace with Mexico could not be gained without an additional year of bloody warfare unless they privately compensated key Mexican dignitaries. He also recognized the difficulty—perhaps the impossibility—of obtaining prior administration approval for such an underhanded "arrangement," to say nothing of the unacceptable delay in waiting for authorization if sought. He was carrying with him a contingency fund of ten-thousand dollars, which was intended for emergencies when regular funds were delayed and rations running low, and this he was willing to gamble in a humanitarian cause. He of course did not suppose that so modest a sum would produce a final settlement; in his judgment at least one-million dollars would have to be distributed among a number of key figures to achieve that goal. Trist was aware that the administration entertained a similar opinion and said that the larger sum would more than likely be obtainable when actual peace appeared near. He supported the smaller bribe as a preliminary necessity to peace talks.

Whether in formal council, as some historians say, or by soliciting individual opinions, as others insist, Scott put forth his plan to Generals Quitman, Shields, Cadwalader, and Pillow. Surprisingly, Pillow approved of the plan, whereas, not so surprisingly, the others opposed it. It is doubtful that their opinions, however strongly expressed, could have deterred Scott, whose mind was already made up but who wanted to avoid a later accusation of acting secretly.[4] Much later Pillow admitted knowing about the scheme but told Polk that Scott had "beguiled him into" endorsing it against his better judgment.

To this day the recipient of the bribe has not been identified, though some speculate that it may have been Miguel Arroyo, later appointed secretary to the Mexican peace commission. However, it is difficult to suppress the suspicion that Santa Anna played a part, for the only result was to delay the American advance, giving him valuable time to prepare defenses, a tactic he had employed effectively from his earliest command.

The settlement of the quarrel between Trist and Scott confused the administration, which was reacting, as usual, to an earlier situation that no longer existed in Mexico. The secretaries of war and state were belatedly scolding Scott and Trist, respectively, and admonishing them to work together sensibly, despite the fact that the two had been getting along famously for several weeks.[5] Pillow, who had reported carefully every detail of the quarrel and who was always careful to place the main fault with the general, now felt obliged to explain the sudden harmony. With his customary ingenuity, he found a solution: Scott, desiring to enhance his political popularity by playing a prominent part in the eventual peace negotiations, must have made the first friendly overture, which Trist, being somewhat in awe of the general, quickly accepted. This theory, although subsequently disproved by a mountain of evidence, fit well enough with the administration's prejudices to make Polk more determined than ever to remove General Scott.[6] Alas, no worthy successor emerged.

The failed attempt to "conquer a peace" (Polk's phrase) by an applied lubricant left the way open to no other course than the original one: assault on the capital. The general had set a deadline of early August to receive a response to his overture, and when none came, his well-rested and now reinforced army prepared to march. On Saturday, August 7, with towering Popocatepetl looming in the dawn light like a glistening silver cone, General Twiggs's Second Division broke camp at sunrise. Soon they formed on the highway, with the rest of the army present to see them off. At a signal from Twiggs, the "Bengal Tiger," his troops gave vent to a mighty cheer and marched away, colors flying, bands playing and every man lustily singing "Green Grows the Laurel." Generals Quitman, Worth, and Pillow followed at one-day intervals. The weather was fair, all spirits high, the scenery breathtaking. The "halls of the Montezumas" (a phrase coined by an inspired newspaper writer) beckoned, and stout hearts would not miss the chance to tread them. Scott delayed his own departure until all divisions were on the highway; then, taking personal command of the engineers, dragoons, howitzer and rocket battery, and staff personnel, with the supply train following, he departed Puebla. Nicholas Trist rode at his side. In all, 10,738 enlisted men and officers moved toward the capital.[7]

For a time the columns passed through farms and range lands, which were dotted with scattered villages and haciendas and differed from earlier scenes only by the awesome presence of the snowcapped peaks. Presently the clear air grew cooler and the road narrower and steeper as they ascended toward the mountains themselves. In places the trail snaked up winding ridges that fell away precipitously on either side, revealing silvery, threadlike watercourses far below. The road now followed the ancient Aztec trail, which its builders had called *coatl*, or "serpent."

After camping near a small alpine lake, Scott and his party, still following the main columns, began the steep ascent toward the summit of the Pass of Cortez, so named for the conqueror who had traced the same course three and one-quarter centuries before them. The twin mountains, Popocatepetl and Iztaccihuatl, were stunningly near, and the morning sun set fire to a spindrift of volcanic steam and powder snow flying from each peak. Streaks of black marred the snowy slopes, the same gritty material that, driven by a chill wind, stung their faces. They discovered it to be volcanic sand. The going was difficult for the horses as they clambered the shoulder of great Popocatepetl, so in places the riders dismounted and soon experienced the shortness of breath that all climbers know.

Abruptly the climb became easy, then leveled into the saddle of the pass. A few yards beyond brought them to the rim of the Valley of Mexico, from which Cortez had surveyed the rich prize that was to be his. The valley three-thousand feet below them stretched fifty or so miles to the north and somewhat less from east to west. It was ringed by towering crags, volcanic cones, and sawtooth ramparts of deep blue and purple. Six lakes, some near and some distant, gleamed like gold in the sun. Countless villages lay scattered among these glistening sheets of water, with fields, orchards, wooded areas, and rock outcroppings interspersed among them. The walls, towers, and steeples of the city loomed in the distance, from which the faint but distinct clanging of hundreds of church bells sounded a continuous alarm, needlessly warning an already aroused citizenry of the invader's approach.

The commander and his party descended the slope and found the army waiting at the village of Chalco on the shore of a large, shallow lake of the same name. From the valley floor the view was less enchanting than it had appeared from the lofty ridge. The ground around the lake was low and marshy, the village a dismal cluster of mud hovels. At this inauspicious place, Scott chose to pause for a few days to plan his next movements. There were those in his company who, when the advance finally occurred, felt certain they could have planned it better.

At Puebla Scott had cultivated the trust of a prisoner in the city jail named Manuel Dominguez, formerly an honest weaver who had turned brigand after being robbed by a Mexican officer.[8] Dominguez, the leader of a band of equally desperate outlaws, impressed Scott as a man of many useful talents. The general played on Dominguez's patriotism and love of adventure to recruit him as chief of a company of spies. From Dominguez, Scott learned much of the enemy's movements as well as the defenses, both military and geographic, protecting the capital. From this vital information, he had a rather exact understanding of the tactical problems facing him. He also understood that, for every spy in his employ, ten of Santa Anna's would be watching him closely enough to take note of all that he shared with his officers. As a consequence, much of what he intended to do was quite different from his announced plans, and orders given were often bewilderingly countermanded at the last moment.[9]

Santa Anna confidently expected the Americans to follow the National Highway all the way to the eastern gate of the city, for it was the only reasonable route from the south, and the mountains effectively cut off a roundabout northern approach. The only alternative was virtually impassable: a circuitous approach along the soggy margins of Lakes Chalco and Xochimilco that would mire wagons and cannon and leave the *yanquis* exposed for miles to sniper fire from nearby promontories. Consequently, he threw his main strength into the fortification of a lofty butte called El Peñon, near the eastern gate and commanding the highway. Should the Americans withdraw from this position and attempt to detour to the north, they would have to circle Lake Texcoco, groping their way over uncharted terrain and exposing their movements at every step. The eastern gate, he felt reasonably certain, would be the one chosen.[10]

For all these reasons and others known only to himself, General Scott launched a feint at El Peñon by Twiggs's Second Division, then veered left with the rest of his force, intending to circle the southern shores of Lakes Chalco and Xochimilco and rest at San Augustin, ten miles south of the city, to reconnoiter. Finding the ground even softer than expected, he initiated other explorations that were partly intended to mystify the enemy before finally plunging ahead with his original plan. The marshy lake shores being closely ringed by rocky hillsides, the entire force was obliged to slog through spongy ground that at times threatened to swallow the entire army, and when they finally arrived at San Augustin, exhausted and covered with mud, more than a few thought their commander had surely become senile.

There soon followed a dazzling series of American victories that earned the admiration of the world. The purpose of this book being to chronicle the life of Nicholas Trist and not to glorify Winfield Scott, the details will be left for the interested reader to discover elsewhere. It is worth mentioning, however, that the seventy-eight-year-old Duke of Wellington, remembering Scott from the War of 1812, had exclaimed on learning of the march on Mexico City, "Scott is lost! He cannot capture the city and he cannot fall back upon his base." After the fall of the Mexican capital the same Iron Duke marveled, "He is the greatest living soldier!"[11] Such was the man whom Pillow, Polk, and other detractors held in disdain.

Final victory did not come speedily or without cost, however. After the bloody battles of Contreras and Churubusco, while all of Mexico was in a frenzy of fear and disorder, Minister of Relations Pacheco addressed a dispatch to James Buchanan proposing initiation of the negotiations that the Americans had repeatedly sought. The message was delivered open to Nicholas Trist by Charles Bankhead, the British minister, with his own earnest appeal that the request be granted. The next morning as General Scott was preparing to resume his assault on the city, General Mora met him at his headquarters at Coyoacan with a proposal for a truce.[12] This, taken together with the message delivered by Bankhead, demonstrated the intense desire of the Mexicans to prevent the American army from entering the city. The truce proposal was unacceptable, but Scott countered with the offer of a "brief" armistice. The duration was deliberately undefined, allowing either side to terminate it. His purpose and fond hope was to allow the elusive peace negotiations to commence. To the Mexicans it was a gift from heaven that Santa Anna quickly accepted. A Mexican commission was speedily assembled, and Trist prepared to carry out the task he had been sent to do. But sinister forces were secretly conspiring, forces that would threaten to wreck the peace process before it was even begun.

The officers and men of the American army were unhappy with the armistice, judging it (correctly, as it turned out) to be nothing more than a stall for time that would be used to strengthen the beleaguered city. They resented giving the Mexicans an advantage that would likely increase American casualties. The widespread unrest within his army annoyed the volatile commander but did not dissuade him from his course. General Pillow, on the other hand, recognized it as a golden opportunity.

Haughty Bill Worth's unhappiness with his chief was, of course, known to Pillow, as it was to every man in the invasion force. Pillow ingratiated himself with the intense and self-centered Worth and soon the two formed a tacit alliance. But Pillow was not satisfied; he needed another confederate.

Lieutenant Col. James Duncan commanded a battery of field artillery in Worth's division. A gallant and resourceful soldier, he had performed with distinction at Resaca de la Palma, Monterrey, and Churubusco; thus, by the time of the armistice, he had probably seen as much action in Mexico as any soldier in the army. It may have been due to the breadth of his experience that he began thinking of himself as more than a mere artillery specialist; in fact, he fancied himself something of a tactician, and worthy of commensurate rank. Some of his newfound self-esteem was based on his role in surveying the route of the army's thrust at the capital.[13] Under orders from Scott to reconnoiter the Chalco route (one of several contemplated for the assault), General Worth delegated the task to a detachment led by Duncan. After reporting to Worth, Duncan returned to headquarters and gave his own and Worth's strong recommendation in favor of the Chalco route and against another strongly supported scheme that would have divided the army. When the final thrust was carried out exactly as he had recommended, Duncan gave himself credit for the grand strategy in a letter published October 8, 1847, in the New Orleans *Daily Picayune*. The truth was that Scott had decided independently (or, more precisely, on other advice) against a divided assault and in favor of the Chalco route. Any indications that he may have thrown out to the contrary were designed to confuse Santa Anna's spies.

After his public boast, Duncan bitterly resented being corrected and admonished for his presumptuous claim. He became an open critic of Winfield Scott and an easy target for Pillow's machinations. Sensing that he had found the one he was looking for, General Pillow began courting Colonel Duncan shamelessly. He mentioned a rich and beautiful widow of his acquaintance and offered to prepare the way for Duncan as her suitor. Suggesting that it was all but certain he would soon be in supreme command, he promised Duncan the post of inspector general. (Although his own elevation eluded him, his promise to Duncan was later made good by President Polk.[14])

Haughty Bill Worth was already firmly established in Pillow's intrigue. His enmity toward Scott and his arrogant pride (he was already entertaining presidential aspirations with the encouragement of influential Democratic politicians[15]) drove him to actions unworthy of such a truly gallant warrior. He faulted Scott for not praising him sufficiently, even though Scott was doing all that he could, short of being unfair to the other division commanders, to regain Worth's goodwill. Sadly, the rupture was complete; Worth was prepared to take serious risks for the sake of injuring his superior and former friend.

On September 10, there appeared in the New Orleans *Delta* a letter exalting to the skies the exploits of General Pillow and depicting Scott as a pathetically inept commanding general. This missive was signed simply "Leonidas," although its writing style bore a striking resemblance to that of the heroic Pillow.[16] The manner of its delivery to the *Delta* was as ingenious as the letter itself, for it seems to have been smuggled into the dispatch pouch of J. L. Freaner (the same reporter who befriended Trist at Veracruz) without his knowledge. Another letter appearing in a Tampico newspaper, as well as in several in the United States, contained a passage that attempted to show how Worth and Duncan had saved Scott from taking the wrong approach to the capital and, thereby, risking the annihilation of the American army. The Leonidas and Tampico Letters, as they came to be known, were widely reprinted in Democratic newspapers throughout the United States. When considerable heat was later applied at army headquarters because of the Leonidas Letter, Pillow found a paymaster in his division who was willing, for a consideration, to take credit for its authorship.[17] But in late August 1847, Nicholas Trist was unaware of these undercurrents as he prepared to enter negotiations.

To understand the monumental task confronting Trist, it is useful to review briefly the tumultuous history of Mexico, for three centuries of strict Spanish rule followed by a chaotic quarter century of independence had produced a people, a form of government, and a national character that were woefully misunderstood by Mexico's northern neighbors. The year the Spanish authorities fled New Spain, 1821, was a year of general Spanish exodus from Latin America, for a crisis raging in Europe had weakened Spain to such an extent that the viceroys who governed the colonies could no longer count on vitally needed support from the mother country. For nearly two decades the monarchy had levied heavy demands to support two wars, against both England and France, bleeding the wealthy by extortionate taxes, imposing heavy military conscription on the poor and, thereby, incurring the resentment of both classes. Crowning these injuries was the disgraceful conduct of a dissolute monarchy, the laughingstock of Europe. When Napoleon contemptuously brushed aside the feeble royalty and placed his brother Joseph on the Spanish throne, the colonies revolted, and one after another proclaimed independence.

During three centuries of rule in New Spain, the Spaniards proved themselves the most dedicated bureaucrats of all the colonial powers by instituting a multitiered social structure based solely on the supremacy of "Spanish blood."[18] At the top of the heap were the *gachupines,* the fortunate ones who were not only of pure Spanish stock but also were born in Spain. The lower aristocracy, the *criollos,* were also purebred Spaniards but suffered the misfortune of being born outside the mother country. These were usually second- or third-generation children of Spanish settlers in New Spain. The *gachupines* held all important power—political, military, and ecclesiastic—but shared social privilege with the *criollos,* while in descending order of rank and fortune came the *mestizos* (persons of mixed Spanish and Indian blood), Indians, mulattoes, and Negroes. The Spanish officials put themselves to the monumentally complex labor not only of recording each person's place on the ladder but also making certain that the innumerable restrictions applicable to each tier were rigorously enforced. Only the aristocracy could hold office, vote, own weapons, ride horses, or educate their children, and other worthwhile privileges were similarly restricted. Penalties for infractions of the caste laws were sufficiently severe to discourage even the boldest from taking liberties.[19]

The bloody eleven-year revolution in New Spain that overthrew the viceroy also swept out virtually the entire governmental structure, leaving only fifteen thousand *gachupines* in the entire nation. The *criollos,* who had hitherto constituted a wealthy but pampered and relatively useless lower aristocracy, inherited most of the task of forming and running a government, for the revolution did not markedly improve or alter the status of the lower orders. The fledgling politicians experimented with their new powers, first by making the ludicrous Augustin Iturbide an emperor,[20] then, when the empire collapsed in less than a year, by forming a republic without comprehending the first principles of democracy.

Iturbide's seizure of power established a pattern for his successors that would endure for more than a century: a bold dash to the capital, gathering supporters along the way until by sheer ruthless force the pretender swept into the presidency, an office for which he was inevitably ill prepared. These would-be dictators were usually men of more ambition than education, born leaders but infants in matters of administration. In the first thirty years of independence the government changed hands fifty times,[21] usually with one *caudillo* (chief) replacing another. Such a man was Antonio López de Santa Anna.

As a young cadet Santa Anna had trained in the royalist forces of the viceroy. When it became apparent that the royalist cause was doomed, he quickly abandoned it and joined Iturbide in the revolt against the throne. He remained loyal to Emperor Augustin I long enough to gain appointment as governor of Veracruz, then, when imperial weaknesses became apparent, he joined a coup of army officers that overthrew and exiled Iturbide. Soon he was promoted to the rank of general; then he turned his boundless ambition in the direction of politics, and by 1833 attained the first of the five presidencies he was to capture over a forty-year career. He found the duties of administration boring and frequently turned the reins of government over to his vice president in order to assume supreme command of the army, justifying his action by explaining that the military threat of the moment transcended mere problems of state.[22]

Despite his erratic performance, which often earned him the wrath of the populace, Santa Anna's uncanny insight into the mood of ordinary Mexicans enabled him to return repeatedly to power. He changed his political orientation rapidly with changing circumstances, declaring himself a monarchist, republican, democrat, conservative, moderate, or liberal depending on the current direction of the tumultuous times in which he lived. Despite his many poses, he was actually a centrist whose natural alliances were with men of power: generals, archbishops, financiers, land barons, and industrialists. In times of supreme danger, the people automatically looked to Santa Anna, even though he might at the moment be in exile and disgrace, and he was always ready to take charge. Despite his notorious opportunism, he was at times capable of singular valor and unselfishness, for which recent historians have viewed him somewhat more favorably than did his contemporaries.[23] Nevertheless, in a land of statues, there are none of Santa Anna.

During the three centuries—1521 to 1821—when Mexico belonged to Spain and was known as New Spain, the territory now known as Texas was virtually unpeopled except by some extremely unfriendly Native American tribes. With the formation of the Republic of Mexico, several settlements were established by Mexican people in this region, but an even greater interest was shown by settlers migrating from Tennessee and other western parts of the United States. These intrusions were legitimized through negotiations initiated by Stephen F. Austin, though they were subject to some conditions imposed by the Mexican government that were agreed to but never strictly observed by the settlers. The influx from the north expanded rapidly, and with the expansion came a growing disregard for the terms of settlement. Greatly offended but unable to enforce compliance, the Mexican government sent two punitive expeditions into the territory. In 1836, Santa Anna led a force of four thousand into Texas to establish permanent military control over the province. The result was the debacle at the Alamo, the subsequent slaughter at Goliad, and finally the total defeat of the Mexican force at San Jacinto. Thereupon the settlers declared Texas an independent republic and elected Sam Houston president. Almost from the first, some citizens sought inclusion in the United States, but it was only in the final hours of the Tyler administration, in March 1845, that annexation became a reality. Mexico refused to recognize the annexation and, therefore, saw no need to define the boundary between Texas and Mexico. Although some historians insist that the Mexican War had nothing to do with Texas, the resolution of the boundary question was central to the larger issue of territorial acquisition. This was the Gordian knot that must be cut before further progress could be made.

The declared purpose of the armistice was to seek to make a peace treaty, and for that purpose Trist now felt himself prepared. Meetings were initiated between himself for the United States and, for Mexico, a commission consisting of ex-President Herrera, J. B. Couto, Gen. Ignacio Mora y Villamil (chief of military engineers), and a lawyer named Miguel Atristain.[24] Unfortunately, the commissioners, given orders to deal as though Mexico had triumphed to that point, were under constraints as severe as those binding Trist. They immediately took up the hotly disputed question of the southern Texas boundary, which Mexico was grudgingly willing to concede at the Nueces River, while the United States held firmly to the Rio Grande. While at Puebla, Trist had dropped a casual and ill-advised remark to the effect that the region between the two rivers might be made a neutral zone, possibly under European oversight.[25] Nevertheless, he now put forth the original demands of his government, including the Rio Grande boundary, but the commissioners wanted to use his earlier statement as a baseline for negotiation. To move the stalled discussion in another direction, he offered the highest monetary figure he had been authorized to grant, but this proved no great enticement. At length he proposed that the armistice be extended forty or forty-five days and offered to obtain a decision from Washington concerning the boundary.[26]

The consequences of Trist's passing the buck to his superiors were profound, and historians continue to question his reasoning in the light of the firm direction he had received to insist on the Rio Grande boundary as *sine qua non*. To President Polk, any departure from this position would be tantamount to abandoning his claim that the Mexicans had started the war when they "invaded our territory and shed American blood upon the American soil," and this he would never do. One view of Trist's action, one that he rather lamely advanced himself, holds that he merely wished to move the negotiations along and for that reason deferred to his superiors a decision that had proved unacceptable coming from him.[27]

With the negotiations stalled, the Mexicans—or more particularly, Santa Anna—viewed the proposed armistice extension as a *yanqui* trick to gain time in which to rebuild military strength. Moreover, the *Puros,* a political party of hawkish disposition, were gaining power and pressuring *el presidente* to desist from all negotiations, which they deemed treasonous.

Reading the signs adroitly, Santa Anna denied ever having entertained thoughts of a treaty and addressed his energies to preparing for a resumption of hostilities. On September 6, General Scott, acknowledging the failure of his magnanimity and, unwilling to be made a fool, notified Santa Anna that the armistice was ended.[28]

The administration, taking its cues from Pillow, also decided that the armistice was a mistake. President Polk condemned it roundly, as if peace were farthest from his thoughts. From a strictly military viewpoint, the armistice was indeed antithetical to American objectives, for it was offered out of compassion, and compassion has no place in war. Polk was especially annoyed that Trist had proposed a forty-five-day extension of the armistice and indignant at his referral of the boundary question for review, believing it would give Mexico the impression that the administration's explicitly stated, nonnegotiable position could easily be modified.[29] Polk confided his displeasure with the emissary to his diary. He told the cabinet that he was thinking of recalling both Scott and Trist.

At about the same time Washington concluded that all was lost, the army, in a brilliantly coordinated series of moves, broke simultaneously through the southern and western gates and seized the capital. Santa Anna fled the city after opening the prisons and loosing hundreds of felons on both the populace and the invaders. Disorder reigned for three days; then Scott restored order by hanging one of his own men, a rapist, and issuing stern warnings to his own men as well as to the populace.

A period of tension and instability ensued. The Mexican army was beaten, scattered and leaderless, yet still extant. The government, still hoping for a miracle, continued its hollow pretense of strength, yet hesitated to resume bargaining. The American troops celebrated a mighty victory and became tourists, but there was no peace. In Washington Daniel Webster spoke for the nation: "Mexico is an ugly enemy. She will not fight—and will not treat."[30] "There seems no hope," said wise old Albert Gallatin, "that a peace will be concluded within the remainder of the Polk administration." The likeliest prospect was for a long, expensive, and thoroughly demoralizing occupation of Mexico while awaiting the emergence of a group of leaders sufficiently resolute to make a bargain. Americans, being generally unable to deal with stagnation, put forth many helpful suggestions. One scheme favored by Zachary Taylor (who was himself stagnant in northern Mexico at the order of the president, who did not wish to brighten Old Rough and Ready's political luster by bringing him back into prominence) was to retire behind a line of defense and wait for the Mexicans to come to their senses. Some experts advocated a permanent blockade of Mexican ports. The most extreme and, to some, the most ominous idea—and the one gaining most rapidly in political strength—called for the occupation, subjugation, and eventual annexation of the entire country. This explosively controversial plan came to be known as the All-Mexico movement.[31]

It was during this hiatus that the Leonidas and Tampico Letters were published, and the newspapers carrying them reached army headquarters a few weeks later. Scott, who had only become fully alerted to Pillow's sabotage in August and had overlooked it in the subsequent heat of the campaign, decided he had endured enough of the cabal against him. He placed Pillow, Worth, and Duncan under technical "arrest," although they were confined only to the city.[32] In his charges against the three, Scott permitted himself, as he frequently did, the luxury of intemperate language, including the following: "pruriency of fame, not earned," "despicable self-puffings," "false credit," and "malignant exclusions of others." Other officers agreed, and the governor of South Carolina rejoiced that Scott had exposed "such quackery, charlatanry, imposture and lying braggadocio."[33] The *National Intelligencer* defended Scott eloquently in an editorial of December 28, 1847: "The duties of a Commanding General in the heart of an enemy country, with an army flushed with victory yet inactive, and under the influences incident to so perilous a position, are very delicate, and can only be met by firmness and the maintenance of rigorous discipline."[34]

During the crisis in the American headquarters and in the wake of Santa Anna's flight and self-exile, the Mexican leaders sought with diligence and wisdom to rebuild a government. Turning to a proven patriot, they prevailed upon elderly Manuel de la Peña y Peña to accept the presidency, at least until an election could be called. Although considered timid by some, Peña was conscientious and honest, and he desperately sought peace. Other leaders were of like mind. In November, to the surprise of the populace, Congress defeated by a vote of 46 to 29 a measure that would have forbidden even the discussion of ceding territories held by Mexico before the war. From these and other signs, Trist thought he detected a break in the war clouds. He was on excellent terms with Peña and the *Moderado* party, and they trusted him because of his dark, almost Latin looks, his impeccable Spanish, and his unfailing courtesy. One could almost forget that he was a *gringo!*

A major sticking point and one on which both nations had hitherto remained immovable was the legitimacy of American annexation of Texas.

Trist felt certain that the passions attending a tumultuous quarter century of Texas history would have to be quieted before progress could be made on the larger issues before him. He forwarded to Minister of Relations Luis de la Rosa a letter he had written two months earlier, during a time when his message would not have been favorably received.[35] In it he stated the background and the de facto basis for Texas independence and, there-fore, its rightful annexation by the United States. From this firm footing he argued that a clearly defined and internationally accepted boundary was essential for lasting security and stability and that in future years such a definite demarcation would be in Mexico's interest as well as that of the United States. Where that boundary should fall had already been deter-mined by the successful separation of the Republic of Texas from Mexico, for the citizens of that new nation had claimed it as the Rio Grande, not the Nueces. This letter, powerful for once in brevity as well as cogency, was delivered by the British legation with its own strong appeal for the renewal of negotiations. Rosa responded favorably if noncommittally but deferred resumption of talks pending the collection of needed documen-tation, a delay for the purpose of sounding public opinion. The winds of peace were blowing perceptibly stronger.

On November 16, two official dispatches from the Department of State were delivered to Trist. One was dated October 4, the other October 25, the latter being essentially a repetition of the former. Both directed him to discontinue all activities previously assigned and return at once to Wash-ington. There would be no further peace offers from the United States, but President Polk would consider any overtures that Mexico might pro-pose. Trist was ordered to inform the Mexicans of the president's decision and specify that they must henceforth tender any peace proposals through General Scott.[36]

Receiving this news, President Peña wept. "All is lost," he lamented.

CHAPTER 10

Guadalupe Hidalgo

"Santa Anna was the most notoriously . . . unprincipled man whom this country holds. . . . And yet we did believe him sincere in his profound desire for peace. Why? For the same reason that a man who, when seen drowning, should he be heard expressing his desire for a plank, might, although he were the most notorious liar that ever existed . . . be believed to be sincere."[1] With this impassioned explanation Trist had sought to convince his superiors that the armistice he and Scott had offered the beaten but still defiant Mexicans was not as insane as it appeared from afar; but to no avail.

At the beginning of his presidency, Mr. Polk regarded the people of Mexico with indifference and mild contempt. Simply stated, he wanted something they possessed, and he was willing to pay for it. Their unwillingness to sell he at first deemed childish intransigence to be dealt with as a parent would deal with a naughty child. But proud Mexico called his bluff, and he soon found himself embroiled in an unpopular war. As his term of office passed its midpoint with his campaign promises unfulfilled and his best efforts thwarted, his annoyance turned to indignation. The focus of his wrath initially was General Scott, but under the influence of Pillow's dispatches, he began to view Scott and Trist together as a single unholy alliance.[2]

As the president waited for an acknowledgment of Trist's recall order, he brooded over what seemed a host of abuses by the commissioner. He began to suspect that Trist, under Scott's influence, was deliberately trying to embarrass the administration to gain a political advantage for the Whigs, a notion that would have amused those who knew Trist to be an ardent lifelong Democrat. In his diary the president gave savage vent to his feelings, for he believed Trist had spoiled all chance for a settlement: "Mr. Trist has managed the negotiation very bunglingly and with no ability. He has done more. He has departed from his instructions so far as to invite proposals from the Mexican commissioners to be submitted to his government for its decision upon them, which can never be accepted by the United States. . . ."[3]

From that day on, the president regarded Nicholas Trist with implacable hatred. In considerable part, his anger resulted from a recent shift on the part of his administration away from the very instructions he now charged Trist with violating. The cost of the war was exceeding all earlier estimates, and influential Democrats were insisting that Mexico be made to pay heavy reparations in the form of vastly greater territory than had originally been considered.[4] Polk was inclined to agree, although he did not favor the idea of total annexation, or "All Mexico" as it was called.

Trist was well aware of the All-Mexico movement, for many of the officers of his acquaintance and not a few highly placed Mexicans with whom he regularly conversed favored the U.S. annexation of Mexico. Sentiment in the United States, however, was changing. In the early months of the war American interest had been light but not insignificant; later, when dispute raged over the impact of the war on the slavery issue, the All-Mexico movement slowed. Then when the war dragged on and its cost in lives and money reached unanticipated heights, there was a growing anger against Mexico and with it a growing inclination to extract reparations in the form of more territory. Trist strongly disapproved of the scheme, considering it both immoral and impracticable, an opinion that was shared by many Americans. Trist's racial views were quite compatible with those of many of his fellow Americans. Like them, he regarded the dark-skinned Mexicans as a "degenerate race" whose absorption by an Anglo-Saxon nation would vitiate the latter without benefiting the former. Although he considered it likely that Mexico eventually would be incorporated into the United States, he believed that either long-term military occupation or forced cession of the entire nation would bring dishonor and worldwide castigation, ending forever what he termed "the Jeffersonian vision" for America. Nevertheless, at first he had no reason to believe that his superiors were considering any terms other than those they had given him when they sent him to Mexico, for he had received no superseding instructions.[5]

At the end of October, Trist, still unaware of his recall orders, reminded James Buchanan that he had been away from his family for five months, twice as long as had originally been estimated, and he strongly desired to return. On the same day, he wrote to Virginia asking her to press the point with the secretary. Then, on November 16, the two recall orders arrived together, granting his urgent request but not in the way he had hoped. Both had been written by Secretary Buchanan. Although in one the secretary noted that the president remained disposed "to treat you kindly," the general tone of the two messages was cold and unfriendly in contrast to earlier communications, which were often informal and encouraging. No words of appreciation, no recognition of dangers and difficulties faced, no sympathy for loneliness and discomfort endured softened the stiff, official language. Trist had tried to forget the hypocrisy of his superior's farewell words and to remember him as a friend, but the two letters destroyed what little remained of his affection for the secretary. He felt abandoned, abused, and resentful.

The two recall orders gave no hint of a lessening desire for peace; therefore, Trist felt certain that a replacement would soon arrive to relieve him. Despite his bitter disappointment, he saw no alternative but to return to Washington; however, two circumstances prevented his immediate compliance. First, he considered it his duty to await the arrival of his replacement and offer that agent all of the information then in his possession, information the administration obviously lacked. Second and most compelling was the impossibility of retracing his steps to Veracruz without a strong escort, which could not immediately be provided. So he waited, intending to return and give a full report in person, which he felt sure would enable the administration to seize the fleeting opportunity that was so evident to him.

As the days passed and still no replacement arrived, Trist was baffled and dismayed. He felt certain that peace was still his government's fervent desire, and now it was Mexico's as well. Why, then, was there no agent present to negotiate? On November 27, he wrote imploring to Buchanan to send someone immediately, explaining that the Mexican Congress would convene January 8, 1848, the last likely assembly of a peace-seeking majority.[6] Having already discussed the terms set forth in the *projet* with the Mexican commissioners, he felt certain that those terms could now be negotiated. All that was wanting was an authorized American representative.

Soon after the arrival of the recall orders and before Trist notified the Mexican government of his removal, Peña y Peña, who had resigned his temporary position as president and was at this time minister of relations, informed Trist in a letter delivered by Edward Thornton that new commissioners had been appointed and would communicate with him as soon as they received instructions. Although on fire for peace, the Mexican government continued to insist that it would respond to an overture initiated by the United States but could not honorably sue for peace as the instructions in Trist's recall order, still unknown to Peña, had suggested. Furthermore, Peña took the position that Trist's proposal to reopen negotiations had bound the United States and could not be revoked. Thornton added a note of his own confirming Trist's opinion that the Mexicans were anxiously seeking peace and urged him to seize the opportunity.

A few days later Trist was visited by one of the leading *Moderados,* a man who had been working tirelessly for peace. With animation he related recent deliberations on the part of Mexican officials at Queretaro and spoke of the "brightening prospects" for peace. Trist described the caller's reaction to his removal: "Upon my saying that it was all too late and telling what instructions I had received, his countenance fell and flat despair succeeded to the cheeriness with which he had accosted me." The *Puros* (war party), on the other hand, received the news with undisguised joy.[7]

In two separate messages dated November 24, 1847, Nicholas informed both Peña and Thornton that his orders had been revoked and that he must now return to Washington. He added in his letter to Peña that he would already have done so but for the lack of an escort to Veracruz. He expressed regret that "another hand than mine" must sign a future treaty, which he sincerely hoped would be done soon. To Thornton he declared boldly (and perhaps suggestively) that he would even have risked disobeying his orders if he could be certain that a treaty would proceed from such action. He hoped that when he reached Washington he would be able to clear up some official misunderstandings. A few days later he wrote to Buchanan explaining the cause of his delayed departure—a special escort could not be spared at the time. The next scheduled supply detachment would leave for Veracruz on December 4, and he planned to avail himself of its protection. In another attempt to gain a replacement, he emphasized the heroic peace efforts of the Mexican government, efforts that would be impossible for anyone distant from the scene to appreciate, and stressed that the Anaya government would surely fall if peace were not soon forthcoming.

There was a second reason to linger in Mexico, one he did not feel free to mention in his letter to Buchanan. The trial of General Pillow for his role in the cabal against Scott was coming up, and Scott had asked Trist to appear as a witness. Trist was happy to oblige, for Pillow had let it be known that a letter from himself to the president concerning the failed bribe attempt had prompted Trist's recall. On November 28, in obvious anguish, Nicholas wrote to Virginia: "I have bid adieu forever to official life. This decision is irrevocable. Say so to Mr. Buchanan, with my kindest regards . . . and my most poignant regret that I cannot again take my post [in Washington] and relieve him from part of his labours. He will soon see the impossibility of this or my having anything to do with Mr. Polk. Say to him from me that a baser villain and dirtier scoundrel does not exist out of the penitentiary or in than Genl Pillow. Say to Mr. B. that if he wants peace and wishes to save the Union to lose not a minute in appointing commissioners. . . . Above all things let him stand out against associating Genl Pillow in the matter. It would do infinite mischief besides deepening the already unfathomable disgrace which he has brought on Mr. Polk and his administration."[8]

Trist had been warned that harsher terms than those he carried in the *projet* might be imposed. He suspected that more territory would be demanded. He disapproved strenuously but realized that now his opinion counted for nothing. It seems probable, however, that his disagreement with the administration on this point may have had something to do with his subsequent actions. Although much has been written about those actions with emphasis on the commissioner's independence and audacity—which were indisputably great—there is evidence that he received encouragement from a number of sources. The Mexican government pretended that the recall had never occurred or would soon be revoked. The British legation urged his independent action in ways that were less than subtle. General Scott offered his opinion that if Trist should make a treaty, it surely would be accepted by the United States. As he wrestled with his thoughts, Trist received a visit from a friend.

On December 4, James Freaner, the same young correspondent for the New Orleans *Delta* who had befriended Trist at Veracruz and who had been the unwitting deliverer of the Leonidas Letter, dropped in for a chat. He was following a pleasant custom that had come about quite naturally, for the two men, though more than twenty years apart in age, were compatible spirits and by now close friends.[9] Freaner frequently shared useful information gleaned in his journalistic rounds, a practice that was helpful to Trist. Freaner was stunned and dismayed to learn of the recall. Then Trist told him something he had shared with no one else: he was thinking of defying the recall order and staying to make a treaty. Freaner's eyes lighted with joy. Trist later recalled the young man's enthusiastic response: "Mr. Trist, make the Treaty. Make the Treaty, Sir! It is now in your power to do your country a greater service than any living man can render her. I know your country. I know all classes of people there. I know them better than you do. . . . They want peace, Sir. They pant for it. They will be grateful for it. Make the Treaty, Sir! You are bound to do it. Instructions or no instructions, you are bound to do it. Your country, Sir, is entitled to this service from you. Do it, Sir! She will support you in it, instructions or no instructions."[10]

The decision was made even while the fiery idealist was speaking. Trist said, "I *will* make the treaty and . . . you stay here to carry it home." With racing pulse and trembling hand, he wrote two messages that same day, December 4. The first was to Edward Thornton, the British diplomat at Queretaro, asking him to notify the Mexican commissioners of his decision and to press upon them a warning: "If they feel able to make and carry through a treaty on this basis, it would be utterly idle to talk or think for an instant of any other and I cannot listen to a single word on the subject; let them say the word and the treaty shall be made. If they do not feel thus able, let them . . . dismiss forever all thought of a treaty for it is the last chance that Mexico can have one equally favorable to her, or indeed for one which any party in this country can accept. I am fully persuaded that its terms would not, by any means, meet the views *now* entertained by my government. . . . It remains to be seen whether the Mexican Government can come up to the mark and give effect to my resolve. 'Now or never' is the word."[11]

His second letter was to Virginia. It must have produced a shocked reaction, then a smile of recognition, for she, more than any other, knew the man who wrote it. "Knowing it to be the very last chance," he wrote, "and impressed with the dreadful consequences to our country which cannot fail to attend the loss of that chance, . . ." he would stay and attempt, with no authority except his own, to make a treaty. He emphasized that the decision was his and his alone.[12] Later he declared that Freaner's enthusiastic response to his tentative plan had been the only influence on his resolve.

Two days later, in a letter to Buchanan, he made full disclosure of his decision to the administration. In all the dry and musty files collected by our State Department in more than two centuries, there can be few as unrestrained as this sixty-one-page outpouring of emotion, patriotism, wisdom, insult, and entreaty. In sustained passages of close-knit logic, it analyzed the real situation, unsuspected or only dimly understood by the government; then the writer's rage and scorn burst forth, excoriating his superiors for their blind pride, ignorance, and unwillingness to be informed. Many frustrated diplomats, abused and neglected by their superiors, must have felt as he did at times, but surely not many have dared to express such thoughts officially.

Although the writer's effrontery could not fail to enrage the president, much in the letter was intended for his benefit. Trist summarized thus: "I place my determination on the ground of my conviction, first, that peace is still the desire of my government; secondly, that if the present opportunity not be seized at once, all chance for making a treaty at all will be lost, probably forever; thirdly, that this (the boundary proposed by me) is the utmost point to which the Mexican Government can by any possibility venture. I also state that the determination of my government to withdraw the offer to negotiate, to which I was made the organ, has been taken with reference to a supposed state of things in this country, entirely the reverse of that which actually exists."[13]

Although by this action he was now utterly cast adrift, Trist continued to file dispatches to Secretary Buchanan almost as though the word "recall" were unknown to him. In these he cheerfully predicted the early signing of a treaty. The same surreal mood gripped the Mexican government. Trist's presence and expressed willingness to treat seemed to them to cancel the previous news of his recall. The commissioners prepared for the encounter with a deliberation that frayed the nerves of the American agent.

Trist allowed the Mexican commissioners to know that he was ready to treat whenever they were prepared to accept, as a baseline for further discussion, the Rio Grande boundary to 32 degrees latitude and thence west to the Pacific. They successfully urged this condition on Peña, but he pointed out that the formal proceedings would have to await confirmation of the commissioners by the Mexican Senate. In due course their confirmation was forwarded from the government, by now situated at Queretaro. On January 2, 1848, and daily thereafter, Commissioners Couto, Cuevas, and Atristain met secretly with Commissioner Trist.

Nicholas Trist's sixty-one-page oracle reached Washington on January

15 and was speedily shown to the president. Polk's reaction was such as could only be shared with his diary: "His dispatch is arrogant, impudent and very insulting to his Government, and even personally insulting to the president. . . . I have never in my life felt so indignant. . . . If there was any legal provision for his punishment he ought to be severely handled. He has acted worse than any man in the public employ whom I have ever known. His dispatch proves that he is destitute of honor or principle and that he has proved himself to be a very base man."[14]

The president was now in a mood to carry out an action that he had long contemplated but had heretofore allowed others to dissuade him from taking. By order of the War Department dated January 13, 1848, General Scott was relieved of his command and replaced by Gen. William O. Butler, a stalwart Democrat if a soldier of limited military experience.[15] He then cut off all of Nicholas Trist's compensation—expenses as well as salary—beyond November 16, the day the recall notice was received, and ordered the discredited emissary to leave Mexico immediately. He refrained from issuing an arrest order only because Butler had not yet arrived in Mexico and the testy General Scott, whose duty it would be to carry out such an order, was likely to prove as fractious as the commissioner.

While peace negotiations were being conducted secretly in Guadalupe Hidalgo, a few miles north of Mexico City, the temporary capital, Queretaro, was a scene of unceasing tumult. Peña, having resigned the presidency in favor of Anaya, found himself unwillingly back in that office when Anaya had to be removed on a technicality; unhappily for him, Peña was at the time president of the Mexican Supreme Court, the position next in line to fill the vacated office as interim executive until an election could be called. His courage, never heroic, was put to a severe test, for powerful enemies clamored for his downfall and some for his life. The *Santanistas* wanted to bring the exiled Santa Anna back and make him a dictator; others favored the total annexation of the country by the United States, insisting that the *Norteamericanos* had brought about the state of anarchy within Mexico and should, therefore, assume responsibility for repairing the damage. This idea was strongly supported by the Catholic Church hierarchy, who sought relief from terrorism and the continual demands on the Church for money to support the war. The *Puros* wanted to continue fighting, and the monarchists hoped for miraculous intervention by Spain. Only the *Moderados* sought peace. But for the absolute secrecy in which they were conducted, the negotiations would never have been allowed to take place.

Despite their eagerness to obtain an agreement, the three Mexican commissioners brought many demands to the table. To avoid bogging down, they began constructing a draft treaty composed of twenty-three articles; thus, they were able to deal with each issue separately. Some of the Mexican demands were substantive, others mere face-saving efforts to appease the various factions that would debate ratification by the Mexican Congress.

Trist was obliged to be his own secretary, lawyer, file clerk, and sole negotiator. Absent was the battery of specialists who assist in treaty-making today: translators, rapporteurs, archivists, recorders, and communications technicians. Struggling manfully, he kept minutes as well as he was able while still carrying on the discussions, which continued with few breaks throughout January. Even under this relentless pressure, his health, which had failed him so often in the past, remained robust except for a toothache that produced a swelling as large as an egg on the side of his face.

Because of the wide divergence between the Mexican demands and the terms of the *projet,* which he regarded as inviolate, Trist was obliged to employ utmost tact, patience, and courtesy. Certain formerly controversial issues, such as the boundary, no longer were contested and could be settled rapidly. Some of the more obviously unacceptable Mexican demands, such as a requirement for the withdrawal of the American military forces from the country during the negotiations, were so absurd and so lamely advanced that Trist was able to dispose of them promptly and firmly without offending the commissioners. The Mexicans found his candor and honesty reassuring. They trusted and liked him, and with growing trust came the speedy resolution of issues for which many good men on both sides had given their lives.

One of the stranger aspects of the negotiation—and one that has prompted confusion to the present time—has to do with the fixing of the western terminus of the international boundary. Even noted scholars have accepted the popular but mistaken view that Trist bungled badly at this point, whereas in truth his persistent efforts spared his superiors the disappointment of losing one of their most cherished objectives. As late as 1952, one American historian wrote to a colleague that "it seems astonishing to me that the serious students missed the solid reasons for freeing Trist from blame for not obtaining Lower California."[16]

From the beginning of his mission Trist had been instructed to obtain both Californias if possible but under no circumstances to yield on Upper California and to treat the thirty-second parallel as the dividing line between the two territories. He was to raise the administration's offer by five million dollars as an inducement to the Mexicans to part with Baja California, but not to jeopardize the negotiations for that purpose alone, whereas any agreement must include Upper California. In this the administration proceeded with great confidence in a map that was to prove faulty. Polk was determined to get San Diego, whose fine harbor was considered nearly equal to San Francisco's; the Mexicans were equally determined to hold it. For Trist, the nub of the question was to establish with certainty where San Diego actually lay and to negotiate a boundary that fell safely to the south of it. In this he received invaluable assistance from Scott's favorite aide, engineering officer Robert E. Lee, and from his own good friend Gen. Persifor Smith. Smith acknowledged his own earlier error and produced documentation showing that San Diego traditionally belonged in Upper California. Trist bent both his instructions and the boundary line, which he drew from the confluence of the Gila and Colorado rivers to a point seven miles south of San Diego. The Mexican negotiators discovered evidence in support of Trist's findings and yielded.[17]

A major sticking point arose when it came time to settle the price that the United States would pay for the territory soon to change hands.[18] The Mexicans had been instructed to demand thirty-million dollars. Although he had earlier mentioned twenty million, Trist now put forth a figure of fifteen million. He rationalized that by prolonging the war after the September negotiations, Mexico had imposed a greatly increased expense on the United States for which it must now be required to pay. The Mexican commissioners referred the matter to their government.

While waiting for a response, the parties took up the question of claims by American citizens against Mexico, claims that in many cases traced back to the settlement of Texas as a territory. Although considered by some modern scholars the principal cause of the Mexican War, these claims were nebulous and hard to prove; no doubt some were inflated and others downright fictitious.[19] Recalling that American ministers had failed in their missions and Mexican governments had fallen because of this issue, Trist put forth the offer that had been given him by Buchanan: the United States would assume liability for up to three-million dollars to settle the claims of its citizens against Mexico provided they had been lodged before May 13, 1847. The Mexicans objected; how could their government be absolved of liability if a limit were imposed on the amount of relief provided? The two conditions seemed incompatible. Seeing that "the Mexican mind was sore and suspicious" and not wishing to jeopardize the excellent gains already made, Trist added a quarter million to the amount of liability to be assumed by his government, feeling fairly sure the claims would not reach that total.[20]

What would be the status of Mexicans living in the ceded territories? Lacking a Solomon to whom the question could be referred, Trist became Solomon. Such persons would be allowed to choose between staying or leaving, and those leaving would not be taxed for the removal of property. Those remaining would automatically become citizens of the United States after one year unless within that time they declared their desire to retain Mexican citizenship. Churches and church property would be inviolable, never to become property of the United States. Controlling troublesome Native American tribes in the region would become the responsibility of the United States government, which would mete out appropriate punishment for Native American incursions into Mexico.[21]

By the end of January, the parties were in accord, needing only concurrence from the Mexican government at Queretaro. Trist had good reason to be impatient, for he knew that General Scott would soon be removed, and his replacement could be expected to arrive at any moment and put a halt to the proceedings at Guadalupe Hidalgo. The only chance for the treaty would be to get it signed, rush it to Washington, and hope that the administration would accept it, however reluctantly, as *fait accompli*. The Mexicans, fully aware of Trist's unauthorized status, were clinging to the same faint hope. To force the government's hand, Trist, perhaps with the quiet encouragement of the Mexican commissioners, handed them a letter stating that because of the continual inexcusable delays, he was terminating negotiations. Before taking this action he visited the new head of the British legation, Percy Doyle, who persuaded Trist to send the letter but delay taking the threatened action until the Mexican commissioners received an answer from their government.

The threat worked; suddenly the Herculean task was done. The Peña government found no objection to the terms Trist demanded nor even to the modest compensation he offered. On February 2, 1848, after a few minor details were cleaned up, the Treaty of Peace, Friendship, Limits and Settlement was signed at Guadalupe Hidalgo. As he prepared to place his name on the document, Don Bernardo Couto turned to Trist and remarked with a sad smile, "This must be a proud moment for you; no less proud for you than it is humiliating for us." Trist's reply was indirect. "We are making *peace*. Let that be our only thought."[22] His real thoughts and feelings he revealed later: "Could those Mexicans have seen into my heart at that moment, they would have known that *my* feeling of shame as an American was far stronger than theirs could be. . . . that was a thing for every right-minded American to be ashamed of, and I *was* ashamed. . . . My object, through out was, *not* to obtain all I could, but on the contrary to make the treaty as little exacting as possible from Mexico, as was compatible with its being accepted at home. In this I was governed by two considerations: one was the iniquity of the war, as an abuse of power on our part; the other was that the more disadvantageous the treaty was made to Mexico, the stronger would be the ground of opposition to it in the Mexican Congress by the party who had boasted of its power to frustrate any peace measures."[23]

His faithful friend Freaner had lingered, as Trist had requested, for the signing of the treaty and now claimed the honor of carrying it to Washington. He made the trip in near record time, delivering the historic document to James Buchanan only seventeen days after it was signed.

CHAPTER II

Washington

Freaner's remarkable dash to the capital received little applause from the administration, for the document he bore was a political hot potato. Many factions were clamoring for Mexican territory greatly in excess of the original Polk demands, while others wanted less and some none at all. The All-Mexico advocates, fully as vocal as the "Fifty-four Forty or Fight" people before them, were gaining broad support despite the opposition of the New England reform crowd, who railed against the manifest immorality of such a scheme. Abolitionists and like-minded folk suspected a plot to expand slave territory. Nearly everyone raised a racial question, albeit in blatantly ironic terms: how could a nation of Anglo-Saxons absorb the "mongrel" Mexicans except by enslaving them all—a patently unthinkable solution?[1]

President Polk was still driven by a relentless determination to acquire California, though some influential voices in his own party were declaring the war unwinnable within the remaining thirteen months of his administration. Although his anger against Scott and Trist inclined him to tear up the presumptuous treaty, a careful examination of its contents convinced him of its faithful adherence to the *projet* he had sent with the commissioner ten months before. He hated to admit that the work of the "utterly unworthy," "arrogant," "impudent," and "very base" Trist may have placed in his hands the only means of making good his objective, but no other conclusion came readily to mind. Reluctantly, on February 20, he referred the detested document to his cabinet.[2]

Some historians have charged Polk with blaming Trist for being *too* faithful in carrying out his instructions. His annoyance, they contend, stemmed from a reluctance to expose the obvious contrast between his earlier goals, so meticulously achieved by his emissary, and his later, expanded objectives.[3] This seems not to be the case, for Polk remained characteristically independent of external pressure and in the end rejected the extremists' position. Still, his failure to interfere with the unauthorized negotiations despite having received early notification of Trist's defiant intentions is puzzling. Could Polk have allowed the proceedings to take place in the hope that something useful might result while preparing to disavow responsibility if they failed? Far-fetched perhaps, though Polk, the consummate politician, anxiously sought peace and would prevent no action that might produce it.[4]

Secretary of State Buchanan, who had sent many amiable and encouraging messages to Trist throughout his long ordeal, opposed the treaty, and for unexpected reasons. Although he had originally opposed any land acquisition (later changing his mind enough to help draft the terms now under consideration), he suddenly decided that *more* territory should be demanded, although he shared the president's view that misconduct by the maker of the treaty should not preclude its acceptance. Secretary of the Treasury Walker also opposed the treaty for similar reasons. Marcy, Mason, Johnson, and Clifford favored sending it on to the Senate with only the recommendation that Article 10 be stricken. (This article guaranteed all land grants made by Mexico in the affected territory.) The president pondered these views overnight. The next day he again called a cabinet meeting and announced his decision to forward the treaty for ratification. He confided to his diary dark misgivings about his secretary of state. Discounting the sincerity of Buchanan's stout insistence that more territory should be demanded, he commented that the secretary was "now a candidate for the presidency, and he does not wish to incur the displeasure of those who are in favor of the conquest of all Mexico." He may also have suspected Buchanan of ambivalence in expecting—perhaps hoping—that the Senate would ratify the treaty although he was on record as opposing it. Polk's diary continued: "No candidate for the presidency ought ever to remain on the cabinet. He is an unsafe adviser."[5]

Polk's reasons for endorsing the treaty were morally and politically sound. He regretted the unanticipated prolongation of the war,[6] with its appalling cost in lives and treasure, and he wished to see it concluded while he was still in office. Also, he knew that the Whigs would pounce on him ferociously if, for personal reasons, he rejected the prize he had pursued so energetically these past three years. That did not mean, however, that he was ready to forgive Nicholas Trist. He sent the treaty to the Senate on February 23 with a recommendation that it be debated on its merits, without reference to the actions of the commissioner. He affirmed the cabinet's opinion that Article 10 should be stricken.[7]

The treaty set off a great debate in the Senate. It was first massaged by the Foreign Relations Committee, which toyed with the idea of discarding it as invalid, then sending a group of notable men to Mexico to negotiate a new treaty, perhaps with the chair of the committee, Ambrose H. Sevier, at its head. When this notion met with an unfavorable reaction, the matter was quickly moved on to the full Senate without recommendation. A clamor immediately arose from those Whigs who had opposed all expansion, some of whom had bitterly opposed the war from its beginning. They now declared that Trist's unauthorized action invalidated an agreement that would strip Mexico of so large a portion of its land. At the other extreme, the cry for all of Mexico was heard from certain powerful Democratic senators. The president waited anxiously, aware that factions even more than parties would hold the key to a two-thirds ratification vote. Although the debate was conducted behind closed doors, the press, already familiar in general with the terms of the treaty, was quick to take sides.

The nearest thing to consensus was a general feeling of relief that a means was at hand to end the hated war, which by now was an embarrassment to most Americans. For this reason alone, many were prepared to excuse the commissioner's irregular behavior and even acclaim him for his success. Few shared the president's sense of outrage, for the injury, if any had been done, affected only him, and little sympathy remained for Polk. Never a beloved executive, Polk in the last year of his presidency was increasingly out of favor with the populace.[8] No one guessed that he was also terminally ill. Many believed that Commissioner Trist would presently return, explain himself, answer questions, and receive a hero's welcome. When this did not happen, some were puzzled and began to wonder if perhaps Trist had good reason to stay away.

The newspapers reflected the views of their more vocal constituents and their most opinionated editors. None was indifferent. Even after, on March 10, the Senate voted 38 to 14 to ratify (with four brave senators abstaining)—barely over the needed two-thirds majority—the newspaper debate raged on. The *National Intelligencer* would have preferred merely to call off the war: no territory, no indemnity, only a gentleman's agreement on permanent peace.⁹ The New Orleans *Daily Picayune* commented unnecessarily that the treaty would be a great disappointment to the All-Mexico faction, then went on to note grudgingly that it would be "very good for the future of both countries."¹⁰ The *Philadelphia Inquirer* called Trist's action in the face of his recall "most commendable."¹¹ The *New York Sunday Dispatch* exulted, ". . . we are overjoyed. We are the first to say—hold, enough."¹² Dozens of others lauded the commissioner for his bravery and patriotism, but the war hawks were dissatisfied. The *New York Herald* thought the only way to keep the Mexicans under control would be by permanent occupation of the whole country.¹³ Maine's *Augusta Age* wanted a harsher peace, with Mexico rather than the United States paying the indemnity.¹⁴

One of the more thoughtful pieces appeared in the *Pennsylvania Inquirer* on March 14. The writer, intrigued by the storm of criticism raised against Trist, approached the subject by asking himself whether the commissioner had had any real choice other than the one he had made, and concluded that he had not. The editor believed that the recall had been ordered, not to remove an unsatisfactory agent (since he was never replaced) but to tighten the screws on the equivocating Mexicans. Trist, being in a position to see and weigh factors that were hidden from his distant superiors, had boldly overruled this maneuver knowing it could not succeed. For this, the writer concluded, Polk would eventually come to forgive his defiant but successful agent.¹⁵ Sadly, the harsh judgment offered more than a half-century later by historian Justin Smith came nearer the mark: "But the president was only Polk the Mediocre after all. His plumage had been ruffled; and instead of giving Trist the high and lucrative post [of American emissary to seek Mexican ratification], he relegated the peacemaker to dishonorable oblivion, and would not even pay him for the time actually spent in the negotiations. To think that a President of the United States could be so small!"¹⁶

Senator Sevier and Attorney General Clifford were appointed commissioners to carry the treaty to Mexico for ratification by the Mexican Congress. They arrived in Mexico on April 15, 1848. That defeated nation quickly became the scene of outcry and wrangling even more clamorous than had occurred in the United States. All the old objections of the war faction were reiterated: shame, treason, economic ruin, permanent bondage, and national oblivion. The peace advocates, however, remained resolute, and they did not neglect honoring the American commissioner who had helped make the treaty that promised peace and recovery. One of the Mexican commissioners read aloud a formal statement: "Your Excellency will permit us to state before concluding that the favorable conception which in the first negotiations was formed of the noble character and high endowments of Mr. Trist has been completely confirmed in the second. Happy has it been for both countries that the choice of the American Government should have been fixed upon a person of such worth, upon a friend of peace so loyal and sincere: of him there remains in Mexico none but grateful and honoring recollections."[17]

The president was nervous about Trist's persistent absence from the country after being ordered to return. He felt sure that the continuing presence of the discredited agent in Mexico would somehow undo the hard-won peace, especially while the two authorized commissioners were in that country. He proposed to his cabinet the forcible removal of Trist. Secretary of War Marcy protested this humiliation of the emissary, but Secretary of State Buchanan, the ex-commissioner's former superior and friend, remained silent. The president resolved to proceed as planned. He ordered the new commander, Gen. William Butler, to remove the troublesome agent by arrest if necessary. This placed Butler, an able and decent man though not a professional soldier, in a difficult position. He was new on the scene and had not yet established himself with either the citizenry or the troops, and he was dealing with a person of some popularity in both affected countries. The general fervently hoped that force would be unnecessary. Unfortunately for him, the commissioner, having defied a president, was in no mood to yield meekly to a mere major general.

In a letter to Virginia about a month after the treaty signing, Nicholas explained that he was unable to leave until the court of inquiry met to consider General Scott's charges against his detractors, and this matter awaited the arrival of witnesses from Washington. His reason, however sincere, seems inadequate. He could have done himself and his cause far more good by presenting himself in Washington during this critical time than by remaining in Mexico as a witness in a military inquiry, the outcome of which was foregone. The question was quickly settled when the president ordered the three defendants released from arrest and, to emphasize his displeasure, bestowed a post of honor on General Worth. Trist wrote that he was uncertain about the amount of remuneration he would receive, and he refused to put the question to the only person who could inform him, for Polk, in his passion for secrecy, had dispatched Nicholas as his personal representative, thus reserving to himself control of all matters pertaining to the mission, including compensation. Bitterly, Trist wrote: "I will accept *nothing*—not even my due—which it depends upon his decision . . . to give me."[18] Still defiant, he now behaved like a man with a death wish.

General Butler, sensing pressure from Washington but reluctant to act in haste, politely advised Trist in writing that he was directed by the president to assist the commissioner's speedy return to the United States. With his customary reliance on written communication, Trist informed the general that the president was abusing his authority. Considering himself no longer an agent of the government, Trist likened himself to any other traveler abroad and declared that he would stay as long as he wished, adding that he would have been ready to leave but now could not do so because it would appear to be "acquiescence in usurped authority."[19] Butler replied in a note that "should it become necessary, which I feel certain it will not, it will be my unpleasant duty to enforce that requirement."[20] Grimly, Trist forced the hapless general to do his duty.

Meanwhile, General Scott was accepting his own removal philosophically. After turning over his command to Butler with all courtesy and no little ceremony, he remained for a time bidding farewell to his comrades in arms. On April 23, 1848, with the thunderous cheers of his troops ringing in his ears, he made his departure. Lt. Col. Robert E. Lee, Scott's valued reconnaissance expert, remarked later that Scott was "turned out as an old horse to die."[21]

Nicholas Trist was not far behind the general. Escorted by a troop of soldiers, he returned over the Pass of Cortez, past remembered scenes of alpine grandeur, past Puebla and Jalapa, where he had made first an enemy and then a friend of proud old Winfield Scott, past hard-won Cerro Gordo and on to battered Veracruz, where his escort marched him aboard a waiting vessel. On May 4 he arrived at New Orleans, where he half expected to be arrested again and clapped in prison. Instead he found himself quite alone. Already he was a forgotten man.

CHAPTER 12

Oblivion

With the benefit of a century and a half in which to reflect on the events described here, most serious students of the Mexican War have concluded that the Polk administration was seriously out of touch with the actual conditions in Mexico. Perhaps this was true because of the growing tension between the president and the secretary of state, but certainly the disservice rendered by General Pillow also played a large part in the administration's ignorance. Moreover, most analysts agree that the action taken by Nicholas Trist not only achieved all of Mr. Polk's objectives but also salvaged what little honor America could rightfully claim while saving thousands of lives. Why, then, did the successful commissioner return to find his career destroyed and his prospects dim? And why has his name been forgotten?

To discover the answers to these questions, it is worth examining the historical events surrounding Trist's own achievements. James Buchanan was distinctly out of favor with the president, so much so, in fact, that he had become ineffective. One wonders, as did Trist, why the secretary remained in so untenable a position.[1] The *New York Herald* printed a series of anonymous letters attacking the president, and Polk, certain they had either been written or inspired by Buchanan, threatened dismissal if he found proof of his suspicions. Buchanan vigorously denied the charge and clung precariously to his post. In this smoldering atmosphere, affairs of state could scarcely flourish. Certainly Buchanan was in no position to defend the discredited commissioner, even if he had been inclined to do so.

Trist returned to a nation gone mad with joy over the results of his labors but curiously indifferent to his personal fortunes. Nine days before he signed the treaty, a worker had found gold in a millrace in the Sacramento Valley, and now half the nation seemed poised for a dash to California. Politicians began feverishly drafting bills for the organization of the new territories. A presidential election was due in the fall, and Zachary Taylor of Buena Vista fame easily captured the Whig nomination, giving that declining party high hopes of regaining the presidency. "Old Rough and Ready" was not the only president whose election traced to Mexican War fame. In 1852, two veteran generals—Winfield Scott and Franklin Pierce—vied for the presidency, and Pierce won easily. A score of future congressmen first came to public notice in Mexico. Artists and poets, previously unknown, emerged from among the veterans to tell the colorful story of the war. And in less than a decade, Col. Jefferson Davis of the acclaimed Mississippi volunteer regiment would become the only president of the Confederate States of America as the tensions over the slavery question, evident during the Mexican War, took center stage once and for all. Throughout the long celebration following the war with Mexico, however, only the Trist and Randolph families rejoiced in the return of the emissary. For him, it was sufficient.

But aside from the tumult and the shouting, what were the real consequences, good and bad, of the war? More importantly, what impact did the treaty have? Most apparent was the enormous increase in the size of the United States, for 592,017 square miles of territory were added, and the troublesome Texas question had been laid to rest.[2] As Polk had foreseen, the acquisition of splendid harbors on the Pacific made this country a first-class trading nation that would soon lead the world in international commerce. The resolution of the international boundary dispute ensured lasting peace and eventually a measure of friendship between two formerly implacable enemy nations. The astonishing efficiency of America's arms, especially its artillery, catapulted the United States into the first rank of world powers and extinguished—at least until the twentieth century—all notions of North American conquest by foreign aggressors. Proven beyond question was the value of the military academy at West Point, many of whose graduates received their baptism by fire in Mexico and went on to distinguish themselves as generals in both armies, Union and Confederate, in the Civil War. And the conflict with Mexico accelerated the onset of that war by exacerbating the slavery question.

It has been widely acknowledged that Trist "abruptly halted" the All-Mexico movement, which some believe came close to success. They point out that the *Puros,* who were rapidly gaining strength during the negotiations, actually favored annexation of Mexico by the United States as the only sure way of quelling anarchy and fostering democratic institutions. Whether that is true may never be known, but ratification of the treaty by the two nations extinguished the All-Mexico movement as instantaneously as a bucket of water quenches a campfire.[3]

Trist found himself in desperate need of funds and with no immediate source of income other than the compensation still due him in payment for his mission, the amount of which was uncertain. The president would not relent from his insistence that Trist was entitled to be paid only to the date when he received the recall notice, November 16, 1847. Trist still insisted that, at a minimum, he should be paid to December 12, the earliest date when it would have been possible to leave Mexico with any reasonable degree of safety.[4] Nevertheless, he stubbornly refused to demean himself by going cap in hand to the White House to plead his case. Nor was the president eager to see him, although a circuitously delivered message hinted that Polk and Buchanan entertained "the most friendly feelings" toward him. He confided years later in a letter to General Scott that this guarded message appeared to be "an invitation to *name my price* for silence and inaction regarding his minion . . . Pillow and other distinct subjects the agitation of which was a terrifying thought for him [Polk]."[5] This dark suspicion is mere conjecture on Trist's part, worthy of no more than passing mention here. However, if such fears did exist, they were groundless, for he refused to injure his adversaries by offering scurrilous testimony to the newspapers in the popular practice of the day. His earlier vow to Virginia to have nothing more to do with official life remained firm.

What then? His brother's question thirty years before seemed just as appropriate now: "What are you going to do now, Nicholas?" Having burned his bridges behind him, he was faced with the daunting question of how to earn a living. Early in July 1848, he moved with his family to Westchester, Pennsylvania. With his rapidly dwindling savings and occasional small remittances from his plantations in Louisiana, he struggled to support his family and put his son Browse through the University of Virginia. At the same time he sought earnestly to help poor Jeff find his way in the world, first as an artist and later as a clerk in a government office. Neither effort succeeded; Jeff presently returned to the institute in Philadelphia, where his care was an additional drain on the family finances. Within a year Trist wrote a friend, "I am at this moment at the last gasp for immediate cash. . . ."[6] Virginia, with Patty's help, opened a boarding school for girls.

Though unsuccessful in his efforts to earn a secure income, Trist was still a figure of some distinction and public acclaim. Veterans writing their war memoirs sought his assistance. Historians importuned him for his recollections of the glory days of Jefferson, Madison, and Jackson. The photographers England & Gunn desired to make his portrait, declaring, ". . . we are anxious to have in our gallery likenesses of all the great men of our nation."[7] These appeals, though flattering, put no food on the table. Meanwhile, the boarding school produced only meager returns.

In the summer of 1851, the family moved to New York, where Trist took a position in the law firm of Fowler and Wells in the Wall Street district. The post proved temporary, and suitable, affordable housing was not to be found. In spite of his dismal circumstances, he plunged into Spartan living and vigorous exercise to keep his spirits up and his health robust. In a long letter to General Scott he boasted that he had put on twenty pounds of muscle by walking up to eight miles a day at four miles an hour and was able to make a perfectly satisfactory breakfast of half a dozen graham crackers. (The Rev. Sylvester Graham, a noted health guru of the day, invented this perennial favorite and made himself hated by the bakers of Boston by preaching against white bread. He also advocated taking cold showers and sleeping with wide-open windows in freezing weather.[8]) Eventually the law job petered out, and the family moved to Philadelphia, a city that held warm memories for the Trists. Virginia again opened a school, this one an academy for young ladies that today would be called a charm school. Again the profits were disappointing; Nicholas and Virginia offered room and board to single ladies and gentlemen, as they had been obliged to do in Havana.

During these difficult years, Trist persisted in speculating with the meager funds that came into his possession, usually on ventures launched by enthusiastic friends. A washing machine business in England, where he went to hunt—unsuccessfully, as it turned out—for the legendary family fortunes; a gold-mining operation in California; a cattle ranch in the West that he hoped to move to Florida; an "improved" steel railroad rail: all came to naught, and each diminished his slender reserves of cash and added to his growing debt. His plan to write the history of his mission to Mexico also failed to materialize, and each passing year dimmed his inspiration for the task. Although he would never admit what his brother Browse had tried to tell him thirty years earlier—that he was no business man—he at last reluctantly concluded that he must seek employment in order to live. For a man in his fifties, job-hunting was not encouraging, but he eventually became a clerk for the Philadelphia, Wilmington, and Baltimore Railroad Company. After a few years, he advanced to the position of paymaster and remained in the employ of this company for twenty years.

Small sums continued to trickle in from the family plantations in Louisiana, never in the amounts envisioned during the early years. From time to time, Virginia and Patty, either together or singly as circumstances allowed, went to Bowdon in Ascension Parish where their holdings were directed by Browse. In 1856, Patty wrote to inform her father of Browse's death at age fifty-four.[9] Trist, though crushed by the news, was by now almost inured to the loss of loved ones. His job, disbursing a monthly payroll of $73,000 to more than two-thousand employees scattered over the vast network of rail, required continual travel. Wrecks were frequent, and Virginia worried constantly that he would be injured or killed. She wrote to a friend, "My . . . heart aches on seeing him come home from his drudgery, looking so worn out and sad. . . ."[10]

But fatigue and discouragement did not diminish his interest in national and world affairs. His library of over six-hundred volumes, including many classics and the better contemporary writings, was considered enormous by the standards of that day. His recollections and opinions continued to be sought by historians and journalists. Despite his reduced station in life and the numbing tedium of his work, his mind was as keen and incisive as ever. His views were considered liberal, even radical. "I am most decidedly a Woman's Rights man," he declared after reading a pamphlet entitled *Woman and Her Wishes*. And though he kept his vow never again to speak to Buchanan, who had disgusted him by remaining in the Polk cabinet and "playing a game" to seize all of Mexico, during the Buchanan presidency he wrote his one-time friend: "This is written by one who in his feelings, both as a citizen and as a man, was once a warm friend of yours—as sincere a friend as man ever had, and who now entertains for you, as a brother man, feelings the reverse of unkind. *Veto that Tariff Bill* . . . do this and you will render to your Country a service that will go far towards making amends for the many errors into which you have fallen."[11]

When, during the same Buchanan administration, the nation drifted inexorably toward war, Trist watched in horror and disbelief. He was a Virginian in his sympathies; his son Browse now lived in Georgia with his Southern wife, and many of their friends and relatives were sworn upholders of the rebel cause; yet he was unswerving in his defense of the Union. In the presidential election of 1860, Trist cast his vote unhesitatingly for Abraham Lincoln, although with his usual forthrightness he declared that his choice reflected his hatred for the Calhoun doctrine of separatism more than any real enthusiasm for Lincoln. His sensitive wife shared his devotion to the Union, but she suffered intensely on account of the division that shattered her circle of friends and family. Her own youngest brother George was secretary of war in Jefferson Davis's cabinet. Out of her anguish she wrote: "My difference of opinion does not make me love less the dear friends of my youth and my blood. No! I shall love them ever, believing as I do that they honestly believe themselves in the right. Tears blind me. I cannot write more."[12]

An earlier letter written during the grim days of impending war reveals her tender love for and understanding of her husband as well as her dread of the coming clash:

The evening is the only time we have to talk over with him the agitating topic of the day, to hear from him the latest news and to know what to think of it. How much I wish that you . . . [had] the advantage of listening to him, he is always well informed, clear headed, farsighted and just and upright in his views. I have little doubt myself that he is perhaps the only man now living in our country who has any real knowledge of the Science of politics as it was understood by Jefferson, Madison and other great minds of their day and his opportunities of information have been so great and his capacity for acquiring knowledge and assimilating it so excellent that I never ask him a question, or listen to what he says, on the subject of politics, without being made to feel how thoroughly he has mastered it and that the light is breaking in upon my own mind from his. I wish to God that we could see any light breaking in upon us from another quarter, but in the black night of the Southern mind in its present state, there is, I fear, nothing to hope.[13]

How perceptively she enunciated the real tragedy of Nicholas Trist's life, for he was already an old-fashioned patriot, even in an era when the nation was still young. Indeed, he seemed to stand alone in understanding "the Science of politics as it was understood by Jefferson [and] Madison." Others quoted the founding fathers to suit their ends, and in doing so corrupted the words and prostituted their intent. It angered him to hear his beloved grandfather-in-law misquoted, whether from ignorance or dishonesty, to further aims that Jefferson never espoused. In his own life he sought to be both a loyal Democrat and a true republican (in the Jeffersonian sense), but he found few in high office who appeared to share his ideals.

Trist's devotion to his family remained the strongest force in his life. He persisted in his efforts to secure a clerkship for Jeff, an intelligent and amiable young man, but the prevailing prejudice against disabled persons defeated his best efforts. Jeff was obliged to remain at the institute, though at some point his talents and familiarity with the place secured him a position on the staff, thus reducing if not eliminating his financial dependence on his parents. Patty lived with her parents until 1862, when she married John Burke and moved to Alexandria, Virginia. Browse studied at the University of Virginia for two years, then transferred to Jefferson Medical College, where he was graduated in 1857. He served as a medical officer, first in the U.S. Navy and then briefly in the Confederate army, though he shortly resigned his commission in favor of private practice in Baltimore.[14]

If Trist refused to make claims on the government in his own behalf, his friends were not reluctant to act for him. In 1858, Winfield Scott, back in Washington as commanding general of the army, received a disturbing letter from another friend of Trist's who had recently visited him in Philadelphia: "I found Mr. Trist engaged in very tiresome employment in the service of a railway company, an occupation altogether unsuitable for a man of his age to say nothing of his abilities and attainments, but which he had felt very happy to obtain. This position in return for very laborious duties yields him $1200 per annum. Twelve hundred dollars a year! For a man like him, and one who has rendered to our country the unrequited service she has received at his hands. . . . Here he is then . . . a man in his 59th year and whose constitution, never at all robust, is undergoing the wear and tear of a degree of drudgery and exposure which would tax quite severely the physical powers of a man half his age."[15]

Scott, who by this time was aged, obese, and plagued by numerous ailments—but still a force in Washington—made repeated efforts to help his one-time enemy and present dear friend, but to no avail. In January 1861, on the eve of the incoming Lincoln administration and shortly before his health forced him to retire, he made one last appeal, this time to Lincoln's secretary of the treasury, Salmon P. Chase. He recounted the wrongs done to Trist by an ungrateful government and urged his appointment as revenue collector in Philadelphia, but this petition, like the others, was ignored.

Trist struggled on at his humble duties until he found himself facing his impending seventieth birthday. Now more than ever mindful of his loved ones and the hardship his death or incapacity would inflict on them, he swallowed his pride and began to listen to his concerned friends. He commenced making certain careful calculations. Then in July 1870, there occurred one of the great ironies of his life: his cause was taken up by a prominent abolitionist.

Senator Charles Sumner of Massachusetts was a scholar of note and a radical lawyer, handsome, eloquent, and in prewar days, a gadfly to the Southern cause. In May 1856, he had treated the U.S. Senate to a blistering diatribe against slavery so vituperative that it had driven a South Carolina congressman to attack Sumner at his desk in the Senate chamber and beat him senseless with a stout stick, leaving him permanently maimed. Now the war was over, and Senator Sumner, recovered in voice if not in body, was using his oratorical gifts in the shaping of Reconstruction. He nevertheless found time to deliver a moving speech to the Senate on behalf of Nicholas Trist. Portions of his address are given here:

> The services of Mr. Trist constitute an interesting chapter in the history of our country. As negotiator of the Treaty of Guadalupe Hidalgo, he exercised a decisive influence in terminating the war with Mexico, by which we were secured in the blessings of peace, and in the possession also of an undisputed claim to Texas, and an addition to the national domain equal in area to the present territory of Mexico, and including in expanse the great and prosperous State of California.
>
> [There followed a detailed account of Trist's commissioning.]
>
> Meanwhile there was at Washington a spirit hostile to negotiation; Mexico was not sufficiently humiliated. In the midst of his negotiation, when a treaty was almost within his grasp, on the 16th of November, 1847, Mr. Trist suddenly received a letter of recall, with the order to return home by the first safe opportunity. After careful deliberation, and with the sure conviction that if his efforts were thus abruptly terminated, the war would be prolonged, while the difficulties of obtaining another commission would be increased, he concluded to proceed, and do what he could for the sake of peace. The Mexicans to whom he communicated the actual condition of affairs united with him, and a treaty was signed on the 2d February, 1848 at Guadalupe Hidalgo. Mr. Trist remained in Mexico until the

18th of April 1848, in order to protect the interests of the United States, and would have remained longer had not an order for his arrest, sent from Washington to our military authorities, compelled him to leave.

It is understood that the president, on the arrival of the treaty, proposed to suppress it; but, unwilling to encounter public opinion, which was favorable to peace, he communicated it to the Senate, when, with certain amendments, it was ratified by a vote of 38 yeas and 14 nays. And thus the war with Mexico was closed.

The commissioner who had taken such great responsibility reached Washington, on his return in June, 1848, only to encounter the enmity of the administration then in power. His mission had been crowned with success, but he was disgraced. By the order of President Polk, his pay stopped at November 16th, 1847, so that the service, as peacemaker, rendered after that date, was left without compensation as without honor. Mr. Trist was proud and sensitive. He determined to make no application at the time for the compensation he had earned, and to await the spontaneous offer of it, unless compelled by actual want. In pursuance of this determination, for more than twenty years, he has worked for his daily bread, most of the time as an employee of a railroad company; but now having arrived at the age of threescore and ten, and, by reason of years and infirmity, being compelled to resign his situation, he naturally turns to this unsettled account, and asks for his due.

[The next paragraph discussed administrative details, the nature of the commission, and the vastly more generous compensation of other emissaries to Mexico (Slidell, Sevier, and Clifford), whose accomplishments were slight in comparison to Trist's.][16]

With his usual meticulous attention to detail, Trist had prepared an accounting of the compensation he had received ($8276.65) and another stating what he believed he should have received ($22,836.55). The difference, the amount now claimed, was $14,559.90. Acting on the favorable report of the Committee on Foreign Relations and impressed by the eloquence of Charles Sumner, the Senate duly (though not until the following April) approved the entire claim. By the time it was paid, the Trist finances had shrunk to almost nothing.

Perhaps embarrassed by its delinquency, the government, having finally paid its long overdue debt, insisted on adding interest. When the position of postmaster became vacant at Alexandria, the postmaster general's office, at the urging of Sen. Simon Cameron of Pennsylvania, offered it to Trist. Rated as a second-class city, Alexandria carried the handsome annual salary of $2900. Trist was happy to accept, especially because it would locate the Trists in the city where their daughter and her husband now lived.

Although many creditors made immediate claims, their bills were soon paid, and life became immeasurably easier. They now saw Patty much more frequently; moreover, Browse and his wife made frequent visits from nearby Baltimore. These were treasured benefits to Nicholas and Virginia, even more precious than the financial relief they now enjoyed. When not at his duties, Trist occupied himself with his books and letters. He was content, and Virginia had never been happier. In the fall of 1871, they attended a dance. Trist, perhaps remembering his daily lessons with Mr. Digrain in New Orleans so long ago, danced the night away simply because "the spirit moved him."[17]

Late in 1873, Trist was felled by a stroke from which he never recovered. He was unable to leave his bed, and the family knew that the end was near, although his demeanor was peaceful and he appeared free of pain. On February 11, 1874, at the age of seventy-three, he breathed his last.

EPILOGUE

Historian Robert Brent notes with some bemusement that American newspapers reacted to the Treaty of Guadalupe Hidalgo by devoting more space to its maker than to the document itself. Every publication aligned itself either for or against the brazen maverick diplomat. Political affiliation had much to do with this taking of sides, but there is evidence of another influence as well. Some Whigs believed that for Trist to resume negotiations after being recalled was a rash assumption of authority that could have had disastrous consequences, but what consequence could have been worse than the real circumstance then existing? Others commended Trist for his courage and initiative. The gulf between detractors and admirers seems to separate those who like to see the underling keep to his place and those whose hearts are cheered by the spectacle of a reckless Don Quixote doing what he knows to be right, whatever the consequences.

By and large, Nicholas Trist has received from historians the sort of handling that President Polk would have approved. "Conceited," "humorless," "timid," "slow-witted," and "high-handed" are among the more acrid epithets hurled at him from the vantage point of hindsight. Like the six blind men who described the elephant, Trist's critics have at least some justification for their charges, for Trist under stress made an easy target. His snobbishness laid him open to the charge of conceit. His ponderous writing style certainly lacked humor, and his reliance on written messages in preference to personal confrontation, especially when he was under attack, indeed smacks of timidity. "Slow-witted" is both unjust and inaccurate, but a man who could quarrel with generals and defy presidential orders well deserves to be called high-handed.

The fiasco at Havana is difficult to assess. Surely it does little to enhance Trist's credentials as a diplomat. The suspicion arises that his distaste for "the herd" caused him to shelter himself from direct contact with rough seafaring men in general, though he had frequent cordial relations with a number of sea captains of "the better sort," as he would have described them. His disdain was probably apparent and surely gave offense, and salty tavern scuttlebutt would naturally fuel a vendetta and perhaps even, as he charged, a "conspiracy."[1] Still, the actions he was accused of by the aggrieved mariners seem not only out of character and outside his jurisdiction but egregiously officious. The flaws in the consular fee system, later removed by Congress, may, in some cases, have influenced his judgment. The dispute with the British abolitionist, though of much greater international significance, is easier to understand. Trist simply lost his temper, as he was wont to do. This incident alone could have wrecked the career of any mid-level diplomat and probably would have cost him his but for the fact that it happened just as one American president was leaving office while another of the opposing party was coming in, and neither was especially friendly to England. Trist succeeded in fighting off both enemies, domestic and foreign, with his trusty pen and in so doing reinforced a habit he would have done well to break.

Clearly, Trist was a changed man when he returned from his eleven-year stay in Cuba. He had ascended the heights, socially at least, then plunged into humiliating poverty for four long years before Andrew Jackson, who had sent him abroad, finally rescued him. He returned to Washington because he had no place else to go. No longer the pampered favorite of an immensely popular president, he was subdued, withdrawn, immersed in menial duties—to all appearances a hardworking, colorless bureaucrat. This must have been the man that Polk saw, and Buchanan, who certainly knew him better, said nothing to change the president's view. His humble station and seeming tractability were exactly what Mr. Polk desired in his secret agent. We shouldn't wonder at the executive's wrath when this drab bird decided to fly with his own wings.

Some thought that a craving for glory—even for the presidency—drove all of his actions in Mexico, including his refusal to leave when recalled. Mr. Polk was the first to dismiss Trist's insistence that he sought no distinction, but he was not the last. Justin Smith wrote with heavy sarcasm that having "sojourned on Olympus and tasted the ambrosia of the

gods . . . gave him queer feelings in the head that were not exactly growing pains, and produced a state of mind that was neither of heaven nor of
earth."[2] Many others sounded the same note, perhaps taking their cues
from Professor Smith. But if a man may be taken at his word, Trist had no
such craving and was even reluctant to accept his mission. He was clearly
apprehensive at the prospect of another long stay in the tropics, where his
health was always at risk. His anxiety about his health drove him into hypochondria, and when he felt especially vulnerable to illness he became
nervous, high-strung, and testy. Such was his state of mind when he arrived in Veracruz and wrote his fateful note to General Scott, yet out of
their famous quarrel grew a lifelong friendship. Buchanan's tempting hint
that the presidency might be his reward for success only repelled Trist by
its obvious insincerity and certainly initiated the slow demise of their friendship. Trist's curious statement to the president that a humble job such as
that of an army storekeeper held more appeal than distinction, though
rejected by both his listeners, was probably the truth.

R. S. Ripley, whose *War with Mexico* appears to be largely an effort to
glorify Gideon Pillow, said of Trist that "no man who so palpably dis-
obeys the direct instructions of his government"[3] could be fit to negotiate
a treaty, a position also taken by some senators in voting against treaty
ratification. But even Polk, who thoroughly detested Nicholas Trist, saw
the folly of this idea and insisted that the treaty be evaluated on its own
merits.

One of the more insidious criticisms of Trist held that he did nothing
more than anyone else could have done. After all, said the advocates of
this view, a treaty draft and detailed instructions had been furnished him,
and the Mexicans by the time he met with them were abjectly desirous of
any peace they could get. This opinion rests on the same flawed premise
as the war itself: that Mexico should be given the same treatment as any
other sovereign nation; that it was—or should be—a stable political en-
tity: monolithic, predictable, and rational. That a wise, just, and steady
U.S. government could stand off at a distance of three-thousand miles,
make a reasonable offer—or if necessary, a threat—and achieve exactly the
results it desired; in short, that a war can be managed like a well-run business. And that a qualified emissary, suitably equipped, transported, and
protected, need be little more than a courier. But reality turned out to be
something quite different. Nicholas Trist, to his credit and considerable
loss, dealt with a reality that was apparent to him but sadly, not to the
administration, and he was equal to the challenge. Many veterans of the

war recognized the imposing magnitude of that challenge. One wrote Trist to offer the opinion that he had done what no other American could have accomplished.

The president and the secretary of state deserve credit for formulating a sound plan and for picking the right man to carry it out. Where they failed utterly was in their handling of the human factor. President Polk's mistrust of Scott naturally colored the thinking of his agent, as did his assumption that a treaty could somehow be obtained without Scott's involvement. He apparently proceeded from the astounding belief that the proud old commander would respond unquestioningly to presidential directions relayed by the chief clerk of the State Department, regardless of the military exigencies confronting him. Even when one places on Trist all the blame that he deserves for his thoughtless treatment of Scott, and on Scott for his preposterously oversensitive reaction, it was Polk, after all, who set their feud in motion.

The quarrel between Trist and Scott would, however, have been of negligible significance had it not put a weapon in the hand of Gideon Pillow. That nefarious character's insidious reports so effectively prejudiced Polk against Scott and Trist that both were eventually removed in disgrace despite achievements that won the approbation of the world. And what of James Buchanan and Secretary of War William Marcy? Had those two officials earned the trust of the president and served him well, they might have prevented or quelled the Scott-Trist feud and even deflected some of Pillow's poison darts. All things considered, James K. Polk was lucky to have ended the war at all. As historian David Pletcher writes: "No one can deny that Polk achieved his goals, but he was favored by good luck, by the steadfastness of American soldiers, and, at the end, by the long-neglected skill of his diplomats."[4]

What sort of man was Nicholas Trist? Louis Sears has called him "laboriously the slave of conscience,"[5] but that striking definition does incomplete justice to its subject. He was also a worrier, a perfectionist, and an idealist. He was obsessed with a need for justice for himself and for others, and he obstinately refused to compromise on principle. He had an intensely analytical mind, an exceptional capacity for detail, considerable erudition, a gift for languages, and more than ordinary charm. Sadly, all of his laudable attributes seemed to desert him when he encountered hostile opposition; at such times he became ill-tempered, defensive, and legalistic, and his all-too potent pen became his trusted weapon. Thomas Jefferson, whom he adored and sought to emulate, never bothered to defend himself when attacked, but in this Trist was his opposite. Perhaps the insecure boyhood of the Trist brothers, which marked Browse in more obvious ways, also left its traces on Nicholas, though outwardly he usually exhibited perfect confidence.

Nicholas Trist, a fiercely independent idealist, lived in a different world from that of the mass of humanity. His values were high-minded abstractions—honor, justice, duty, civility, and responsibility—which, though not unusual in well-bred gentlemen of his day, preoccupied him to such an extraordinary degree they may have made him excessively fastidious about the sort of activities in which he was willing to engage. But he did not rail against hardships (as did his equally sensitive father before him) nor cry out against obscurity and poverty. He refused to engage his enemies in a "newspaper war" or publicly disparage those at whose hands he had suffered. In dire adversity he exhibited courage, patience, and a character of gold. And he brought honest emotion, like a breath of fresh air in a mausoleum, to the cloistered chambers of diplomacy.

When Trist died, the Washington *Sunday Herald* published a laudatory obituary. The writer predicted that Trist would "fill a larger place in the future history of his country than he has of late in the eyes of his countrymen."[6]

The prediction has not been fulfilled. Perhaps it still can be.

NOTES

The Trist correspondence cited here is stored on microfilm at the University of North Carolina as part of the Southern Historical Collection under the major heading *Southern Women and Their Families in the 19th Century: Papers and Diaries.* In the following notes, an entry under each chapter head will identify the reel number, series, and subseries of the *Nicholas Philip Trist Papers,* from which the correspondence cited in the chapter is quoted.

INTRODUCTION
1. Louis Martin Sears, "Nicholas P. Trist, A Diplomat with Ideals," *Mississippi Valley Historical Review* (June 1924): 98.

CHAPTER I
(See Reel 1, Series 1, Subseries 1.1)
1. Fawn M. Brodie, *Thomas Jefferson: An Intimate History,* p. 177.
2. H. B. Trist to Mary Trist, n.d., 1802.
3. H. B. Trist to Mary Trist, Mar. 3, 1803.
4. H. B. Trist to Mary Trist, June 1, 1803.
5. H. B. Trist to Mary Trist, Aug. 5, 1803.
6. Ibid.
7. Samuel Eliot Morison, *Oxford History of the American People,* p. 366; Alf J. Mapp, Jr., *Thomas Jefferson: Passionate Pilgrim,* p. 51; J. Christopher Herold, *Age of Napoleon,* pp. 300–304.
8. Mapp, *Thomas Jefferson,* p. 56.
9. H. B. Trist to Mary Trist, Dec. 2, 1803.

10. Elizabeth Trist to Thomas Jefferson, Mar. 1, 1804.
11. Elizabeth Trist to Caroline House, Aug. 31, 1804.
12. Elizabeth Trist to Thomas Jefferson, Sept. 9, 1804. The recipient of this letter could readily empathize with the writer's grief. Of the seven children born to Thomas and Martha Wales Jefferson, only two survived early childhood, and of those two, Maria Eppes died in childbirth at age twenty-five.
13. Elizabeth Trist to Thomas Jefferson, Oct. 27, 1807.
14. Mapp, *Thomas Jefferson,* pp. 120–21; Morison, *Oxford History,* pp. 369–70.
15. Nicholas Trist to Elizabeth Trist, Dec. 11, 1808.
16. Elizabeth Trist to Nicholas Trist, June 3, 1810.
17. Ibid; Elizabeth Trist to Thomas Jefferson, Sept. 9, 1804; Elizabeth Trist to Caroline House, Aug. 31, 1804.
18. H. B. Trist (the younger) to Elizabeth Trist, Nov. 20, 1814.
19. Harnett T. Kane, *Plantation Parade: The Grand Manner in Louisiana,* p. 218.
20. Mary Trist Tournillon to Nicholas Trist, Feb. 7, 1816.
21. J. F. Dumoulin to Nicholas Trist, Apr. 12, 1817.
22. H. B. Trist to Nicholas Trist, Oct. 30, 1817.
23. Brodie, *Thomas Jefferson,* p. 378.
24. Mapp, *Thomas Jefferson,* p. 191.
25. Robert Arthur Brent, "Nicholas Philip Trist: Biography of a Disobedient Diplomat," (Ph.d. diss., University of Virginia, 1950), 11.
26. The above descriptions of the Trist brothers' visit to Monticello derive from the factual account in Brent, "Nicholas Philip Trist," pp. 11–15 and in Robert W. Drexler *Guilty of Making Peace,* pp. 20–22. Accounts of domestic, social, and recreational life at Monticello are derived from biographies of Thomas Jefferson, in particular those by Fawn M. Brodie and Alf J. Mapp.
27. Brent, "Nicholas Philip Trist," 13.
28. Nicholas Trist to Martha Jefferson Randolph, Sept. 18, 1818.
29. Martha Randolph to Nicholas Trist, Sept. 20, 1818.

CHAPTER 2
(See Reel 1, Series 1, Subseries 1.1 and 1.2; Reel 2, Series 1, Subseries 1.2)
1. Elizabeth Trist to Nicholas Trist, Nov. 1, 1818.
2. Thomas J. Fleming, *West Point: The Men and Times of the United States Military Academy,* p. 3.
3. Wilson Fairfax to Nicholas Trist, Dec. 18, 1818.
4. Fleming, *West Point,* p. 43.
5. R. Ernest Dupuy, *Men of West Point,* chap. 1.

6. Fleming, *West Point,* pp. 26, 27.
7. Ibid., p. 32.
8. Brent, "Nicholas Philip Trist," 19.
9. Elizabeth Trist to Nicholas Trist, Jan. 2, 1819.
10. H. B. Trist to Nicholas Trist, Jan. 30, 1820.
11. H. B. Trist to Nicholas Trist, Nov. 17, 1818.
12. H. B. Trist to Nicholas Trist, Jan. 26, 1819.
13. H. B. Trist to Nicholas Trist, Sept. 24, 1819.
14. H. B. Trist to Nicholas Trist, July 6, 1820.
15. Fleming, *West Point,* p. 49.
16. Ibid., p. 49.
17. Mary Tournillon to Nicholas Trist, Jan. 20, 1820.
18. Lewis Livingston to Nicholas Trist, June 6, 1819.
19. Elizabeth Trist to Nicholas Trist, Feb. 9, 1820.
20. H. B. Trist to Nicholas Trist, Jan. 30, 1820.
21. H. B. Trist to Nicholas Trist, Jan. 13, 1821.
22. Nicholas Trist to H. B. Trist, Apr. 23, 1821.
23. Elizabeth Trist to Nicholas Trist, May 10, 1821.
24. Nicholas Trist to Thomas M. Randolph, May 14, 1821.
25. Fleming, *West Point,* p. 52.

CHAPTER 3
(See Reel 2, Series 1, Subseries 1.2)

1. Nicholas Trist to Virginia Randolph, July 12, 1821.
2. H. B. Trist to Nicholas Trist, July 25, 1820.
3. H. B. Trist to Nicholas Trist, July 27, 1821.
4. Mapp, *Thomas Jefferson,* p. 103.
5. Nicholas Trist to Virginia Randolph, Jan. 1, 1822.
6. Nicholas Trist to Virginia Randolph, Jan. 16, 1822.
7. Ibid.
8. Brodie, *Thomas Jefferson,* pp. 458–59.
9. Ibid.
10. Nicholas Trist to Virginia Randolph, Jan. 16, 1822.
11. Milton Meltzer, *Andrew Jackson and His America,* p. 40.
12. Brodie, *Thomas Jefferson,* p. 474.
13. Clarence P. Hornung, *The Way It Was in the U.S.A.,* pp. 406, 416.
14. Nicholas Trist to Virginia Randolph, Mar. 22, 1822.
15. Ibid.
16. Nicholas Trist to Virginia Randolph, July 7, 1822.
17. Elizabeth Trist to Nicholas Trist, Jan. 1, 1822.
18. Nicholas Trist to Virginia Randolph, Aug. 22, 1822.
19. Nicholas Trist to Virginia Randolph, Feb. 24, 1822.

20. Virginia Randolph to Nicholas Trist, Dec. 10, 1822.
21. H. B. Trist to Nicholas Trist, n.d.
22. Nicholas Trist to Virginia Randolph, May 5, 1823.
23. Brent, "Nicholas Philip Trist," 30.
24. Nicholas Trist to Virginia Randolph, June 24, 1823.
25. Nicholas Trist to Virginia Randolph, Oct. 23, 1823.
26. Martha Randolph to Nicholas Trist, June 25, 1823.
27. Nicholas Trist to Virginia Randolph, Nov. 4, 1823.
28. Virginia Randolph to Nicholas Trist, Jan. 8, 1824.
29. Nicholas Trist to Virginia Randolph, Mar. 3, 1824.

CHAPTER 4
(See Reel 2, Series 1, Subseries 1.2 and 1.3)

1. Mapp, *Thomas Jefferson*, p. 308.
2. Brent, "Nicholas Philip Trist," 31.
3. Drexler, *Guilty of Making Peace*, pp. 32–33.
4. Mapp, *Thomas Jefferson*, pp. 335–36.
5. Ibid., p. 293.
6. Brodie, *Thomas Jefferson*, pp. 456–57; Mapp, *Thomas Jefferson*, p. 348.
7. Page Smith, *The Shaping of America: A People's History of the Young Republic*, pp. 802–10.
8. Brent, "Nicholas Philip Trist," 34.
9. Brodie, *Thomas Jefferson*, pp. 207–208.
10. Smith, *Shaping of America*, p. 7; Brodie, *Thomas Jefferson*, p. 44.
11. Mapp, *Thomas Jefferson*, p. 193.
12. Brodie, *Thomas Jefferson*, p. 279.
13. Ibid., p. 23.
14. J. C. Furnas, *Goodbye to Uncle Tom*, pp. 84–85.
15. Brodie, *Thomas Jefferson*, p. 287.
16. Mapp, *Thomas Jefferson*, p. 330.
17. Brodie, *Thomas Jefferson*, p. 465. Jefferson once remarked that whenever he saw three physicians together, he looked around to see if the buzzards were gathering.
18. Mapp, *Thomas Jefferson*, p. 336.
19. Ibid., p. 350.
20. Ibid., pp. 345–50.
21. Drexler, *Guilty of Making Peace*, p. 35.
22. Mapp, *Thomas Jefferson*, p. 355.
23. Ibid., p. 357.
24. H. B. Trist to Nicholas Trist, Mar. 9, 1826.
25. H. B. Trist to Nicholas Trist, Apr. 10, 1826.
26. H. B. Trist to Nicholas Trist, Apr. 26, 1826.

27. Brent, "Nicholas Philip Trist," 39.
28. Ibid., pp. 44–45.
29. Mapp, *Thomas Jefferson*, p. 358.
30. Martha Randolph to Nicholas Trist, Aug. 2, 1827.
31. Mapp, *Thomas Jefferson*, p. 337.
32. Thomas Mann Randolph to Nicholas Trist, Mar. 10, 1828.
33. Nicholas Trist to Thomas Mann Randolph, Mar. 11, 1828.
34. Joshua Baker to Nicholas Trist, Feb. 27, 1828.
35. Smith, *Shaping of America*, p. 578.
36. Brent, "Nicholas Philip Trist," 45.
37. Ibid., pp. 41–42.
38. H. B. Trist to Nicholas Trist, May 12, 1828.
39. Brent, "Nicholas Philip Trist," 55.
40. Ibid., pp. 56–57.

CHAPTER 5
(See Reel 2, Series 1, Subseries 1.3; Reel 3, Series 1, Subseries 1.3)

1. Thomas R. Hietala, *Manifest Design: Anxious Aggrandizement in Late Jacksonian America*, p. 1.
2. Virginia Trist to Nicholas Trist, Dec. 3, 1828.
3. Brent, "Nicholas Philip Trist," 64, 66.
4. Ibid., 66.
5. Nicholas Trist to Virginia Trist, Jan. 20, 1829.
6. Brent, "Nicholas Philip Trist," 42, 66–67; Sears, "Nicholas P. Trist," 86; Drexler, *Guilty of Making Peace*, p. 44.
7. Virginia Trist to Nicholas Trist, Jan. 13, 1829.
8. Nicholas Trist to Virginia Trist, Feb. 17, 1829.
9. Nicholas Trist to Virginia Trist, Mar. 29, 1829.
10. Nicholas Trist to Virginia Trist, Apr. 11, 1829.
11. Nicholas Trist to Virginia Trist, June 10, 1829
12. Virginia Trist to Nicholas Trist, June 14, 1829.
13. H. B. Trist to Nicholas Trist, July 16, 1829.
14. Brent, "Nicholas Philip Trist," 68–69.
15. Ibid., 70–71.
16. Morison, *Oxford History*, pp. 435–36.
17. Ibid., pp. 427–29.
18. Brent, "Nicholas Philip Trist," 77–80.
19. Notation on memo, Andrew Jackson to Nicholas Trist, May 19, 1831.
20. Brent, "Nicholas Philip Trist," 83.
21. Drexler, *Guilty of Making Peace*, pp. 33–34.
22. Ibid., p. 48.
23. Virginia Trist to Nicholas Trist, July 1, 1831.

24. Martha Randolph to Virginia Trist, July 5, 1831.
25. Martha Randolph to Nicholas Trist, Apr. 17, 1833.
26. Drexler, *Guilty of Making Peace,* p. 45.
27. Nicholas Trist to Virginia Trist, Sept. 18, 1831.
28. H. B. Trist to Nicholas Trist, Dec. 28, 1831.
29. H. B. Trist to Nicholas Trist, May 8, 1832.
30. Virginia Trist to Mrs. Thomas Jefferson Randolph, Sept. 9, 1832.
31. H. B. Trist to Nicholas Trist, Nov. 7, 1832.
32. Brent, "Nicholas Philip Trist," 90.

CHAPTER 6
(See Reel 3, Series 1, Subseries 1.3; Reel 4, Series 1, Subseries 1.4; Reel 5, Series 1, Subseries 1.4)

1. H. B. Trist to Nicholas Trist, Apr. 25, 1833.
2. William Hodge et al. to Nicholas Trist, June 21, 1833.
3. Brent, "Nicholas Philip Trist," 92, 97.
4. Hietala, *Manifest Design,* pp. 89–90.
5. Nicholas Trist to Virginia Trist, Dec. 18, 1833.
6. Nicholas Trist to Virginia Trist, Dec. 22, 1833.
7. Virginia Trist to Nicholas Trist, Jan. 4, 1834.
8. Virginia Trist to Nicholas Trist, Jan. 29, 1834.
9. Meriwether Lewis Randolph to Virginia Trist, Jan. 24, 1834.
10. Nicholas Trist to Virginia Trist, Mar. 2, 1834.
11. Brent, "Nicholas Philip Trist," 95.
12. H. B. Trist to Nicholas Trist, Aug. 4, 1834.
13. Virginia Trist to Nicholas Trist, Jan. 11, 1835.
14. Virginia Trist to Nicholas Trist, Feb. 3, 1835.
15. Nicholas Trist to Virginia Trist, Mar. 14, 1835.
16. Nicholas Trist to Virginia Trist, Mar. 23, 1835.
17. Virginia Trist to Nicholas Trist, May 25, 1835.
18. H. B. Trist to Nicholas Trist, July 17, 1835.
19. Virginia Trist to Mary Randolph, Aug. 7, 1835.
20. Virginia Trist to Nicholas Trist, Jan. 26, 1836.
21. Nicholas Trist to Virginia Trist, May 13, 1836.
22. Ibid.
23. Virginia Trist to Andrew Jackson, Dec. 11, 1837.
24. Sears, "Nicholas P. Trist," 88.
25. Brodie, *Thomas Jefferson,* pp. 236–37.
26. Martha (Patty) Trist to Virginia Trist, June 8, 1838.
27. Virginia Trist to Nicholas Trist, Apr. 7, 1839.
28. Virginia Trist to Nicholas Trist, June 12, 1839.
29. Virginia Trist to Nicholas Trist, Aug. 15, 1839.

30. Peter Crusoe to Nicholas Trist, Aug. 12, 1839.
31. Nicholas Trist to Virginia Trist, June 20, 1839.
32. Virginia Trist to Nicholas Trist, Aug. 18, 1839.
33. Virginia Trist to Nicholas Trist, Sept. 26, 1839.
34. Brent, "Nicholas Philip Trist," 111.
35. Drexler, *Guilty of Making Peace,* p. 56.
36. Hietala, *Manifest Design,* pp. 13, 17.
37. Nicholas Trist to Virginia Trist, Nov. 30, 1839.
38. Trist's note scribbled on a letter, Sarah Easton to Nicholas Trist, July 21, 1840.
39. Brent, "Nicholas Philip Trist," 112.

CHAPTER 7

1. James C. N. Paul, *Rift in the Democracy,* pp. 82–83.
2. Hietala, *Manifest Design,* pp. 26, 69.
3. Walter LaFeber, *The American Age: United States Foreign Policy at Home and Abroad Since 1750,* p. 104.
4. Paul, *Rift in the Democracy,* p. 89.
5. Ibid., p. 140.
6. Charles Vevier, "American Continentalism: An Idea of Expansionism," *American Historical Review* (1960): 325–26; Paul H. Bergeron, *The Presidency of James K. Polk,* p. 68; Norman A. Graebner, *Empire on the Pacific: A Study in American Continental Expansion,* p. 218; LaFeber, *American Age,* p. 109; W. Dirk Raat, *Mexico and the United States: Ambivalent Vistas,* p. 62.
7. David M. Pletcher, *The Diplomacy of Annexation: Texas, Oregon, and the Mexican War,* pp. 334–37.
8. Brent, "Nicholas Philip Trist," 115.
9. Drexler, *Guilty of Making Peace,* p. 60.
10. Milton Meltzer, *Bound for the Rio Grande, the Mexican Struggle: 1845–1850,* p. 54.
11. K. Jack Bauer, *The Mexican War, 1846–1848,* p. 11.
12. Meltzer, *Bound for the Rio Grande,* p. 69.
13. Pletcher, *Diplomacy of Annexation,* pp. 334–35.
14. Ibid., p. 600.
15. Ibid., p. 376.
16. Henry Steele Commager, *Documents of American History,* pp. 310–11.
17. John R. Collins, "The Mexican War: A Study in Fragmentation," *Journal of the West* 11, no. 2 (Apr. 1972): 227–29; Pletcher, *Diplomacy of Annexation,* p. 231.
18. Graebner, *Empire on the Pacific,* pp. 191–92.
19. Pletcher, *Diplomacy of Annexation,* p. 233.

20. Ibid., p. 499; Drexler, *Guilty of Making Peace,* p. 11.

21. Drexler, *Guilty of Making Peace,* p. 12.

22. Justin H. Smith, *The War with Mexico,* vol. 2, p. 127–28.

23. Pletcher, *Diplomacy of Annexation,* pp. 500–501.

24. Smith, *War with Mexico,* vol. 2, p. 128; Drexler, *Guilty of Making Peace,* p. 13.

25. Sears, "Nicholas P. Trist," 93; Nicholas Trist to W. Scott, Jan. 12, 1861, as cited in Drexler, *Guilty of Making Peace,* p. 13.

26. Smith, *War with Mexico,* vol. 2, p. 127.

27. Pletcher, *Diplomacy of Annexation,* p. 501; Jack Nortrup, "Nicholas Trist's Mission to Mexico: A Reinterpretation," *Southwestern Historical Quarterly* 71, no. 3 (1968): 341–46; Eugene Keith Chamberlin, "Nicholas Trist and Baja California," *Pacific Historica Review* 32, no. 1 (1963): 57; Kenneth M. Johnson, "Baja California and the Treaty of Guadalupe Hidalgo," *Journal of the West* 11, no. 2 (Apr. 1972): 347; Graebner, *Empire on the Pacific,* p. 206. The range of opinions expressed by these historians illustrates well the mixed reaction to Trist. Graebner writes, "Trist's diplomacy secured a treaty . . . when American generals, politicians, the press, members of the cabinet, and the President himself believed it impossible." At the other extreme, Nortrup treats him as a consummate bungler and dupe of the Mexicans; however, Professor Nortrup's reinterpretation is placed in some jeopardy by his persistent substitution of "project" for "*projet.*"

28. Graebner, *Empire on the Pacific,* pp. 195–96; Brent, "Nicholas Philip Trist," 132–33.

29. Brent, "Nicholas Philip Trist," 133.

30. Graebner, *Empire on the Pacific,* p. 195.

31. Drexler, *Guilty of Making Peace,* p. 3.

32. Nicholas Trist to Virginia Trist, May 8, 1847.

CHAPTER 8
(See Reel 8, Series 1, Subseries 1.5)

1. Jeffrey N. Stafford, "The Role of Nicholas Philip Trist in the Mexican War" (diss., University of South Carolina, 1968), 8–9.

2. Graebner, *Empire on the Pacific,* p. 175.

3. Bergeron, *Presidency of James K. Polk,* p. 71.

4. Graebner, *Empire on the Pacific,* p. 177.

5. Winfield Scott to Nicholas Trist, May 7, 1847.

6. Ibid.

7. Stafford, "Role of Nicholas Philip Trist," 12; Brent, "Nicholas Philip Trist," 146.

8. Brent, "Nicholas Philip Trist," 148.

9. Stafford, "Role of Nicholas Philip Trist," 10.
10. Donald Barr Chidsey, *The War with Mexico*, p. 143; Smith, *War with Mexico*, vol. 2, p. 377.
11. Drexler, *Guilty of Making Peace*, p. 4.
12. Stafford, "Role of Nicholas Philip Trist," 15; Brent, "Nicholas Philip Trist," 149–50.
13. Brent, "Nicholas Philip Trist," 151.
14. Stafford, "Role of Nicholas Philip Trist," 19, 20.
15. Ibid.
16. Smith, *War with Mexico*, vol. 2, p. 130. The title "Generalissimo," as applied to Santa Anna, is of dubious authenticity. Like many of his grandiose titles, it may have been self-bestowed; however, it is sometimes used by historians and has at least the useful function of distinguishing him from other Mexican generals of lower rank.
17. Stafford, "Role of Nicholas Philip Trist," 21–22; Brent, "Nicholas Philip Trist," 187.
18. Bauer, *Mexican War*, p. 285.
19. Graebner, *Empire on the Pacific*, p. 199.

CHAPTER 9
1. Bauer, *Mexican War*, p. 371.
2. Smith, *War with Mexico*, vol. 2, p. 361.
3. Ibid., p. 131; Bauer, *Mexican War*, pp. 284–85.
4. Bauer, *Mexican War*, p. 285; Bergeron, *Presidency of James K. Polk*, pp. 99–100.
5. Bergeron, *Presidency of James K. Polk*, p. 99; Graebner, *Empire on the Pacific*, p. 199. As mystified as everyone else, Secretary of War Marcy wrote drily to a friend, "This is a changeable world. . . ."
6. Bergeron, *Presidency of James K. Polk*, p. 99.
7. Smith, *War with Mexico*, vol. 2, p. 93.
8. Ibid., p. 362.
9. Ibid., pp. 95–97; Bauer, *Mexican War*, p. 290; Thomas J. Farnham, "Nicholas Trist and James Freaner and the Mission to Mexico," *Arizona and the West* 11, no. 3 (autumn, 1969): 247–60.
10. Bauer, *Mexican War*, p. 288.
11. Ibid., p. 322.
12. Pletcher, *Diplomacy of Annexation*, pp. 513–14.
13. Bauer, *Mexican War*, pp. 290, 371.
14. Smith, *War with Mexico*, vol. 2, p. 187; Bauer, *Mexican War*, p. 210.
15. Smith, *War with Mexico*, vol. 2, p. 186.
16. Bauer, *Mexican War*, p. 372.
17. Smith, *War with Mexico*, vol. 2, p. 435; Bauer, *Mexican War*, p. 372.

18. Pletcher, *Diplomacy of Annexation,* p. 515.

19. W. Dirk Raat, *Mexico and the United States,* p. 31; Pletcher, *Diplomacy of Annexation,* p. 32.

20. *The Spanish West* (Time-Life Books), p. 98.

21. Meltzer, *Bound for the Rio Grande,* p. 29; Pletcher, *Diplomacy of Annexation,* pp. 333–34; Chidsey, *War with Mexico,* p. 17.

22. Oakah L. Jones, Jr., *Santa Anna,* p. 60.

23. Raat, *Mexico and the United States,* p. 65; Bauer, *Mexican War,* pp. 201, 393; Wilfrid H. Calcott, *Santa Anna: The Story of an Enigma Who Once Was Mexico,* p. 256.

24. Smith, *War with Mexico,* vol. 2, p. 135.

25. Pletcher, *Diplomacy of Annexation,* p. 518; Graebner, *Empire on the Pacific,* p. 199; Jesse S. Reeves, *American Diplomacy under Tyler and Polk,* pp. 320–21.

26. Smith, *War with Mexico,* vol. 2, p. 136.

27. Farnham, "Nicholas Trist and James Freaner," 249.

28. Smith, *War with Mexico,* vol. 2, p. 137; Bauer, *Mexican War,* p. 308.

29. Reeves, *American Diplomacy,* p. 316; Bergeron, *Presidency of James K. Polk,* p. 101.

30. Smith, *War with Mexico,* vol. 2, p. 235.

31. Graebner, *Empire on the Pacific,* p. 203; Bergeron, *Presidency of James K. Polk,* pp. 105–106.

32. Smith, *War with Mexico,* vol. 2, p. 436; Sears, "Nicholas P. Trist," 93.

33. Smith, *War with Mexico,* vol. 2, p. 436.

34. Ibid.

35. Bauer, *Mexican War,* p. 381; Stafford, "Role of Nicholas Philip Trist," 50.

36. Bauer, *Mexican War,* p. 382; Graebner, *Empire on the Pacific,* pp. 200–201; Stafford, "Role of Nicholas Philip Trist," 38–39.

CHAPTER 10
(See Reel 8, Series 1, Subseries 1.5)

1. Drexler, *Guilty of Making Peace,* p. 92.

2. Pletcher, *Diplomacy of Annexation,* p. 529; Reeves, *American Diplomacy,* p. 324; Bauer, *Mexican War,* p. 385.

3. Stafford, "Role of Nicholas Philip Trist," 41.

4. LaFeber, *American Age,* p. 113; Bauer, *Mexican War,* pp. 368–70.

5. Farnham, "Nicholas Trist and James Freaner," 257; Raat, *Mexico and the United States,* p. 76.

6. Drexler, *Guilty of Making Peace,* p. 110; Robert A. Brent, "Reaction in the United States to Nicholas Trist's Mission to Mexico," Ensayos y Documentos, *Revista de Historia de America,* nos. 35–36 (1953): 106, 112.

Brent and others have noted that at this time Polk was revising his opinions rapidly. Actually, the president was falling back on the firm policy he felt had served him well vis-à-vis Great Britain in the Oregon dispute.

7. Drexler, *Guilty of Making Peace,* p. 110.
8. Nicholas Trist to Virginia Trist, Nov. 28, 1847.
9. Farnham, "Nicholas Trist and James Freaner," 252–54.
10. Drexler, *Guilty of Making Peace,* p. 113.
11. Ibid., pp. 113–14.
12. Nicholas Trist to Virginia Trist, Dec. 4, 1847.
13. Drexler, *Guilty of Making Peace,* p. 115.
14. Ibid.
15. Bauer, *Mexican War,* p. 373; Smith, *War with Mexico,* vol. 2, pp. 188, 438.
16. Guy Stanton Ford to Eugene Keith Chamberlin, Jan. 14, 1952, as reported by Chamberlin, "Nicholas Trist," 49.
17. Graebner, *Empire on the Pacific,* pp. 207–208; Chamberlin, "Nicholas Trist," 58–62. The treaty boundary east of the two rivers–Gila and Colorado–followed the channel of the Gila River to the western boundary of what is now the state of New Mexico, then due south the thirty-second parallel, then due east to the Rio Grande and along the Rio Grande to its mouth. The Gila River ceased to be the international boundary in 1853 with the negotiation of the Gadsden purchase, an acquisition made to facilitate railroad construction.
18. Pletcher, *Diplomacy of Annexation,* 545–46.
19. Graebner, *Empire on the Pacific,* 112–13; Curtis R. Reynolds, "The Deterioration of Mexican-American Relations, 1833–1845," *Journal of the West* 11, no. 2 (Apr. 1972): 213.
20. Stafford, "Role of Nicholas Philip Trist," 65.
21. Ibid., 65–66.
22. Drexler, *Guilty of Making Peace,* pp. 129–30.
23. Ibid.

CHAPTER 11

1. Meltzer, *Bound for the Rio Grande,* pp. 225–33; Bergeron, *Presidency of James K. Polk,* p. 106.
2. LaFeber, *American Age,* p. 114; Graebner, *Empire on the Pacific,* p. 214.
3. Pletcher, *Diplomacy of Annexation,* pp. 559–60; Reeves, *American Diplomacy,* p. 326.
4. Graebner, *Empire on the Pacific,* p. 215; Paul F. Lambert, "The Movement for the Acquisition of All Mexico," *Journal of the West* 11, no. 2 (Apr. 1972): 327; Pletcher, *Diplomacy of Annexation,* p. 560.

5. Pletcher, *Diplomacy of Annexation,* pp. 558–59; Brent, "Nicholas Philip Trist," 214.
6. Farnham, "Nicholas Trist and James Freaner," 250.
7. Pletcher, *Diplomacy of Annexation,* p. 559; Reeves, *American Diplomacy,* p. 327.
8. Hietala, *Manifest Design,* pp. 248–49.
9. *National Intelligencer,* Feb. 28, 1848.
10. New Orleans *Daily Picayune,* Feb. 4, 1848.
11. *Philadelphia Inquirer,* Feb. 18, 1848.
12. *New York Sunday Dispatch,* Feb. 20, 1848.
13. *New York Herald,* Feb. 8, 1848.
14. *The Augusta Age,* Feb. 4, 1848.
15. *Pennsylvania Inquirer and National Gazette,* Mar. 14, 1848.
16. Smith, *War with Mexico,* vol. 2, pp. 248–49.
17. Drexler, *Guilty of Making Peace,* p. 126.
18. Ibid.
19. Ibid., p. 131.
20. Ibid.
21. Smith, *War with Mexico,* vol. 2, p. 188.

CHAPTER 12
(See Reel 8, Series 1, Subseries 1.5; Reel 12, Series 1, Subseries 1.7; Reel 16, Series 1, Subseries 1.9)

1. Bergeron, *Presidency of James K. Polk,* pp. 34, 163–66. Polk and Buchanan wrangled bitterly throughout the former's administration, with the secretary frequently offering his resignation. The president did not take these gestures seriously, once commenting, "There was not the slightest danger of his resigning."
2. Nortrup, "Nicholas Trist's Mission to Mexico," 345.
3. Lambert, "Movement for the Acquisition of All Mexico," 317, 319, 326.
4. Ibid.
5. Drexler, *Guilty of Making Peace,* p. 135.
6. Nicholas Trist to Beverly Randolph, May 2, 1849.
7. Brent, "Nicholas Philip Trist," 236–37.
8. Morison, *Oxford History,* p. 519.
9. *Southern Women and Their Families in the 19th Century, Part 4: Nicholas Philip Trist Papers,* Southern Historical Collection, 8.
10. Drexler, *Guilty of Making Peace,* p. 137.
11. Ibid., pp. 138–39.
12. Virginia Trist to a niece (name unknown), Aug. 24, 1862.
13. Virginia Trist to a sister (name unknown), Jan. 4, 1861.
14. Brent, "Nicholas Philip Trist," 240–41.

15. Drexler, *Guilty of Making Peace,* p. 137.
16. Brent, "Nicholas Philip Trist," 243–46.
17. Virginia Trist to Patty Trist Burke, Oct. 8, 1871.

EPILOGUE

1. Nicholas Trist to Virginia Trist, Nov. 11, 1839. The suspicion of a cabal against Trist was the subject of frequent speculation within the Trist family as well as by friends and supporters. In a letter to her husband (Dec. 2, 1840) Virginia alluded to "the Clique at Havana" and even included mention of an indignant remark by little Browse about "the bad Captains." On April 27, 1841, Hermogene Brown wrote to Nicholas: "I see with pain you are troubled by Sailors the worst class to deal with, they are very ignorant & malicious but with a strong nerve. You will be able to master them."
2. Smith, *War with Mexico,* vol. 2, p. 127.
3. Ibid., p. 467.
4. Pletcher, *Diplomacy of Annexation,* p. 610.
5. Sears, "Nicholas P. Trist," 85.
6. Washington *Sunday Herald,* February 12, 1874.

BIBLIOGRAPHY

Angle, Paul M., and Fairfax Downey. *Texas and the War with Mexico.* New York: Harper & Row, 1966.

Bauer, K. Jack. *The Mexican War, 1846–1848.* Lincoln: University of Nebraska Press, 1974.

———. *Surfboats and Horse Marines.* Annapolis, Md.: U.S. Naval Institute, 1969.

Bergeron, Paul H. *The Presidency of James K. Polk.* Lawrence: University Press of Kansas, 1987.

Brent, Robert A. "Reaction in the United States to Nicholas Trist's Mission to Mexico, 1847–48." Ensayos y Documentos, *Revista de Historia de America,* nos. 35–36 (1953): 105–18.

Brent, Robert Arthur. "Nicholas Philip Trist: Biography of a Disobedient Diplomat." Ph.D. diss., University of Virginia, 1950.

Brodie, Fawn M. *Thomas Jefferson: An Intimate History.* New York: W. W. Norton & Company, Inc., 1974.

Calcott, Wilfrid H. *Santa Anna: The Story of an Enigma Who Once Was Mexico.* Norman: University of Oklahoma Press, 1936.

———. *Church and State in Mexico.* Durham, N.C.: Duke University Press, 1927.

Chamberlin, Eugene Keith. "Nicholas Trist and Baja California." *Pacific Historica Review* 32, no. 1 (1963): 49–63.

Collins, John R. "The Mexican War: A Study in Fragmentation." *Journal of the West* 11, no. 2 (Apr. 1972).

Commager, Henry Steele. *Documents of American History.* 3d ed. New York: F. S. Crofts & Co., 1946.

Chidsey, Donald Barr. *The War with Mexico.* New York: Crown Publishers, 1968.

Dana, Richard Henry, Jr. *Two Years before the Mast: A Personal Narrative of Life at Sea*. N.p.: World Publishing Co., 1946.

Donavan, Frank. *The Thomas Jefferson Papers*. New York: Dodd, Mead & Co., 1963.

Drexler, Robert W. *Guilty of Making Peace*. Lanham, Md.: University Press of America, Inc., 1991.

Dupuy, R. Ernest. *Men of West Point*. New York: William Sloane Associates, 1951.

Ewing, R. C. *Six Faces of Mexico*. Tucson: University of Arizona Press, 1966.

Farnham, Thomas J. "Nicholas Trist and James Freaner and the Mission to Mexico." *Arizona and the West* 11, no. 3 (autumn, 1969): 247–60.

Fehrenbach, T. R. *Fire and Blood*. New York: Macmillan, 1973.

Fleming, Thomas J. *West Point: The Men and Times of the United States Military Academy*. New York: William Morrow, 1969.

Furnas, J. C. *Goodbye to Uncle Tom*. New York: William Sloane Associates, 1956.

Graebner, Norman A. *Empire on the Pacific: A Study in American Continental Expansion*. New York: The Ronald Press Company, 1955.

Herold, J. Christopher. *The Age of Napoleon*. New York: American Publishing Company, 1963.

Hietala, Thomas R. *Manifest Design: Anxious Aggrandizement in Late Jacksonian America*. Ithaca, N.Y.: Cornell University Press, 1985.

Hornung, Clarence P. *The Way It Was in the U.S.A.* New York: Abbeville Press, 1978.

James, Marquis. *Andrew Jackson the Border Captain*. New York: Garden City Publishing Co., Inc., 1940.

———. *Raven: A Biography of Sam Houston*. Indianapolis, Ind.: The Babbs-Merrill Company, 1929.

Johnson, Kenneth M. "Baja California and the Treaty of Guadalupe Hidalgo." *Journal of the West* 11, no. 2 (Apr. 1972).

Jones, Oklah L., Jr. *Santa Anna*. New York: Twayne Publishers, 1968.

Kandell, Jonathan. *La Capital: The Biography of Mexico City*. New York: Random House, 1988.

Kane, Harnett T. *Plantation Parade: The Grand Manner in Louisiana*. New York: Bonanza Books, 1955.

LaFeber, Walter. *The American Age: United States Foreign Policy at Home and Abroad Since 1750*. New York: W. W. Norton & Company, 1989.

Lambert, Paul F. "The Movement for the Acquisition of All Mexico." *Journal of the West* 11, 2 (Apr. 1972).

Lavender, David. *Climax at Buena Vista*. Philadelphia and New York: Lippincott, 1966.

Mapp, Alf J., Jr. *Thomas Jefferson: Passionate Pilgrim*. New York: Madison Books, 1991.

Meltzer, Milton. *Andrew Jackson and His America*. New York: Franklin Watts, 1993.

——. *Bound for the Rio Grande, the Mexican Struggle: 1845–1850*. New York: Alfred A. Knopf, 1974.

Merk, Frederick. *Manifest Destiny and Mission in American History*. New York: Alfred A. Knopf, 1963.

Morison, Samuel Eliot. *The Oxford History of the American People*. New York: Oxford University Press, 1965.

Nevin, David. *The Mexican War*. Alexandria, Va.: Time-Life Books, 1978.

Nortrup, Jack. "Nicholas Trist's Mission to Mexico: A Reinterpretation," *Southwestern Historical Quarterly* 71, no. 3 (1968): 921–46.

Paul, James C. N. *Rift in the Democracy*. Philadelphia: University of Pennsylvania Press, 1951.

Pletcher, David M. *The Diplomacy of Annexation: Texas, Oregon, and the Mexican War*. Columbia: University of Missouri Press, 1973.

Pratt, Julius W. *A History of United States Foreign Policy*. New York: Prentice-Hall, 1965.

Raat, W. Dirk. *Mexico and the United States: Ambivalent Vistas*. Athens: University of Georgia Press, 1992.

Reeder, Red. *The Story of the Mexican War*. New York: Meredith Press, 1967.

Reeves, Jesse S. *American Diplomacy under Tyler and Polk*. 1907. Reprint. Gloucester, Mass.: Peter Smith, 1967.

Reynolds, Curtis R. "The Deterioration of Mexican-American Relations, 1833–1845." *Journal of the West* 11, no. 2 (Apr. 1972).

Sears, Louis Martin. "Nicholas P. Trist, a Diplomat with Ideals." *Mississippi Valley Historical Review* (June 1924): 85–98.

Simpson, Lesley Bird. *Many Mexicos*. Berkeley: University of California Press, 1966.

Smith, Justin H. *The War with Mexico*. Vols. 1 and 2. New York: The Macmillan Company, 1919.

Smith, Page. *The Shaping of America: A People's History of the Young Republic*. Vol. 3. New York: McGraw-Hill, 1980.

Southern Women and Their Families in the 19th Century: Papers and Diaries, Series A—Part 4: Nicholas Philip Trist Papers. Southern Historical Collection. Chapel Hill: University of North Carolina, Microfilm Reels 1–7.

The Spanish West. New York: Time-Life Books, 1976.

Stafford, Jeffrey N. "The Role of Nicholas Philip Trist in the Mexican War." Diss., University of South Carolina, 1968.

"The White House: An Historic Guide." 12th ed., 2d printing. Washington, D.C.: White House Historical Society, rev. 1975.

Vevier, Charles. "American Continentalism: An Idea of Expansion, 1845–1910." *American Historical Review* (1960): 323–35.

Werstein, Irving. *The War with Mexico*. New York: W. W. Norton & Co., 1965.

Wright, Marcus J. *General Scott*. New York: D. Appleton & Co., 1897.

INDEX

Tournillon, St. Julien (the elder), 12, 33, 39–42, 51

Tournillon, St. Julien (the younger), 33, 51, 74

treaty. *See* peace treaty

Trist, Elizabeth, 3, 7–11, 14–15, 23, 27–28, 38, 60

Trist, Hore Browse (brother of NPT), 9–12, 15, 51, 81, 83; as Trist's advisor, 23–24, 32, 56, 60–61; as Trist's business partner, 57, 66, 74, 78

Trist, Hore Browse (father of NPT), 3–7

Trist, Hore Browse (son of NPT), 74, 90, 155, 162

Trist, Martha ("Patty"), 50, 87–90, 162

Trist, Nicholas (grandfather of NPT), 3

Trist, Nicholas Philip, 4; appearance, 11, 15, 102; arrest, 151–52, 161; with British officials, 93–95; death, 167; finances, 39, 51, 52, 53, 70, 73, 74, 76–77, 98, 142, 151, 155, 156, 159–62; friendships, IX–X, 60, 61–62, 66, 108, 118, 150–51, 156, 159, 164; get-rich schemes, 66, 83, 156; health concerns, X, 18, 21, 34, 49, 53, 76, 79, 80, 81, 83, 91–92, 108, 113, 117, 143, 156, 165; relations with Jackson, IX–X, 66, 69, 70, 71, 73, 75, 77, 80, 82; relations with Jefferson, 8, 34, 46, 73; Jefferson's estate, 49, 51–53, 55; law, 8, 11, 13, 16, 32, 36, 39–42, 44, 53; linguistic skills, 9, 10, 11, 60, 80, 102, 166; peace negotiations, 131–32, 134, 135, 139–46; personality and character, IX–X, 11, 13, 35, 37, 38, 39, 71, 86, 95, 112, 143, 161, 163–67; phi-

losophy, 4, 46–47, 136, 157, 158–59; relations with Polk, 136, 141, 142, 155; public view, 153–54, 163; quarrel with Scott, 109–18, 119; railroad clerk, 156–57, 159, 161; recall, 134, 135–42, 160–61; religious opinions, 39, 42, 64–66, 89, 114; with sea captains, 83, 91, 92–93; social skills, 80, 143, 166; writing, 56–58, 61, 70, 86, 95, 98, 112, 134, 164, 166

Trist, Thomas Jefferson ("Jeff"), 81, 85–86, 88, 92, 155, 157, 159

Trist, Virginia (née Randolph), X, 60, 72, 78, 86–87, 89–92; during courtship, 15, 16, 17, 24, 31–32, 36, 38–39, 44; as a mother, 56, 84–85, 89–90; religious beliefs, 64–66, 89

Twiggs, David E., 121, 123

United States Military Academy. *See* West Point

Van Buren, Martin, 61, 66, 69, 96–97

Virginia (state), 13, 23

Virginia University of, 28, 48–49

War Department, 109, 142

Washington D.C., 59, 66–67, 78

Webster, Daniel, 67, 98, 132

West Point, 17–30, 118

Whigs, 97, 136, 163

White House, 68, 69, 71

Wilkinson, James, 8, 9

Worth, William J., 25–26, 118, 120–21, 126–27, 133

yellow fever, 7, 13, 74, 107, 113